INSURANCE BROKERS
An Industry Accounting and Auditing Guide

INSURANCE BROKERS

An Industry Accounting and Auditing Guide

Robin G Oakes BCom, FCA

Neville Russell

Accountancy Books
Gloucester House
399 Silbury Boulevard
Central Milton Keynes
MK9 2HL
Tel: 01908 248000

© 1995 The Institute of Chartered Accountants in England and Wales.
ISBN 1 85355 545 2

First edition published 1990.

British Library Cataloguing-in-Publication Data.
A catalogue record for this book is available from the British Library.

Typeset by J&L Composition Ltd, Filey, North Yorkshire
Printed in Great Britain by Bell and Bain

Contents

Contents

PART VI
TAXATION

List of abbreviations

The following is a list of abbreviations commonly used in the insurance broking profession.

ABI	Association of British Insurers
ACH	Associate of the Chartered Insurance Institute
AIA	1 Associate of the Institute of Actuaries
	2 American Insurance Association
ANC	Absolute Net Claims
ANP	Absolute Net Premiums
AO	All Other
AOL/aol	Any One Loss
AP	1 Additional Premium
	2 Annual Premium
ASB	Accounting Standards Board
BACS	Bankers Automated Clearing System
BC	Burning Cost
BIBA	British Insurance Brokers' Association
BIBC	British Insurance Brokers' Council
BIIBA	British Insurance and Investment Brokers' Association
BORD or bord	Bordereau
CA	1 Central Accounting – as used by the main bureaux, Lloyd's, ILU and LIRMA
	2 Companies Act
CAAT	Computer-assisted Audit Technique
Cap.Ap.	Capital Appreciation of Investments
CAR	Contractors' All Risks
CC	Ceding Commission
CHAPS	Clearing House Automated Payment System
CIF	Cost, Insurance, Freight
CII	Chartered Insurance Institute
CL/CON LOSS	Consequential Loss
CMR	Convention on the Contract for the International Carriage of Goods by Road (CMD 3455)
CMR Form	Lloyd's goods in transit (CMR) policy

C/N or CN	1 Cover Note
	2 Credit Note
COINS	Co-insurance
CTL	Constructive Total Loss
Dep	Deposit, e.g. deposit premium
D/N	Debit Note
DTI	Department of Trade and Industry
EEL	Each and Every Loss
EER	Each and Every Risk
E & O	Errors and Omissions (insurance) – equivalent to professional indemnity
E & OE	Errors and Omissions Excepted
ECO	Extra Contractual Obligations
EML	Estimated Maximum Loss
EMPL	Estimated Maximum Probable Loss
EMU	European Monetary Unit
EPS	Electronic Placing Support
ESA	Early Signings Account
EUA	European Unit of Account
Ex R/I	Excess of Loss Reinsurance
Excl	Exclusion
Fac	Facultative
Fac/Oblig	Facultative/Obligatory
FDO	For Declaration Only
FGU	From the Ground Up
FIL	Foreign Insurance Legislation
FIMBRA	Financial Intermediaries. Managers and Brokers Regulatory Association
lst S	First Surplus Treaty
FOB	Free on Board
FRED	Financial Reporting Exposure Draft
FRS	Financial Reporting Standard
FSA	Financial Services Act 1986
FSL	Full Signed Line
FWL	Full Written Line
GIT	Goods in Transit
GPI	Gross Premium Income
GPUL	Gross Premium Underwriting Limit
IBA	Insurance Broking Account
IBNR	(Losses) Incurred but not Reported
IBRA	Insurance Brokers (Registration) Act 1977
IBRC	Insurance Brokers Registration Council
IITC	Insurance Industry Training Council
ILU	Institute of London Underwriters

IMRO	Investment Managers Regulatory Organisation
L/A	Lloyd's Agent
LAN	Local Area Network
LACC	Lloyd's Aviation Claims Centre
LATF	Lloyd's American Trust Fund
LAUTRO	Life Assurance and Unit Trust Regulatory Organisation
LC	Letter of Credit
LCA	Lloyd's Central Accounting
LCO	Lloyd's Claims Office
LCTF	Lloyd's Canadian Trust Fund
LIBC	Lloyd's Insurance Brokers Committee
LIMNET	London Insurance Market Network
LIRMA	London Insurance and Reinsurance Market Association
LMX	London Market Excess
LOA	Life Offices' Association
LOC	Letters of Credit
LPC	London Processing Centre
LPSO	Lloyd's Policy Signing Office
LUCRO	Lloyd's Underwriters Claims and Recoveries Office
LUNCO	Lloyd's Underwriters Non-marine Claims Office
M & D	Minimum & Deposit (Premium)
MAT	Marine, Aviation and Transport
MIA	Marine Insurance Act 1906
MFL	Maximum Foreseeable Loss
NCA	Net Current Assets
NCB	No Claims Bonus
NM	Non-marine
NMA	(Lloyd's) Underwriters Non-marine Association
NPI	Net Premium Income
NRL	Net Retained Line
NTA	Net Tangible Assets
NTU	Not Taken Up
OCA	Outstanding Claims Advance
OGP	Original Gross Premium
OGPI	Original Gross Premium Income
OGR	Original Gross Rate
ONPI	Original Net Premium Income
ONR	Original Net Rate
O/R or OR	Overrider

Ors	Others
O/S	1 Outstanding
	2 Outside the Scope (VAT)
PAN	Premium Advice Note
P & I	Protection and Indemnity
PD	Property Damage (third party)
PI	1 Premium Income
	2 Professional Indemnity (insurance)
PIA	Personal Investment Authority
PIL	Premium Income Limit (of a Name at Lloyd's)
PL	Public Liability
Pm	Premium
PML	1 Probable Maximum Loss
	2 Possible Maximum Loss
PPI	Policy Proof of Interest
PR	Pro Rata (in proportion)
Q/S	Quota Share (reinsurance)
Reinst	Reinstatement
Retro	1 Retrospective Rating
	2 Retrocession
RI or R/I	Reinsurance
R/Id	Reinsured
R/Irs	Reinsurers
RITC	Reinsurance to Close (a Lloyd's syndicate's year of account)
ROA	Reinsurance Offices Association
RP	Return Premium
RPB	Recognised Professional Body
RTBA	Rate to be Agreed
SAS	Statement of Auditing Standards
2nd S	Second Surplus Treaty
SFA	Securities and Futures Authority
SG	Ship and Goods
SIB	Securities and Investments Board
SL	Stop Loss Reinsurance
SORP	Statement of Recommended Practice
SRO	Self Regulating Organisation
SSA	Statement of Standard Accounting Practice
ST	Short Tail
Syn or Synd	Syndicate
TBA	1 To be Advised
	2 To be Agreed
3rd S	Third Surplus Treaty
TL	Total loss

TLO	Total loss only
TP	Third party
TPFT	Third party, Fire and Theft
U/A	1 Underwriting Account
	2 Underwriting Agent
UITF	Urgent Issues Task Force
U/O	Use and Occupancy Insurance
UNL	Ultimate Net Loss
U/W	Underwriter
WBS	Without Benefit of Salvage
XL or XS	Excess of Loss Reinsurance

Preface to the first edition

The original idea for this publication came from Nick Tarrant of the Institute Publications Department (now Chartac Books) in 1985. Nick has now moved on to new ventures, as have a number of my colleagues at Neville Russell who have helped me in drafting.

At that first discussion with Nick, we agreed it would be inappropriate to publish until we knew the changes Lloyd's were going to make to the regulation of Lloyd's brokers. At the time, a discussion document was expected early in 1986 with the byelaws being passed later that year. In the event the byelaws came into force during 1988. The new rules are covered in Chapter 4 insofar as they concern accountants and auditors.

A direct consequence of the delay in publication is the inclusion of a brief chapter on the Financial Services Act; legislation which has had such impact on the industry. FIMBRA, however, keep changing their rules, and only those extant at November 1989 are covered. For the chapters on financial management in brokers, we went to friends in the industry. Those who helped most with Chapter 6 on high street brokers are John Smeaton of Fielding, Smeaton, Jones (Agencies) Ltd and John Brosche of Mansbrook, Brosche & Co Ltd. Chapter 7, covering the London market and international scene, draws heavily on material provided by Mike Rossor and Clifford Dear at J H Minet Limited.

Section IV was substantially the responsibility of John Hughesdon, one of my fellow broking partners. He also drew on Neville Russell in-house information, accounting and audit guidance. Section V was prepared by members of Neville Russell Consultancy who have wide practical knowledge of the application of information technology in the insurance market. Mark Fennell, head of our VAT consultancy, contributed Chapter 13, and Stephen Andrew, a corporate tax partner, Chapter 14. These chapters reflect tax legislation following the Finance Act 1989. Jane Lyons, our Information officer, has helped with the Bibliography. Drafting assistance came from Jo Bright (now with P&O), Steve Hawkes (with Walsh International) and Ian Chrystie, an audit manager who has spent time on secondment to the Brokers department at Lloyd's.

I also appreciate the help given by David Drummond-Tyler, the Neville

Russell Insurance Technical Manager, staff at BIIBA, personnel in the Brokers department at Lloyd's and the IBRC, and other colleagues and friends who have completed technical reviews of the book.

Finally, I have had the help of several secretaries during the gestation period, but the Central Text Processing Department at Neville Russell and my current secretary, Philippa Saxby, have borne the brunt of the typing, for which I am very grateful.

I hope you will find the book of interest whether you are involved in insurance broking management, regulation or advice. However, neither Neville Russell nor the Institute can, of course, take any responsibility for any loss resulting from the material in this publication.

Robin Oakes
May 1990

Preface to the second edition

Much has happened in the past four years in the world of insurance broking. In particular, the speed of change in regulatory and accounting matters has significantly increased. I have tried, in this edition, to reflect the current status of various issues and to indicate how I believe outstanding matters may be resolved. There is, however, a requirement on us all to remain constantly alert to changes and pronouncements.

This edition reflects the replacement of LAUTRO and FIMBRA by the PIA and gives guidance on the accounting and audit implications of the PIA Rulebook. It also addresses the changes in Lloyd's regulations, which now require quarterly solvency reporting, and the review of operating practices at Lloyd's, which may further weaken the traditional exclusive access Lloyd's brokers have had to that market. Anticipated changes in IBRC Rules are considered although details are not yet to hand.

UK legislation has been influenced by EC developments and, in particular, the ABI and IBRC Codes of Practice will be subject to change. The old codes have not therefore been reproduced in this edition. Money laundering is now an area where brokers have statutory reponsibilities and compliance officers have to take on yet another onerous task. I address these matters.

Accounting and taxation have also changed in the past four years. The introduction of financial reporting standards affects insurance brokers as it does all other corporate entities. One of the potentially most significant changes to the face of brokers' financial statements will arise through the implementation of FRS 5. The debate generated from this standard may lead in due course to an industry SORP. Brokers are also affected by the new UK tax on insurance premiums. Guidance is included on its implications.

Not surprisingly in the light of all these changes, I have again drawn on the help of colleagues, clients and friends. In addition to those mentioned in the preface to the first edition, many of whom have helped again, particular thanks go to my Neville Russell colleagues – Andrew Judt (now with NIG Skandia) and James Owen, who have helped considerably with the drafting, Debbie Lovell, who has extensively researched the PIA,

Chris de Silva and David Jordorson, who have updated the chapters on information technology and VAT and IPT respectively, and Barbara Stirling, who has been responsible for the word processing. In addition, I would like to thank Colin Robinson of Ernst and Young who has provided technical review on behalf of Accountancy Books and Alan Hodder of Bain Hogg, who has provided current LIBC thinking at various points.

The health warning at the end of the first preface, of course, remains in force. I trust, however, that this new edition will continue to help all of us better serve the insurance broking industry, in all its diversity.

Robin Oakes
December 1994

Foreword

I believe Robin Oakes' second edition is both timely and instructive given the enormous changes taking place in our industry. This edition is certainly required reading by many of our members whether they be the owners of their companies, financial directors or market practitioners.

Whilst the complexity of regulation makes ever increasing demands on our time, we have to accept that standards in our industry must be improved thereby increasing the efficiency of our day-to-day practices.

This helpful guide will certainly go a long way to providing a useful addition to every broker's reference library.

Simon R Arnold
Chairman
BIIBA

PART I

Introduction

Chapter 1 – The insurance industry

1.1 Introduction

To appreciate the role of the insurance broker in an insurance environment it is necessary to have a basic understanding of the operation of the insurance industry as a whole. It is a world-wide industry and the basic principles by which it operates are universal. However, national rules and practices differ, and the emphasis of this chapter is on the evolution and operation of the insurance market in the United Kingdom. The remainder of the book will discuss the role of the insurance broker in Britain, the impact of regulation, management control and, in particular, the financial accounting and audit implications.

In its simplest form, insurance involves one party (the insured) paying a sum of money (the premium) to another party (the insurer or underwriter). For this consideration, the insurer bears the risk – the possibility of loss or damage arising from a particular happening. If the event covered by the insurance policy occurs, the insurer agrees to pay the claim arising up to the sum insured, which in some instances may be unlimited. The insurer keeps the premium whether or not a claim is paid. Generally, a number of risks are accepted and the premiums are invested in a fund from which claims are met as they arise. The insurer expects that his total premiums, and an investment return on the cash representing those premiums, will exceed his total claims and expenses.

The primary function of insurance is therefore to spread the financial losses of a few insureds over many who have no losses. Contributions made to the fund from which these losses will be met are related to the possibility and frequency of their occurrence. Insurance also allows:

(a) release of financial and management resources for the insured, which would otherwise be occupied with risk management;
(b) economies of scale for the insurer;
(c) benefits to all parties from specialisation;
(d) opportunity to invest funds to provide added security to the insured;
(e) society as a whole to benefit by easing the burdens on social security schemes; and
(f) a business to continue trading after a potentially catastrophic event.

3

The main elements of insurance are:

(a) an insurance contract: a legally binding agreement between two or more parties setting out the terms of the insurance and the object or liability insured;

(b) an insurable interest: a financial involvement in the risk insured, which may be personal, in connection with assets owned directly, or by a third party, arising from some contingent liability or other event in which the insured has rights or an interest;

(c) *uberrima fides*: utmost good faith by both parties, which involves a full disclosure of all material facts of which a prudent underwriter should be aware in assessing the risk;

(d) indemnity: the insured should be restored to the same financial position as existed before the loss occurred subject to the amount of the sum insured and other terms written into the contract; and

(e) subrogation: the insurer can assume another's rights against a third party, or has the right to make a claim in the name of another person. Thus the insurer provides an indemnity to the insured and recovers the loss from the third party.

1.2   Development of classes of insurance

Insurance in one form or another has been a feature of commercial life for at least 4,000 years. It developed initially where goods were transported by sea. One of the earliest recorded insurance arrangements was described by the Greek prosecutor, Demosthenes, over 2,000 years ago. He told the court in Athens that two men had advanced 3,000 drachmas, which they would lose should a cargo of wine be lost or shipwrecked during its journey through the Bosphorus. The arrangement was that if the cargo was safely delivered the full sum assured would be repaid, together with a bonus, the amount of which depended on the time of year and thus the risk of shipwreck. Insurance has developed over the centuries in order to satisfy the changing needs of individuals and businesses seeking protection against financial loss. As a result, in the United Kingdom there are now a number of recognised classes of business, of which the most important are the general classes of marine, fire, accident and health, liability, other property and pecuniary losses, motor and aviation, and the special class of life assurance. Each of these types of business has its own particular features, which are introduced in the following paragraphs.

1.2.1   Marine

The Lombards, merchants from northern Italy, introduced marine insurance to Britain in the fourteenth and fifteenth centuries.

However, their domination of business caused considerable public resentment and led to the imposition of severe restrictions during the reign of Elizabeth I. The Lombards emigrated and British underwriters were able to capitalise on the marine insurance expertise they left behind. Marine business was therefore the first class of insurance to develop in Britain. The oldest surviving British insurance policy dates back to 1547 and relates to a voyage from Cadiz to London. The number of marine insurance transactions increased rapidly, and by 1575 a register of marine policies was introduced through the Chamber of Assurances. This in turn led to the standardisation of policy wordings. The Chamber of Assurances provided the venue for the Court of Arbitration, which was established in 1601 to consider disputes on marine policies.

Marine insurance today is largely governed by the Marine Insurance Act 1906, which was a codification of previous case law. The Act is fundamental to an understanding of marine insurance but its importance is increased because it is the only code of commercial insurance which has been enacted by Parliament.

The function of marine insurance is to cover the risk of damage, injury or other losses caused by collision, fire or similar 'perils of the sea'. There are three elements of risk: hull (the vessel itself), cargo (the goods consigned to be carried by the vessel) and freight (the charges for transporting the goods). Policies may be written to cover a period of time, a particular voyage or a combination of the two.

1.2.2 Fire

Financial protection for property became particularly important with urban growth. Fire insurance developed towards the end of the seventeenth century after the Great Fire of London in 1666. The first fire insurance company was established in 1680. The early fire insurance companies affixed metal fire marks to the outside wall of policyholders' premises so that the fire brigades, which were by and large controlled by the insurance companies, could identify with whom the property was insured. The Tooley Street fire of 1861 caused immense damage to the warehouses along the Thames in the middle of London, resulting in claims totalling £1,000,000, and led to a reappraisal of the basis for computing premiums. The reappraisal included a penalty for policyholders with poor fire precautions. Parliament also passed an Act establishing a fire service for London, run by the City.

Fire policies today are in standard form and cover damage to property caused by fire, lightning or explosion. They are also subject to a number

5

of standard exclusions. It is possible to obtain cover for special perils, such as natural events, or to cover consequential loss.

1.2.3   Accident and health

The Industrial Revolution brought with it specific personal risks, which provided the opportunity for the emergence of accident and health insurance. This began in 1848 with insurance in respect of railway accidents and developed to provide compensation for all accidents and sickness. The main cover provided today is for personal accident, sickness and permanent health.

1.2.4   Liability

The growth of liability insurance was also precipitated by the Industrial Revolution. There are two main categories of liability insurance – employers' and public.

In the early days of industrialisation, employers did not accept much responsibility for sickness or injuries sustained by workers in the course of their employment, on the principle that the employee had agreed to accept the risk of being injured by accepting employment. There was also a legal defence known as 'common employment', which meant that the law protected employers from liability where one employee was injured as a result of another employee's actions. Liability could be avoided if an employee contributed, in even the smallest way, to his own injury. In 1880 the Employers' Liability Act gave some workers additional legal rights, but it was only in 1972 that employers were compelled to take out insurance to cover the cost of compensation where an employee is injured by the employer's fault.

Public liability insurance covers the insured where:

(a)   others suffer loss to person or property through the insured's careless or negligent actions;
(b)   the loss results from the insured's defective goods; or
(c)   the liability is imposed by statute.

1.2.5   Other property and pecuniary losses

Theft cover was first provided in 1887 as an extension of a fire policy. In the following decade, theft insurance developed as a separate form of business and may now cover damage to buildings caused during a burglary, in addition to loss of goods by stealing.

Fire and theft policies cover claims arising from specific perils but not from accidental damage or loss. A logical progression was the 'all risks' policy, which covers specified property against loss or damage from almost any cause. All risks cover was first introduced at the end of the nineteenth century.

1.2.6 Motor

The first motor vehicle appeared in Britain in 1894 and within a few years insurance cover became available to motor vehicle owners. The Road Traffic Act 1930 made it compulsory to have insurance against injury to third parties (except passengers). The Road Traffic Act 1960 extended that requirement to include passengers, and the Road Traffic Act 1988, implementing the EC Second Motor Directive, requires insurance against third party property damage. The normal minimum motor insurance is 'third party only', which provides cover against damage to the property of others in addition to personal injury as required by statute. However, fully comprehensive cover is available to cover damage to the insured's vehicle caused by fire, theft, accidental collision or malicious damage.

1.2.7 Aviation

Aviation insurance is the most recent major class of business. It has developed since the First World War. It is complex and highly specialised and covers damage to aircraft, cargo and air travellers' baggage, and personal accident, public liability and product liability. Parliament has imposed strict controls over this class of business.

1.2.8 Life

Life assurance, like marine insurance, has ancient historical roots. For example, Romans and Greeks formed associations known as funeral clubs, to which they paid contributions and out of which burial costs were met.

The first recorded instance of life assurance in Britain relates to a policy written in 1583 in respect of a William Gibbons. A group of individuals agreed to provide cover for him for a period of 12 months. At the bottom of the policy they added the words: 'God send the said William Gibbons health and a long life'. Unfortunately, Mr Gibbons died after 11 months.

For the next century there was little change in the type of life assurance provided, with most policies being for the short term. In the mid-eighteenth century policies were introduced which guaranteed that a minimum sum would be paid in the event of death. At about the same time, actuarial principles evolved based on the work of mathematicians who produced what became known as mortality tables. These tables compute in mathematical terms the likelihood of the death of a person of a given age. Actuarial principles gave insurers a scientific basis for calculating premiums, depending on the age of the individual when the policy was taken out. The Life Assurance Act 1774 introduced a degree of regulation to the life assurance market, in particular prohibiting insurances upon lives 'except in cases where the persons insuring shall have an interest in the life or death of the person insured'.

Life assurance provides financial security and protection for dependants by the payment of a lump sum or other benefits on the death of the insured. This is known as term business. Life assurance is, however, a unique class of insurance business because it may also be used for long-term investment purposes. Such policies may be described as endowment, and are linked to particular forms of investments such as unit trusts. Variants of such policies provide annuities and pensions.

The principal differences between life assurance and general insurance business may be summarised as shown in the table below.

Life	*General*
Contracts cover a long period	Contracts are usually made for a short period of one year or less
The premium is usually set at the beginning of contract	The premium varies on renewal
The size of a claim is determined at the beginning	The size of a claim varies, dependent on the loss arising
The risk of a claim being made increases throughout the contract	The risk exists at the same level throughout the contract
A policy may acquire a surrender value, in return for the policyholder surrendering his rights	Payment arises only in the event of the insured risk occurring
Payment of a claim completes the contract	More than one claim can arise

1.3 Direct and reinsurance business

The classification of insurance business into direct and reinsurance is quite separate from, and is superimposed upon, any analysis by class of business. Direct insurance involves acceptance by an insurer of up to 100 per cent of the risk placed from the general public. A variation is co-insurance, where a number of insurers each bear a proportion of the risk under separate contracts. Reinsurance literally means 'insuring again' and is the practice by which the direct insurer 'lays off' to another insurer a proportion of the risk he has accepted from the initial insured. It is a contract between insurers and does not involve the general public who first placed the insurance.

Reinsurance thus serves to spread the impact of financial loss between insurers in the event of a claim. Consequently, it reduces the financial effect of uncertainty of future events for the direct insurer and may, depending on the terms of the contract, replace a variable, unpredictable cost with a fixed maximum cost. It cannot, however, prevent a claim arising from an initial insured. Since the direct insurers can reinsure part of their risks, they are able to accept more of the original risk or to accept more risks and thereby spread their loss exposure over a wider range of business.

Insurers can accept reinsurance and direct business or they may specialise and write reinsurance only. A reinsurer may also reinsure part of the reinsurance risks written.

Reinsurance contracts may be divided between facultative and treaty. In both cases the underwriter seeking reinsurance is said to 'cede' the amount of risk and is called the 'cedant' or 'ceding company'. The underwriter to whom the risk is ceded is called the reinsurer. Under a facultative contract the cedant is free to choose whether or not to offer a particular direct risk written to a reinsurer, who may refuse to accept it. A treaty contract, on the other hand, requires a cedant to cede, and a reinsurer to accept, all covers falling within the scope of that treaty. There are two main types of treaty – proportional and non-proportional.

Proportional treaties may be quota share, where a fixed proportion of all risks of a given class are ceded to the reinsurer, or, more usually, surplus treaties, where the cedant retains an agreed proportion of a particular class of business or part of a risk. Non-proportional treaties include excess of loss, stop loss and aggregate excess of loss treaties. With excess of loss, the cedant's direct liability in respect of any one event is covered beyond an agreed amount, usually up to a specified limit. Stop loss treaties provide that, where the loss ratio on a given class of business exceeds a specified percentage in any one period, the reinsurer will reimburse the cedant the excess up to a given limit. Aggregate excess of loss treaties are similar to stop loss treaties, except that cash amounts are used in place of percentage loss ratios. In principle, proportional

9

business involves the reinsurer paying the claim in the same proportion as the premium he received, whereas with non-proportional treaties he does not. A more detailed explanation of reinsurance terminology will be found in the glossary in Appendix 5.

1.4 The insurance market

The United Kingdom insurance market is made up of three basic elements: the buyer or insured, the intermediary and the seller, insurer or underwriter. The latter category may be subdivided into direct sellers and reinsurers. Figure 1.1 illustrates the relationships between these three elements.

1.4.1 Sellers: the insurer

Insurers or underwriters have formed themselves into several different types of organisation, some of which are unique to the insurance industry. In the UK, there are insurance companies with various types of constitution, involved in either general or life business or both (a 'composite' insurer) or specialising in a particular type of risk. The Society of Lloyd's ('Lloyd's') is a feature of the United Kingdom market. Members of the society are known as 'Names' and are grouped in underwriting syndicates.

In essence the insurers bear or underwrite the risk under an insurance policy, whatever the nature of their organisation. In this book, the generic terms 'insurer' and 'underwriter' are used to refer to both insurance companies and Lloyd's syndicates.

The quality of the security behind an insurer is important to the insured. If the insurer's underwriting and investment are unsuccessful and other assets become eroded, settlement of claims will depend on the nature of the investment backing the insurer. Corporate insurers may be proprietary or mutual companies, or various forms of associations.

The majority of insurance companies are proprietary companies which have limited liability and are owned by shareholders. These companies are now incorporated under the Companies Acts, although in the past they have been created by Act of Parliament, Royal Charter or Deed of Settlement. The profits of these companies, being essentially the excess of premiums plus investment income over claims, expenses and claims reserves movements, belong to the shareholders. Profits may be distributed by way of dividend or retained within the company to finance future expansion or to provide a further general reserve to improve the security of policyholders.

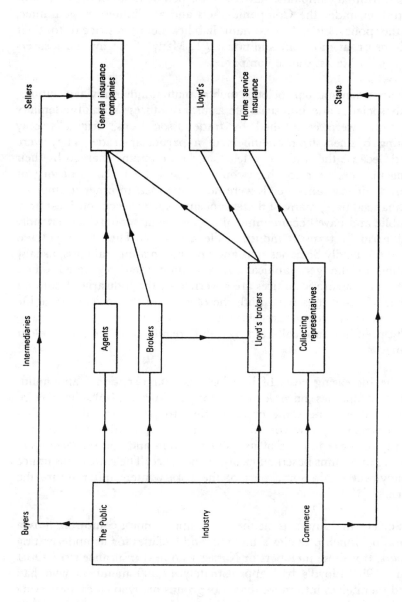

Figure 1.1 Elements of the insurance market. From GCA Dickinson and JT Steele, Introduction to Insurance, M & E Business Studies Services, 1984.

11

Mutual insurance companies are owned by the policyholders, who share in any profits made by way of lower premiums or higher life assurance bonuses. Mutual companies have been formed by Deed of Settlement or Registration under the Companies Acts and are limited by guarantee, with the policyholders' maximum liability being restricted to their premiums or, at most, an additional £1. Many of the mutual insurers are specialist life assurance companies.

There are other mutual societies such as mutual indemnity associations, friendly societies and industrial life assurance offices. Mutual indemnity associations were established by trade associations, originally only accepting business from members of a particular trade. They were formed because the tradesmen felt that the premiums charged by their existing insurers were too high compared with their claims history, or because their insurance needs were not being met. In order to improve their financial base, many of these associations now accept business from the public and have become mutual or proprietary companies. Friendly societies usually transact industrial life assurance. They are registered under the Friendly Societies Acts and are run on a mutual basis, usually operating in the geographical areas around their registered office. Industrial life assurance offices are governed by the Industrial Assurance and Friendly Societies Acts. Both the offices and the societies issue life policies, generally for modest sums and to lower income groups. Traditionally, premiums are collected by calling regularly on the policyholder at home.

With the increasing costs of insuring risks, large national and multinational companies have formed captive insurance subsidiary companies to underwrite some or all of the group's insurable risks. This saves contributing towards direct insurers' overheads and allows a company to make full use of its risk evaluation and control techniques by paying premiums based on its own experience. The captive insurance company will retain some part of the risks written and reinsure the balance.

The Society of Lloyd's is neither a company nor an insurer. It is a corporation which provides a building and facilities for its underwriting members. It is these members or Names who bear insurance risks. On 1 January 1994 Lloyd's had approximately 17,500 members who had formed themselves into more than 179 groups or 'syndicates' of varying sizes. In 1993 there was a significant reduction in the number of individual Names underwriting at Lloyd's and as a result corporate capital vehicles were established in order to strengthen the capital base. On 15 July 1994 there were 95 such corporate bodies in existence providing 15 per cent of the market's capacity. For the 1995 year of account this has increased to 23 per cent and it is possible that the majority of underwriting capacity will soon be provided by underwriters with the protection of limited liability.

The historical roots of Lloyd's lie in the seventeenth century, when merchants used to meet and transact business in coffee-houses around the City of London. One such coffee-house, owned by Edward Lloyd, became popular with businessmen having an interest in maritime undertakings, including insurance. The date on which this coffee-house was opened is unknown, although it was certainly in existence in the 1680s. Edward Lloyd became a source of information on maritime intelligence and in 1696 started publishing *Lloyd's News*. This publication was the forerunner of *Lloyd's List*, which is London's oldest newspaper.

Even after the death of Edward Lloyd, his name continued to be associated with insurance, despite the fact that the insurance market had moved to a new coffee-house. In 1771 a committee was formed to look for larger premises, with the result that the running of Lloyd's was transferred from the coffee-house owner to the insurers themselves. The Society of Lloyd's was incorporated in 1871 by Act of Parliament. The provisions of the Act included the objects of the Society, the right to make byelaws for its control, and the formation of a committee to administer it. As Lloyd's developed within a changing insurance market, further Acts were passed in 1911, 1925, 1951 and 1982. The most recent statute, the Lloyd's Act 1982, followed an enquiry under Sir Henry Fisher into the constitution and self-regulation of Lloyd's. The Act established a new Council, which has overall responsibility for and control of affairs at Lloyd's, including all rule-making and disciplinary powers.

Lloyd's is the centre for the world's marine insurance and shipping intelligence, but it now transacts all types of insurance except long-term life business.

Lloyd's insurances (with the exception of motor business) are generally transacted in the 'Room' in the Lloyd's building where each syndicate is represented by an underwriter. The underwriter assesses the various risks presented to the syndicate from the risk details set out on a document called a 'slip' and supporting documentation provided by the broker. The underwriter enters on the slip the proportion of the risk the syndicate is willing to carry. The underwriter then signs the slip underneath his 'line' – hence the term 'underwriter'. The introduction of computer systems has had a significant impact on Lloyd's and the handwritten slip is beginning to be replaced by electronic placing. These matters are discussed in Part V. Every underwriting member is committed by the underwriter for the proportion of the risk accepted on his behalf. He has to demonstrate adequate assets and make a deposit to support the volume of business transacted. This provides additional policyholder protection.

1.4.2 The State

The State also acts as an insurer under the National Insurance Acts, which require all employees to contribute to the national insurance scheme. This scheme was introduced with the Beveridge Report in 1948 and was an extension of the Poor Laws, which began with the Elizabethan Poor Law Act 1601. National insurance has only been mentioned here for completeness; it is not within the scope of commercial insurance.

1.4.3 Intermediaries

Although insurable risks can be placed direct by the insured with insurers, many risks are placed by intermediaries who act as an interface between the two parties. These are 'brokers' or 'agents'. One of the earliest historical references to insurance intermediaries was in 1575, when mention was made of 'those' who assisted the merchants in buying and selling, and in their contracts, and who were concerned also in the writing of insurances and policies. At first, when there were few people requiring insurance and relatively few underwriters, it was simple for the prospective insured to go direct to the underwriter. However, as ventures became more numerous, hazardous and complex, the services of a trusted and experienced intermediary became necessary. Similarly, because the potential losses being insured became so large that they exceeded the capacity of a single insurer, a skilled intermediary was employed, who would know how and where the risk could best be shared.

The early intermediaries differed from the brokers of today in that they were often engaged concurrently in other business activities. They charged fees to the insured according to the work involved, whereas today the broker is remunerated by a commission (brokerage) received from the underwriter, although the broker's method of remuneration is currently changing again. This is discussed fully in Chapter 10.

Intermediaries include individuals, partnerships or companies who trade as insurance brokers, and building societies, banks, estate agents, solicitors and accountants. Since the Insurance Brokers (Registration) Act 1977 (IBRA) has placed statutory limitations on the expressions 'insurance broker', 'assurance broker', 'reinsurance broker' and 'reassurance broker', many intermediaries refer to themselves as insurance consultants or agents, or use other terms which enable them to avoid registration under the IBRA. Many of these are now, however, subject to the financial services legislation.

In the same way as insurers may either specialise or deal in a variety of risks, so intermediaries may act for only one class of business, such as life assurance or marine, or for many. There are also intermediaries who specialise in direct or reinsurance business, and who operate internationally or nationally from single offices, in London or other towns and cities, or from a network of offices abroad or in the United Kingdom.

The main types of intermediary currently operating in the United Kingdom are insurance brokers, Lloyd's brokers who operate at Lloyd's, insurance agents and collecting representatives. These are discussed briefly in the following paragraphs, but a detailed treatment of the types and role of insurance brokers is given in Chapter 2.

Insurance brokers

An insurance broker is a person or firm who brings buyers and sellers of insurance or reinsurance together with a view to their entering an insurance or reinsurance contract. Insurance brokers act independently of insurers and have freedom of choice within the market on where to place business, subject to limitations set by the insured. They act as agents for the insured. Since December 1981, only those who have registered with the Insurance Brokers Registration Council (IBRC), a body established under the IBRA, may legally describe themselves as 'insurance brokers'. However, the IBRA does not contain a definition of an insurance broker. Those who advised Parliament in drafting the Act accepted the definition of brokers set out in Article 2(1)(a) of the EC Directive on insurance agents and brokers of 13 December 1976. This describes 'brokers' as:

> 'persons who, acting with complete freedom as to their choice of undertaking, bring together, with a view to the insurance or reinsurance of risks, persons seeking insurance or reinsurance and insurance and reinsurance undertakings, carry out work preparatory to the conclusion of contracts of insurance or reinsurance and, where appropriate, assist in the administration and performance of such contracts, in particular in the event of a claim'.

Lloyd's broking companies are a particular type of insurance broker who, in addition to placing business in the company market, can place business at Lloyd's. Indeed, staff from the broker are the only people who can enter the Room to place business. In order to act as a Lloyd's broker, the company must satisfy the Council of Lloyd's as to its staff's expertise, integrity and financial standing.

There is also a significant class of intermediary which has the independence of a broker but is not registered under the IBRA. This is the independent non-broker intermediary who acts between the various other bodies in the market.

Insurance agents

Insurance agents are appointed by the insurer and act only for those organisations which have appointed them. They are basically insurance salesmen operating primarily in those sections of the non-marine markets where the sums insured and premiums are smaller and therefore of less interest to brokers. Since there is less need to spread risks between insurers, the broker's role is less important. Agents are remunerated by means of a commission which is paid every time a policy is renewed, and which therefore acts as an incentive to ensure renewal.

People such as solicitors, estate agents, garage proprietors and accountants, although not directly connected with insurance, are well placed to identify clients who might require insurance cover and introduce them to the insurance company for which they act as agents. The EC Directive on insurance agents and brokers defines 'agents' as follows:

> 'persons instructed under one or more contracts or empowered to act in the name and on behalf of, or solely on behalf of, one or more insurance undertakings in introducing, proposing and carrying out work preparatory to the conclusion of, or in concluding, contracts of insurance, or in assistance in the administration and performance of such contracts, in particular in the event of a claim'.

This is similar to the definition of insurance brokers given under the previous heading, but brokers act with complete freedom as to their choice of insurer, whereas the agent is restricted to dealing with those insurers with which he has a contract.

Home service collecting representatives are also agents in strict legal terms. They are employees of insurance companies who visit the homes of their policyholders to collect the weekly premiums and attempt to sell additional policies. They are normally paid a basic salary plus overriding commission.

16

Chapter 2 – The broker's world

2.1 Introduction

The difference between a broker and other agents has been set out in
1.4.3. However, brokers themselves conduct their business in a variety of
ways. Figure 2.1 illustrates some of the fundamental differences between
brokers. Brokers may perform one, two or all three of these roles,
although most specialise in one.

Whatever the broker's position on the graph, carrying out his role will
involve matching the requirements of his client to the market by negotiating a 'best fit' relationship with an underwriter. This requires the
broker to have a clear understanding of the business which is being
placed so that he can advise the insured in the light of his knowledge
of the insurance market and present the risk properly to the insurer. Part
of the broker's function is to explain the advantages and disadvantages of
the policy wording to the insured and to negotiate the terms, including
the premium rating.

In the event of a claim arising under a policy, the broker will probably be
involved in arranging settlement. A Lloyd's broker handling a risk at

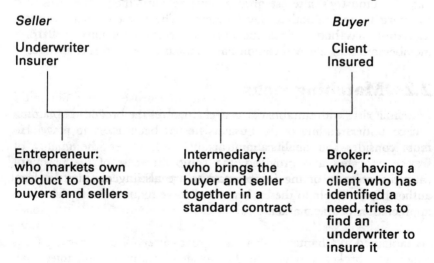

Figure 2.1   Different types of broker

Lloyd's is responsible for claims handling. These matters are dealt with in more detail in subsequent paragraphs.

Brokers adopt a structure best suited to the role they have identified for themselves. Some are sole traders, others are partnerships or private or public limited companies. They may be based regionally, in London or internationally. They may deal primarily with composite insurance companies or specialist insurers, such as Lloyd's syndicates, with London-based international or overseas companies, or with other types of insurance agents, such as pools. The type of business placed will also vary – direct, reinsurance, domestic, corporate, personal financial planning, including life assurance and pensions, are examples. These aspects of the insurance broking industry are considered later in this chapter.

The size of a broker and the nature of his business will determine the appropriate organisation. The smallest direct broker or personal financial planning consultant requires little more than an office and a secretary. Large international brokers will have specialist sections or subsidiaries by type of business and geographical location. Sections will then be split by function between the producers of business, brokers, technicians, claims brokers, administration and finance.

Brokers and other insurance intermediaries have also formed trade associations, both to protect their interests and to provide mutual support. The first association was established in 1906, and the most recent is the British Insurance and Investment Brokers' Association (BIIBA). Since the environment in which the intermediary operates is constantly evolving, the industry's interest groups have to vary their objectives and structure to accommodate developments. The latest financial services legislation has had a dramatic effect on certain sections of BIIBA's membership and the Association has adapted to meet this challenge.

2.2 Matching risks

Matching risks with suitable risk bearers involves the broker in obtaining a clear understanding of the business he has been asked to place. He must consider the qualifications of the underwriter, the quality of service expected and provided, the competitiveness of the premium rate, the security of the insurer and the possibility of using binding authorities available to the broker. All of these require a comprehensive appreciation of the market.

As explained in Chapter 1, there is a great variety of underwriters from which the broker can choose. Composite insurance companies may provide a full service, writing almost any risk presented to them, but there are insurers who are recognised as specialists in particular areas. The freedom shown by an insurer in setting the terms and conditions which apply to its policies, or the way in which standard policy wordings are interpreted, will influence brokers. If a client has unusual insurance requirements, the broker might wish to approach an insurer who is prepared to be innovative.

Reinsurance arrangements will generally be made with specialist reinsurers – companies, pools consisting of a number of underwriters or Lloyd's syndicates.

The broker will advise his client on the best way to present the risk. He will analyse the business, perhaps drawing on the expertise of specialist brokers or obtaining surveys or other expert information. The more entrepreneurial broker will design policies for his client or identify a new niche in the market for which he will create a policy. He then has to sell to both insureds and insurers. An example is insurance against liabilities arising under the five-year guarantee on white goods which is now freely available.

Assessing the quality of the service provided by insurers will include examining the speed with which insurers give quotations and handle claims, their standard of documentation and their general efficiency in dealing with transactions. Geographical factors may also be relevant where the client has overseas connections or the adequate servicing of a risk requires specialist local knowledge.

As in all business, price is important and the broker will seek a premium which is competitive compared with the rest of the market. This may involve seeking a number of quotations and balancing the level of premiums against the terms and extent of the insurance cover pro-vided. This balance will vary according to the type of insurance being sought. For example, with private motor business and other small risks placed in a strongly competitive market, a low premium can be obtained. Larger or more unusual risks will be insured by a specialist underwriter who can provide cover to suit the client's requirements but who may also require a significant premium. Negotiations to obtain the most generous terms will take into consideration factors such as the client's history of claims, steps taken to reduce risks, excess limits and the amount of business placed by the client with the insurer. In all types of insurance, any reduction in price must be compared with any consequent loss in cover. The broker has a duty to protect his client's interest.

Most private insurances have high handling costs and earn small amounts of brokerage per policy, and on the face of it appear unattractive

19

to brokers. Such business may therefore be subject to a handling charge payable by the client in addition to the commission paid by the insurer. Where the broker raises a handling charge he must inform the client.

Although the type of cover, service provided and premium rates charged by insurers are important, it is essential that the broker is satisfied that, in the event of a client having to make a claim, the insurer has the resources to settle it. There are strict requirements imposed by the Government aimed at ensuring the solvency of UK insurance companies and Lloyd's syndicates. European legislation is changing the regulatory framework for branches of EU insurers located other than in the company's home country. Nevertheless, rising claims pose an increasing threat to the security of insurance companies. Regulation is not so effective in some foreign countries or in relation to insurance pools.

Large broking houses will often have a security committee responsible for vetting all underwriters with whom they deal. The membership of this committee and its operation are described in Chapter 7. Its decisions will be based on market intelligence, discussions with other brokers and reviews of published information and intelligence reports. Where such controls exist, it is important for the broker to ensure that they cannot be countermanded, resulting in bad debts and dissatisfied customers.

Legal opinion also has an impact on security. The cases of *Bedford Insurance Co. Ltd* v *IRB* (1985), *Stewart* v *Oriental Fire and Marine Insurance Co. Ltd* (1985) and *Phoenix General Insurance Co. of Greece* v *ADAS* (1986) are all concerned with the legality and enforceability of insurance contracts where the insurer is not properly authorised under United Kingdom regulations to act as an underwriter. Brokers should satisfy themselves expressly that the insurers or reinsurers with whom they are placing business are authorised. If they do not, they may have failed in their duty of reasonable skill and care to their clients. This is a significant new area of risk affecting the selection of insurers and may prove especially difficult in a foreign country where the broker is unfamiliar with the law. Use of a local broker may be valuable.

The IBRC and Lloyd's monitor a broker's spread of business over a number of insurers to identify undue reliance on any one underwriter. They therefore need to have an effective procedure for assessing the security of a large number of insurers.

A broker may have an authority (a binding authority or cover) given by an underwriter to grant cover on the underwriter's behalf within agreed limits. Such authorities are used more in the non-marine and aviation markets than the marine, but they are common in both the Lloyd's and insurance company markets. Regulations at Lloyd's control business written under binding authorities.

Because the authority legally binds the insurer, it is usually only given to brokers with whom the underwriter has a well-established relationship and who are trustworthy. The broker is given guidelines and limits as to what business he may accept on behalf of the insurer. With motor insurance, for example, the broker might not be given the authority to insure drivers aged under 25. The extent of the broker's authority may be expressed or implied. Where the broker issues cover notes under a binding authority he must inform the insurer of a risk written within an agreed time period. The insurer has a responsibility for ensuring the authority is being used in accordance with its terms. Brokers may in certain instances, especially motor insurance, issue cover notes on behalf of the insurer but without being subject to a binding authority.

A binding authority is valuable to a broker, as it can speed up the matching process. It may, however, mean that the client's business is not always placed with the most competitive insurer. Since the broker is acting as agent for the insured in placing the business through the binding authority, and as agent for the insurer in accepting it, he must be careful of conflicts of interest. The broker should be satisfied that the insured knows that the business is being placed on a binding authority.

2.3 Placing risks

Having established a good match, a broker does not normally place an insurance with the insurer until the client has accepted a quotation. Provisional insurance cover may be obtained pending an insurer's survey or where established clients require immediate additional cover. The broker has a responsibility to inform his client when insurance cover has been effected, advising him of the principal details of the cover and the date from which the insurer accepted the risk.

While most private insurance is placed with a single insurer, much insurance business is written using 'slips'. The slip is a document containing particulars of the risk to be placed. The broker will take the slip to an underwriter, who signifies his acceptance by initialling the slip, indicating the share of the risk he will take (his 'line'). The broker then takes the slip to other underwriters who also take a share, until ultimately the whole risk is written. As discussed in Chapters 8 and 11, computers are increasingly used to facilitate this process. By using the slips, a complex, large or unusual risk can be spread over a number of insurers, and any losses are shared between them in proportion to the line they have written.

The slip may be spread among all types of underwriter – at Lloyd's, companies or insurance pools. The broker's skill involves identifying the lead underwriter. The 'lead' is so described by virtue of being the first to initial the slip, even though subsequent underwriters may subscribe for larger proportions of the risk.

The lead underwriter will set the terms of the contract, especially the premium. If subsequent underwriters will not complete his slip on those terms, the broker has to advise the lead of changes. However, many following underwriters will decide how much, if any, of the risk they will accept on the basis of their confidence in the lead. If a claim arises under the policy, the lead is often the only underwriter to see the details and to determine whether or not the claim is valid and should be settled. He will initiate on behalf of all the underwriters on the slip any necessary investigations or the appointment of specialist assessors. There is, however, no legal requirement for other underwriters to follow the lead's decision, although such action is unusual.

It is possible for a broker to get more than 100 per cent of a risk underwritten on a slip, if insurers are enthusiastic to be involved. In this case, the broker has to scale down the lines of each underwriter proportionately to the oversubscription. However, once an underwriter has initialled the slip, he has entered into a binding contract of insurance. There are no circumstances in which the line an insurer has written can be increased without his consent.

When an insurance cover comes up for renewal, the broker will generally approach the same lead underwriter to start the slip.

If a broker is completing a slip or not selling a standard insurance policy, he will be responsible for ensuring the policy is prepared. This is particularly so at Lloyd's. It is therefore important for the broker to understand the law of insurance in order to ensure that the various parties have a secure contract conforming to their expectations.

2.4 Claims

As a matter of market practice, the broker's duties extend beyond placing the insurance. In the event of a claim arising under the policy, the broker might advise the client and act on his behalf in dealing with the insurer.

Although there is doubt as to whether the broker has a legal duty to assist in servicing claims, with insurances placed at Lloyd's there is no alternative. The client, under Lloyd's rules, does not generally have direct access to the underwriter, or the market accounting, claims processing or policy clearance houses. The broker has to deal with the claim on the insured's behalf. If a Lloyd's broker either:

(a) processes claims very poorly and thereby seriously affects his clients and prejudices the name of Lloyd's; or
(b) refuses to process claims on behalf of clients

the regulatory authorities at Lloyd's would investigate. Suspension might follow, or Lloyd's might require corrective action to be taken by the broker.

With certain types of insurance, in particular motor policies, the broker will state what the claims procedure is when the policy is taken out. In many cases, the client will be advised to pursue any claims with the insurer direct. In instances where the claims procedure is not discussed at inception, the broker's role will depend upon any terms of the insurance agreement, either written or implied, or his previous conduct in the event of claims. Because the broker has been instrumental in negotiating the insurance contract, it may be argued that he should ensure that the terms of the contract are fulfilled.

Where the broker has responsibility for claims handling, his first step on notification of a claim will be to check that the circumstances giving rise to the claim are covered by the insurance policy and that the premium has been paid. He should notify the insurer immediately of the claim. The insured will generally complete a claim form, with which the broker may assist.

The procedures which are involved in processing a claim will vary according to the size and nature of the claim. Accounting policies are dealt with in Chapter 10.

In the Lloyd's market and among other specialist insurers, claims offices have been established. The offices are not responsible for agreeing terms of settlement – the underwriters themselves must agree these. However, the offices are responsible for progressing claims settlement and may have delegated authority to agree detailed terms. Lloyd's has established the Lloyd's Claims Office (LCO), which has taken over the responsibilities of the offices which formerly specialised in particular markets – Lloyd's Underwriters Claims and Recoveries Office (LUCRO) in the marine market, Lloyd's Underwriters Non-marine Claims Office (LUNCO) and Lloyd's Aviation Claims Centre (LACC).

The broker should keep in touch with the progress of claims and if necessary provide assistance. This may include:

(a) advising the client on the completion of relevant forms and on any special documentation which may be required, such as medical certificates, engineers' reports, estimates;

(b) instructing the client where action is necessary, such as informing the police in the event of theft or motor accident;

(c) in the event of a motor accident where a third party appears to be responsible, recovering uninsured losses;

(d) in the event of large losses on insured property, liaising with the loss adjuster;

(e) dealing with solicitors and surveyors or other appropriate specialists; and

(f) arranging settlement, collecting cash and paying the insured expeditiously.

Risk management or administration is becoming important for large or complex risks. This will often be provided by the broker and include claims servicing, loss funding, inspection services and industrial testimony.

In some instances, especially where risk management is involved, the broker will charge a claims handling fee. This will be payable by the client, who must be told about and agree to the amount at the outset of the claim being dealt with.

The qualities that a broker must have are therefore objectivity, imagination and technical ability. He must use these skills within the market and legal environment in which he operates.

2.5 Brokers and the law of agency

The law which primarily governs the relationship between insured, broker and insurer is that of agency. An agent is a person employed for the purpose of bringing his principal into a contractual relationship with a third party. He does not make contracts on his own behalf. The legal doctrine which applies is 'qui facit per alium facit per se' (he who does something through another does it himself).

It is in the matter of agency that the distinction between types of insurance intermediaries – brokers and 'agents' – again becomes relevant. For the purpose of this subsection on agency, the word 'agent' will be used when referring to that type of insurance intermediary.

The broker is an agent employed to buy or sell on behalf of another. He is not liable to his principal for the failure of the buyer to pay the price. However, in performing his role, he owes a duty of care to his principal. The level of care expected will vary; a higher level of care will be expected from a professional broker than from a part-time insurance agent.

It is sometimes a matter of uncertainty whether an insurance intermediary is agent for the insurer or the insured. In general, a broker is the agent of the insured with the aim of finding suitable insurance cover, whereas an insurance agent is the agent of the insurer with the responsibility of finding a client to purchase insurance. In both cases, however, the intermediary receives his income from the insurer.

The intermediary's legal status is often confused during the course of an insurance transaction, since he may become the agent for both his client and the insurer. For example, where a broker has a binding authority, he is his client's agent in effecting the insurance, but when he issues a cover note under the binding authority, he is the insurer's agent. This could give rise to an unacceptable conflict of interest and all parties should be made aware of the nature of this conflict.

Duties of an agent are to:

(a)   exercise diligence in the performance of his duties and display any special skill he professes to have; and
(b)   render an account when required;

but not to:

(c)   become a principal as against his employer;
(d)   make a profit behind the commission or other remuneration paid by the principal;
(e)   delegate authority; or
(f)   disclose confidential information or documents entrusted to him by the principal.

The broker's status as agent of the insurer was illustrated in *Stockton* v *Mason* (1978) when a motor policyholder's wife telephoned their broker to inform them of a change in cars under the insurance. She was told '. . .that will be all right. We will see to that'. A number of days later a letter was received from the broker saying that the insurance company would only cover the new car if the insured was driving it. However, between the dates of the telephone call and receiving the letter, the policyholder's son had had an accident in the new car, injuring a third party. In the Court of Appeal it was held the third party claim should be paid by the insurance company. The brokers had given the impression that cover was granted, not that they would merely seek to arrange it, and the Court found that there was implied authority given to the broker by the insurer to provide cover notes, i.e. insurance for a temporary period.

25

This decision is not considered satisfactory because of the reasoning. The broker does not start as agent of the insurer and therefore he cannot have implied authority. No doubt the law will be clarified in due course.

Another example might arise where a proposal form is prepared by the broker. In this instance, he is not the agent of the insurer although he is paid commission for business introduced. Such business is, however, accepted or rejected by the insurer and there the broker is acting as agent for the proposer in this instance. Erroneous answers signed by the proposer without reading or checking the form may result in the policy being voidable at the insurer's discretion.

Thus in the event of a dispute, the court will look at the function the intermediary was performing in deciding whether he was acting as the agent for the insured or the insurer at the time.

The agency relationships may appear more confused at Lloyd's. The underwriter looks to the Lloyd's broker, not the insured, for payment of the premium. Where business is written under the Marine Insurance Act 1906, any insurer is entitled to act similarly. As already explained, claims on policies placed at Lloyd's are handled by the broker for most classes of business. The broker negotiates on behalf of his client with the underwriter. He may be involved in negotiating with loss or average adjusters, or other assessing specialists appointed by the underwriter. Since the broker is agent for the insured and must disclose all material facts to his principal, assessors' reports should be sent direct to the underwriter and not via the broker.

2.6 Errors and omission

Brokers registered under the IBRC or at Lloyd's have to meet minimum requirements for professional indemnity, or errors and omissions insurance cover. These requirements are discussed in Chapters 3 and 4. This cover is required because of the legal position in which the intermediary finds himself.

Most claims under this insurance arise where insureds fail to collect a perceived valid claim under a policy broked by an intermediary. The problems often arise because the broker has inadequate systems of management control and management supervision. The specific weaknesses are discussed in **3.3.1**.

Third parties may find grounds for errors and omissions claims where brokers have a conflict of interest in any business in which they are involved. Lloyd's has formalised this by divestment – the separation of brokers from underwriters. Managing agents who employ the under-writers of Lloyd's syndicates may not be owned by a Lloyd's insurance broker, nor be part of the same group as a broker. There are, however, many brokers both in the UK and elsewhere which have an interest in a corporate insurer, including corporate vehicles at Lloyd's. Brokers in this situation must be aware of conflicts of interest.

Brokers must also, as has been discussed, ensure that policy wording is sufficiently precise, the security of insurers is sound, and management procedures in the broking house are at their most efficient.

2.7 Corporate structure

All insurance brokers operating in the UK are subject to regulation by the IBRC. In addition, brokers doing business within the Lloyd's insur-ance market have to be registered by the Council of Lloyd's. The detailed regulatory environment for brokers is set out in Part II. These regulatory authorities place requirements on the capital structure of an insurance broker which are a prerequisite of registration and thus business. In May 1994, for example, out of 15,000 individuals registered as insurance brokers, 2,100 were carrying on business on their own account as sole traders or partnerships operating through 1,270 insur-ance broking businesses. Many of these were provincial, or 'high street', brokers. Generally, however, the larger brokers have taken the advantage of limited liability and 2,605 corporate bodies are registered by the IBRC. Most of the remaining registered individuals will work for these companies.

Just as the legal structure of insurance brokers varies, so too does the size of insurance broking firms, which range from the sole trader to large international companies and groups employing more than 3,000 mem-bers of staff. Few brokers attempt to provide a full range of services across all markets, although some of the major groups have a wide diversity of expertise.

The broking organisations may conveniently be classified as inter-national, national, London or small high street. The management structure of such businesses is considered in Chapters 6 and 7, but some of their features are described in the following paragraphs.

The international category includes the largest listed insurance broking groups of companies with world-wide representation and operations. The business of such a group may include not only insurance and reinsurance broking and claims handling in all classes of business, but also underwriting agencies, insurance companies and other companies whose activities may not be directly related to insurance, such as estate agency, tourist agency and employee benefits. There is a heavy concentration of these organisations towards only two countries – the USA and the UK.

The attraction of this size of broker is that it can handle all aspects of insurance for large, particularly international, commercial enterprises. It gives comprehensive advice on risk management and self-insurance, as well as placing world-wide risks and giving geographical cover. However, competition is intense and most international brokers have secure bases on both sides of the Atlantic.

Generally, the large groups are structured so that subsidiary and associated companies are best able to deal with the broking activities on a geographical, class of insurance and industry basis. Other subsidiaries will provide services for the rest of the group, such as personnel functions or treasury management. Separate subsidiaries will enable the group to maintain specialisation in different areas. It is also an aid to the delegation of authority, organising work and establishing accountability for performance.

Since broking is very much a matter of trust, an individual broker will build up close business relationships with underwriters and clients. It is very common for a team of brokers (the producing and renewal brokers and their technical support) to be poached by a competing broking organisation. They will take with them their expertise and their market contacts, attracting business from their previous employers. One way in which companies try to retain loyalty is to establish incentive companies, profit-sharing schemes and share options.

Most of the international groups have a Lloyd's broker as a subsidiary. This enables any other company in the group to channel business through that broker into Lloyd's. Such access is essential if the organisation is to service its clients efficiently, because of the nature of risks that Lloyd's underwriters are prepared to accept.

However diverse the group, top management must ensure that the objectives of the individual companies are consistent with the objectives of the group as a whole.

National or London brokers generally confine their activity to dealing with risks originating or being insured in the UK. The larger national brokers will be organised in a similar group structure to international insurance brokers. Some national brokers, such as those associated with the motoring organisations or the clearing banks, will have a wide geographical spread of offices competing with locally-based high street or provincial brokers. They will handle personal and commercial business, such as household, motor, employers' liability and so on.

London brokers are often specialists in a particular market – for example, American medical malpractice reinsurance or excess of loss reinsurance. In this case, the broker will join a niche market, and often attract and hold business as a result of his personal charisma.

The vast majority of insurance brokers in the UK are relatively small, provincial, high street brokers. The steps taken by large firms in organising their business are equally relevant to smaller brokers. Objectives need to be determined from which sub-goals and plans can be deduced. The firm needs to be organised with a chain of authority, responsibility and accountability.

Such brokers deal primarily with the general public, often with casual, off-the-street enquiries. Their business is usually placed with the major composite insurance companies. Often they will handle general and life and pensions business. The latter constitutes some 20 per cent of smaller brokers' business and may lead to investment advice through unit-linked policies. Many such brokers are therefore subject to the financial services legislation, along with some of their larger colleagues. This is considered in Part II. The general business of smaller brokers is mainly in motor (30 per cent of total business), general non-marine (40 per cent) and marine and reinsurance (10 per cent).

2.8 Types of insurance broker

Brokers have been classified in this chapter in terms of their structure; they may also be categorised according to the type of insurance they arrange. Generally, the size of the broker is not a determining factor.

Typically, smaller brokers sell direct to the public, often from high street premises. They are 'retail' brokers, who then may place their business on the insurance market through specialist wholesale brokers.

Most insurance brokers deal only with direct business such as motor, life and pensions, general property and household business. Their clients have little knowledge or understanding of the insurance market and will be guided by their broker. Often, these brokers have no experience or need of expertise in more complex types of business. Many of them are dealing with 'certificate' business for large composite insurance companies.

Reinsurance is the business of insuring the insurer. Brokers who arrange reinsurance tend to specialise in this business. They are invariably based in London and operate in both UK and international markets. Reinsurance brokers are often independent subsidiaries in a larger insurance broking group.

Reinsurance broking differs from direct insurance broking, since both the broker's client, the cedant and the reinsurer are experts in insurance. Consequently, insurers often place their reinsurance with brokers in the hope that some reciprocal business will follow.

The international scope of reinsurance is important to the world-wide insurance market in that risks can be ceded to and received from most parts of the world. In some parts of the world, the reinsurance broker's role might be extended if there is no locally qualified representative of the insurer. In such cases the reinsurance broker could be appointed as underwriting agent if he has local connections. Such a broker would have extensive authority to underwrite reinsurances and settle claims, sometimes without prior reference to his principals in the UK.

In recent years, particularly since the 1975 Pensions Act and the introduction of greater flexibility for personal pensions plans, there has been a rapid growth in the market for life assurance, pensions and personal financial planning. There are a number of insurance brokers and companies which operate only in this market. It is a highly specialised market, and brokers are in competition with other professional advisers, such as accountants and solicitors, and direct mail shots from life assurance and unit trust companies. Such business is attractive because, once the policy has been established, there are few costs associated with its ongoing management or with claims when they arise.

This particular market has led into portfolio management and self-administered pension schemes, and this too links with stockbrokers and actuaries. In the current political climate it will become even more significant to the insurance broking industry.

2.9 Trade associations

The first association representing the interests of insurance brokers was established in 1906 by a group of leading brokers seeking to prevent unfair competition and to establish brokers and agents as a more widely recognised class. This association became the Corporation of Insurance Brokers and Agents in 1910, when it received its certificate of incorporation from the Board of Trade.

Although initially membership was on the basis of practical experience, membership later came to depend upon success in examinations set by the Corporation. After several years the Corporation of Insurance Agents was established as a separate section.

Two other representative bodies were subsequently formed – the Association of Insurance Brokers in 1948 and the Federation of Insurance Brokers in 1966. The Corporation, Association and Federation had similar objectives, their main difference being in respect of membership requirements. In 1976 these three broking bodies, together with Lloyd's Insurance Brokers' Association, formed the British Insurance Brokers' Council (BIBC) in order to present a united front in making representations to the Government, which was drafting legislation which resulted in the IBRA.

The BIBC was disbanded in 1977, as were the four broking bodies. In their place, the British Insurance Brokers' Association (BIBA) was formed in January 1978. BIBA is not a statutory body and membership is voluntary. However, by 1983 nearly 83 per cent of insurance broking firms had become members. The increasing importance of life assurance, pensions and investment advice has resulted in a further change of name, and on 1 January 1988 the Association became the British Insurance and Investment Brokers' Association (BIIBA).

Until that time, the main requirement for membership of BIBA was registration under the IBRA. Now insurance brokers have to meet high standards of qualification, experience and conduct before being accepted by BIIBA.

BIIBA, apart from seeking to protect its members' interests, also undertakes commercial and promotional support including advertising, consumer leaflets, seminars and the provision of information to the public. Its committee structure reflects the areas where it assists its members.

The Corporation of Insurance and Financial Advisers (formerly the Corporation of Mortgage Brokers and Life Assurance Consultants) was formed in 1968. Its membership is open to individuals or companies carrying on the bona fide business of insurance and mortgage broking, life assurance and tax planning, pensions, investments and general financial advice, or such associated professions where these activities represent a substantial part of the business. The Corporation provides members with political contacts, professional interchange, information on sources of mortgage finance, client references and advertising opportunities.

The Life Insurance Association was formed in 1972. Its members must be individuals actively involved in the full-time selling of life insurance, and they include many registered brokers.

PART II

Regulation

Chapter 3 – Regulation and the Insurance Brokers (Registration) Act

3.1 Introduction

For many years the insurance broker has been subject to regulation – imposed by either Government or the insurance industry. It continues to be a matter of debate whether the current proliferation of regulatory bodies meets the requirements of the insurers or the insured, whether professionals in the market or the general public. Regulation has so far been on a national basis although the influence of the European Union is already being seen in the United Kingdom's legislative framework.

The Government has intervened when it has considered intervention to be in the interests of the insurance market and more especially the public at large. The earliest instance of such intervention came in 1575 with the establishment of the Chamber of Assurances, where marine policies were required to be registered.

It has always been in the insurance industry's interests to supervise the activities of its own members and modern regulation has generally come from within. The aim has been to limit the amount of interference from outside and to promote a professional attitude within the market, thus increasing public confidence in the services offered. Self-supervision developed from the trade associations, which were formed to protect the interest of their members.

In this Part, the development of regulation from the Insurance Brokers (Registration) Act 1977 (this chapter), through to the Financial Services Act 1986 (Chapter 5) and the byelaws governing the operation of Lloyd's brokers promulgated in 1988 (Chapter 4), will be explored. However, it is not the purpose of this book to provide a detailed analysis of the legislation or the bodies responsible for monitoring its application. Reference should be made to the Acts and byelaws themselves, and the rules of the appropriate bodies.

Under the financial services legislation, the rules of the Personal Investment Authority (PIA) and their impact on auditors are examined. Some larger London market insurance brokers will find it more appropriate to be members of the Investment Managers Regulatory Organisation (IMRO). Others may not have sufficient 'investment' business to justify registration with a supervisory regulatory organisation. In this connection, the guidance given on the Insurance Brokers Registration Council (IBRC) includes its role as a recognised professional body. While some background to the legislation is provided, the main purpose of Chapters 3 to 5 is to help accountants and auditors identify those aspects which affect them.

3.2 Insurance Brokers (Registration) Act 1977

The most significant piece of legislation aimed specifically at insurance intermediaries is the Insurance Brokers (Registration) Act 1977 (IBRA). Before the implementation of the IBRA in December 1981, any individual or firm could set up in business without experience in the insurance industry. People were free to describe themselves as insurance brokers, or to use any other title implying that they were in a position to advise members of the public on insurance matters.

Those established and reputable brokers who had a proper knowledge and understanding of the insurance markets were keen to promote the standing and conduct of those who called themselves insurance brokers, aware of the damage being done to their profession's reputation by unqualified 'advisers'. For this reason the four insurance broking representative bodies described in Chapter 2 were willing to co-operate with the Secretary of State for Trade when he approached them in May 1975.

The four bodies were asked to formulate proposals for a self-regulatory body, which could establish and enforce standards and control admission. They were also asked to draft a code of conduct to be met by insurance brokers. In addition to restricting the operations of unsuitable insurance brokers, the Government needed to legislate in order to bring British law in line with other European countries as part of the EC 'harmonisation' process.

The broking organisations established the BIBC, which was the forerunner of the BIBA, now known as the BIIBA. In August 1976 the BIBC sent a report to the Department of Trade entitled 'Consultative Document on the Regulation of Insurance Brokers'. On the basis of this report a Private Member's Bill was laid before Parliament and the IBRA was passed on 29 July 1977. It describes itself as 'An Act to provide for the registration of insurance brokers and for the regulation of their professional standards; and for purposes connected therewith'.

3.3   Insurance Brokers Registration Council

Section 1 of the Act established the Insurance Brokers Registration Council (IBRC) 'which shall be a body corporate with perpetual succession and a common seal and shall have the general function of carrying out the powers and duties conferred on them by this Act'. The schedule to the IBRA deals with the constitution, powers and functions of the IBRC.

The Council comprises both insurance brokers and other professionals. The brokers are elected by the registered brokers and the other members are nominated by the Secretary of State for Trade. The Council has the power to take almost any action which, in its opinion, is calculated to facilitate the proper discharge of its functions. It also has some specific administrative functions.

The Council's main function is to maintain a register of persons who satisfy the requirements of character, suitability, insurance broking experience and approved qualifications.

In addition to the register of individual insurance brokers, the IBRA requires that the Council establish and maintain a list of bodies corporate operating as insurance brokers. In order to enrol in this list the body corporate must satisfy the IBRC:

(a)   that a majority of its directors are registered insurance brokers; or
(b)   in the case of a body corporate having only one director, that he is a registered insurance broker; or
(c)   in the case of a body corporate having only two directors, that one of them is a registered insurance broker and that the business is carried on under the management of that director.

There are rights of appeal.

Once applicants have been successful and become registered, they must take steps to maintain their status as insurance brokers. Registration of individuals is renewable each 1 January and listing of companies is renewable each 1 May.

3.3.1   IBRC Rules

The IBRC has used its rule-making powers to produce a number of sets of rules which are the subject of statutory instruments. The most important are dealt with below.

The IBRC (Registration and Enrolment) Rules 1978 (SI 1978 No. 1395) set out the initial and annual registration or enrolment fees for individuals, partnerships and companies. The fees have since been increased.

The IBRC (Code of Conduct) Approval Order 1978 (SI 1978 No. 1394) provides a guide to the professional conduct of insurance brokers. There are three principles set out in this code which are fundamental to the maintenance of the required professional standards:

(a) Insurance brokers must at all times conduct their business with utmost good faith and integrity.
(b) Insurance brokers must do everything possible to satisfy the insurance requirements of their clients and place the interests of those clients before all other considerations. Subject to these requirements and interests, insurance brokers should have proper regard for others.
(c) Statements made by, or on behalf of, insurance brokers when advertising must not be misleading or extravagant.

The IBRC (Accounts and Business Requirements Rules) Approval Order 1979 (SI 1979 No. 489) covers requirements for carrying on business necessary to retain registration or a listing. These include a minimum working capital requirement that the aggregate of current assets less the aggregate of current liabilities must be at least £1,000 at all times. These requirements are considered more fully under the headings Accounts Rules and Audit and solvency returns on pages 39 and 40.

The IBRC is currently undertaking consultation on various changes proposed to these Rules. It is anticipated that these will require the IBA to have full trust status but the date of implementation is not yet determined. As a result of these anticipated changes the IBRC has declined to give permission for forms to be reproduced in this book. Copies of current returns may be obtained from the IBRC at 15 St Helen's Place, London, EC3A 6DS.

The IBRC (Indemnity Insurance and Grants Scheme) Rules Approval Order 1987 (SI 1987 No. 1496) replaces an earlier order of 1979 and requires brokers to maintain professional indemnity (errors and omissions, or E & O insurance). The Council has also set up a grants scheme to which all registered brokers pay a levy if called upon to do so. Grants may be made in connection with anyone who has suffered loss arising from the negligence, fraud or dishonesty of an insurance broker in connection with a UK direct insurance policy. More details of E & O insurance will be found later in this chapter.

The requirements of the IBRC (Conduct of Investment Business) Rules Approval Order 1988 (SI 1988 No. 950) are discussed later in this chapter. They allow registered brokers to carry out investment business regulated by the Financial Services Act, under certain circumstances.

The IBRC can consider cases against brokers through its investigating and disciplinary committees and the latter can erase a name from the register pursuant to such disciplinary proceedings.

The IBRA limits the use of the terms 'insurance', 'reinsurance', 'assurance' and 'reassurance' when used to describe a 'broker' (as in 'insurance broker') as a trading title or description to those registered in accordance with the Act.

Accounts Rules

On application for or renewal of registration, audited accounts must be supplied to the IBRC including a balance sheet, a profit and loss account and the auditors' report. The profit and loss account must:

(a) show the total revenue of the business, dividing such revenue between that directly derived from insurance broking business and all other revenue;
(b) classify expenditure grouped under appropriate headings; and
(c) show or disclose by way of a note the total brokerage contained in the account.

If the revenue in (a) above includes non-insurance broking income, the nature of each business giving rise to such income should be disclosed.

Brokers also have to complete a questionnaire intended to reveal any undue dependence on a particular insurance company. Where an insurance broker, in its last accounting period, placed insurance with fewer than ten companies, or if more than 35 per cent of brokerage results from insurance placed with a single company, it must explain to the IBRC why it is not unduly dependent on any of those insurers with whom business has been placed.

A broker's accounting records must show and explain the transactions of the business and they must be sufficient to disclose at any time, with reasonable accuracy, the financial position at that time. Any accounts prepared should be capable of giving a true and fair view of the state of affairs of the business and of its profit or loss for the period.

In particular, the accounting records must contain entries from day to day of all sums of money received and expended in the course of the business, the matters in respect of which the receipt and expenditure take place and a record of the assets and liabilities of the business. It must be possible to demonstrate compliance with the IBRC Rules at any time and the accounting records must be preserved for at least three years from the date of the last entry made.

In addition to the minimum working capital requirement of £1,000, insurance brokers must ensure that at all times the value of the assets of the business (excluding intangible assets) exceeds the liabilities of the business (excluding long-term liabilities) by at least £1,000 ('any day' solvency).

Payments and receipts in respect of insurance transactions, including commission received, must go through approved bank accounts registered in the broker's name and specifically designated insurance broking accounts (IBAs). This requirement ensures that money due to and from clients and insurers is kept separately from other monies. The insurance broker must obtain a written acknowledgement from the bank that the insurance broking account is correctly designated, that it is being opened to comply with the IBRC Rules and that the bank is not entitled to any charge, encumbrance, lien, right of set off, compensation or retention against approved short-term money or any assets standing to the credit of the insurance broking account of the insurance broker. The only exception to this final point arises where the bank has made an advance on an insurance broking account to the same broker.

These accounting requirements impose on the broker somewhat more onerous requirements than the Companies Acts. Indeed, it is a requirement of the IBRA that all registered insurance brokers should submit accounts audited by appropriately authorised auditors. There is no distinction between sole trader, partnership or company accounts in this matter.

Audit and solvency returns

Compliance with the IBRC Accounts and Business Requirements Rules, described above, involves an annual return (form 5) to the IBRC. This 'Statement of Particulars' includes an accountant's report, which it is the responsibility of the insurance broker's auditor to complete. It includes confirmation that Rules 6 and 7 of the Accounts and Business Requirements have been complied with. These rules are reproduced in Appendix 4. Hence the scope of the audit is extended and at the planning stage this must be properly scheduled.

The return has to be submitted within six months of the date to which the broker makes up his accounts. Upon receipt by the IBRC it is passed to a firm of independent chartered accountants for review. A number of questions may arise from this examination which will be directed to the broker. He may well consult his auditors in considering his response and the auditors may be asked to confirm those responses to the IBRC.

The Statement of Particulars, or solvency return, includes a section setting out the broker's assets and liabilities. It is based on the figures given in the audited balance sheet with adjustment for the following:

(a) tangible fixed assets, which are included at the lower of net book value or net realisable value;
(b) intangible fixed assets, which are not included;
(c) insurance debtors, where debits in excess of nine months old must be separately disclosed and are included only if the broker and his auditor are satisfied as to their recoverability;
(d) current liabilities, which are those falling due within 36 months, other than insurance liabilities which must all be included as current; and
(e) contingent liabilities, which must be included as quantified after considering all the relevant facts and circumstances. This is taken to indicate that, if the contingency is unlikely to crystallise, no entry needs to be made. The following items should be specifically considered:
   (i) dilapidations under leases;
   (ii) brokerage repayable;
   (iii) contingent taxation arising from the realisation of any asset included in the statement at its realisable value ((a) above); and
   (iv) capital expenditure contracted for but not provided on intangible assets.

Before signing his report, the auditor should be satisfied that all amounts are correctly included in the statement in accordance with the Rules. In addition, he must obtain written independent confirmation from his client's bank that IBA designated accounts have been properly maintained in accordance with their status.

The broker should have established procedures for opening IBAs and acquiring IBA short-term assets. Payments made from the IBA must be monitored by a responsible official to ensure they are not for non-IBA purposes, other than the withdrawal of brokerage, fees and commission. The auditor should be satisfied that adequate controls exist and should carry out substantive tests to ensure that the controls operate properly.

These will include verifying the nature and validity of transactions passing through the IBA.

The auditor also has to be satisfied that the broker's accounting system is adequate to enable transactions to be properly monitored and matched, in accordance with the Rules. This includes 'any day' solvency, which requires a broker to have an excess of IBA assets over liabilities at all times.

Errors and omissions

Although the auditor has no obligation to report on E & O insurance, it is necessary to be satisfied with compliance in this area as part of the contingent liability and going concern reviews. Many claims against these policies arise because the original assured or reinsured fails to collect what they consider to be a valid insurance claim. A survey of the underwriters of insurance brokers' E & O indicates that a high proportion of these failures arise from inadequate management controls by brokers.

The most common circumstances giving rise to error on the part of the broker are set out below:

(a) *Contact with clients*
   - instructions not carried out
   - discussions not recorded
   - proposal completed on behalf of client
   - cover confirmed before completion
   - incorrect or insufficient advice to client regarding terms of cover
   - renewals overlooked
   - duty of disclosure

(b) *Contact with underwriter*
   - non-disclosure or deliberate ambiguities
   - obligations during policy period
   - unsatisfactory market practice

(c) *Documentation and accounting muddles*
   - placing slip ambiguities or defects
   - gaps or conflicts between layers and consecutive policies
   - cover note defects and ambiguities
   - wording defects and ambiguities
   - accounting

(d) *Fraud and dishonesty*
   - by the broker
   - by another intermediary
   - by the client

(e)   *Defective security*

(f)   *Administration of binding authorities*

(g)   *Failure to notify claims and excess layer claims*

(h)   *Sub-brokers, umbrella arrangements, joint ventures and overseas offices*
  - lack of supervision and control
  - failure to adequately resource overseas offices.

Fraud or dishonesty may arise by:

(a)   manipulating the market to maximise brokerage;
(b)   setting up bogus schemes;
(c)   deliberately withholding adverse information;
(d)   wilfully breaching warranties; or
(e)   straight 'cooking' of the figures or forgery.

3.3.2   IBRC Conduct of Investment Business Rules

As mentioned in the introduction to this chapter, the IBRC has recognised professional body status under the Financial Services Act. In compliance with the requirements of this status, the Council has approved Conduct of Investment Business Rules applying to all insurance brokers authorised to carry on investment business under its auspices.

Authorisation may be given by the IBRC to those who:

(a)   provide investment advice and/or arrange transactions only in relation to long-term insurance contracts and/or unit trust schemes; and
(b)   in the course of such business do not handle clients' money or funds; and
(c)   do not earn income from such business in excess of 25 per cent of total income.

The Rules are supplemented by, and should be read in conjunction with, certain guidance notes and compliance procedures. The principal matters are set out below.

The Council has the following requirements for compliance:

(a)   the broker must establish and maintain such procedures as will enable each employee to comply with the Rules;
(b)   these compliance procedures must generally be in writing;
(c)   although a 'small firm' (as defined below) need not record its

procedures in writing, it is strongly advised to do so and must still comply with the Rules and have the appropriate procedures in place; and

(d) the broker firm must arrange at least once a year for:

    (i) a review of its compliance procedures to ensure they are still effective;

    (ii) a review of a representative sample of client files by a registered insurance broker who is both a competent and reliable officer or employee of the firm, but has no direct responsibility for the clients selected; and

    (iii) a review of a representative sample of its relevant investment business (and that of its appointed representatives) to ensure that the Rules have been properly complied with during the period under review.

A return has to be made to the IBRC confirming compliance. For all (except small) brokers, a copy of the firm's compliance procedures must be kept at every office from which investment business is carried out and must also be made available to every officer, employee and appointed representative (a microfiche copy is acceptable).

A 'small firm' is defined as a broker where the number of persons involved in investment business does not exceed ten in total of the employees or officers of:

(a) the firm;
(b) an appointed representative;
(c) any connected firm authorised to carry on investment business; and
(d) any appointed representative of such a connected company.

The broker's accounting records must show readily that brokerage earned from providing investment advice and arranging transactions in connection with long-term insurance contracts and unit trust schemes does not exceed 25 per cent of total annual income. In the first instance it is the responsibility of the broker's compliance officer to ensure that the 25 per cent level is not breached. The Council has agreed with the Securities and Investment Board that, where firms are already authorised by the IBRC, they may continue to be so authorised if their percentage of investment income exceeds the 25 per cent threshold but does not exceed 49 per cent of their total income.

Where a firm believes that the 25 per cent threshold may be breached it must take the following actions:

(a) alert the Council if it appears that in any one year income from investment business will exceed 25 per cent of the total income and provide details of the estimated income from investment business as a percentage of its total income;

(b) if it appears that the income from investment business will exceed 40 per cent of the total income but remain under the 49 per cent level, the firm will be required to monitor its income from invest-ment business internally on a monthly basis and advise the Council if the percentage income is likely to exceed 45 per cent of the total income;

(c) in respect of those firms whose income from investment business may exceed 45 per cent of their total income but remain under 49 per cent, a six-monthly submission must be made to the Council providing details similar to those required for the annual return (form 11). Firms should apply to the Council directly for the appropriate form. These firms will also be subject to *annual* monitoring visits by the Council's panel accountants or staff to ensure that the internal control systems are such that the firm does not exceed the 49 per cent level; and

(d) if a firm believes that it will exceed the 49 per cent threshold level in any particular year, it should take *immediate* steps to notify the Council and seek authorisation through another appropriate body.

Form 11 has to be submitted at the same time as form 5, currently within six months of the balance sheet date.

Any document of title received by the broker on behalf of his client must either be forwarded to the client as soon as is practicable, or else be dealt with in accordance with the client's instructions. Any documents held on the client's behalf must be kept in safe custody. The broker must not keep such documents of title unless in practice this is unavoidable. In this instance, a register of client's documents of title is to be main-tained, updated as necessary and reconciled every three months with the documents held, under the supervision of the compliance officer. Although these Rules do not apply to a life assurance policy, brokers are encouraged to maintain the same procedures for these documents.

'Client money' is any money payable by or to the client via the broker in respect of investment business. Such money is paid to the broker for onward transmission and not for its own account. It excludes money properly held in an IBA account in respect of general insurance business.

A broker firm is registered on the understanding that it will not hold client money. Arrangements will therefore have to be made for money due to or from clients under investment contracts (e.g. life policies) to be settled directly between the parties involved, except where the broker acts as a 'post box' for forwarding cheques.

A broker may receive clients' money under certain circumstances. Client money received in the form of a cheque made out in the firm's name must be endorsed by the firm rather than being allowed to pass through the broker's bank account. If it receives a cheque made payable to the client or a third party, this must be forwarded immediately. If client money is received in any other form, it must be returned at once, with the request that such money be paid direct to the third party in question. It must also be recorded in the client money register maintained by the broker.

3.4   Other legislation

There are several other pieces of legislation which affect the insurance broker. Two of the Insurance Companies Acts (1974 and 1981) deal with:

(a)   misleading statements made to induce people to enter into insurance contracts;

(b)   the disclosure of any connection with the insurer to be made by the intermediary; and

(c)   the provision of a 'cooling-off' period in connection with long-term business such as life insurance.

The Consumer Credit Act 1974 affects insurance brokers who are involved in credit broking and debt adjusting, counselling or collecting. Above certain *de minimis* provisions the broker will need a licence from the Office of Fair Trading unless he does not have a formal agreement with the provider of credit.

Although, as its title suggests, the Marine Insurance Act 1906 is primarily concerned with marine business, many of the principles it embodies extend to non-marine insurance as well. The law imposes a duty of utmost good faith on parties to an insurance contract. This is necessary because an insurer may not be aware of all material facts which are relevant to a proposed risk, unless brought to his attention by the insured.

This Act imposes a duty to disclose material facts when an insurance is proposed. Section 18(2) states that:

'Every circumstance is material which would influence the judgement of a prudent insurer in fixing the premium or determining whether he will take the risk'.

Section 19 extends the duty of disclosure of material facts to an agent effecting insurance. This catches the insurance broker, who must declare every known material circumstance; further, he is deemed to know every circumstance which in the ordinary course of business ought to be known by him.

The duty of utmost good faith applies equally to insurers as to proposers or their agents. If utmost good faith is not observed by either party, the contract may be avoided by the other party.

Another area of the Marine Insurance Act which applies to insurance brokers concerns the liability to pay premiums. The result is that in the Lloyd's insurance market generally, and in marine insurance elsewhere if the Act applies, premiums are considered as paid when the policy is issued, even if the broker has not received the due amount from the insured. The broker is always assumed liable to the insurer for the premium and this is reinforced by the automatic settlement procedures in the market. Outside Lloyd's and where the Act does not apply, the broker is not liable to pay a premium to the insurer which he has not yet received himself.

The introduction of the Policy Holders Protection Act 1975 followed the collapse of several insurance companies. It provides protection to policy-holders where insurers become unable to meet their liabilities. The Act established the Policyholders Protection Board with power to impose a levy on various parties, including insurance brokers, in insurance trans-actions. The DTI has prepared a consultation paper on the workings of this Act following several further well-publicised company failures which involved significant compensation payments.

One of the aims of the Fair Trading Act 1973 was to control or eliminate restrictive practices, which were seen to be hindering competition, contrary to the interest of consumers. Prior to the Act, at least one of the trade associations had a regulation forbidding incorporated insur-ance brokers to approach clients of other brokers uninvited. Such regulations were outlawed under the provisions of the Act. Example 12 of the IBRC Code of Conduct embodies the principles of the Fair Trading Act, stating: 'Insurance brokers shall have proper regard to the wishes of a policyholder or client who seeks to terminate any agreement with them to carry out business'.

The Unfair Contract Terms Act 1977 excluded insurance policies from its scope, on the condition that the insurance industry issued 'Statements of Insurance Practice'. Two statements were issued as a result – one relating to non-life business and the other to long-term business. These statements relate directly to insurance brokers to the extent that they are involved in drafting policies and handling claims. In accordance with the spirit of the Unfair Contract Terms Act, the statements are intended to ensure that terms and conditions of insurance contracts are reasonable.

The purpose of the Data Protection Act 1984 is to establish guidelines for the way in which personal data can be used and to ensure compliance with the guidelines. Personal data should only be obtained and processed lawfully and it should be held or disclosed only for lawful purposes. Non-personal or manually processed or publicly available data, such as share registers, are outside the scope of the Act.

Businesses which process personal data are required to register with the Data Protection Registrar, disclosing the type of data they keep. It is an offence to use and process personal data without being registered and it is also an offence to change the data usage without informing the Registrar.

Once a business has been registered with the Data Protection Register it must ensure that the personal data is:

(a) obtained and processed fairly and lawfully;
(b) kept for the purpose(s) specified in the Register;
(c) adequate, relevant and not excessive, given the purposes for which it is kept;
(d) kept accurate and up to date;
(e) made available to data subjects on request;
(f) protected against loss or disclosure; and
(g) kept only for as long as necessary.

Insurance brokers may also need to be aware of provisions covering their activities included in legislation such as the Misrepresentation Act 1967, Sale of Goods Act 1983 and Supply of Goods (Implied Terms) Act 1973 which govern most commercial contracts. Insurance broking bodies corporate are also subject to the Corporate Bodies Contracts Act 1960.

Insurance brokers are subject to the law relating to the avoidance or recognition and reporting of money laundering, particularly arising from the Money Laundering Regulations 1993 (SI 1993 No. 1933). These Regulations came into effect on 1 April 1994. Money laundering has been defined as 'the process by which criminals attempt to conceal the true origin and ownership of the proceeds of their criminal activities. If undertaken successfully, it allows them to maintain control over those proceeds and, ultimately, to provide legitimate cover for their source of income'.

The aim of the Regulations is to make it more difficult to conceal the origin of funds obtained through terrorism, drug dealing and other serious crimes. Insurance brokers should comply with the requirements of the Regulations when providing any services that might be of use to money launderers. This might, for example, be through providing insurance and investment services.

The Regulations create new criminal offences, which may be committed by individuals, employees and organisations, of failing to maintain appropriate procedures for the prevention or reporting of money laundering. The reporting (in good faith) of money laundering suspicions, under the legal provisions, is specifically exempted from all confidentiality requirements. This ensures that no action can be taken against the reporter even where the suspicions are later proved to be ill-founded.

There are specific procedures required to be established and maintained under the Regulations:

(a) for identification of clients;
(b) for record keeping;
(c) for internal reporting; and
(d) as may be reasonably necessary for the purposes of forestalling and preventing money laundering.

Insurance brokers need to ensure such procedures are in place and all employees are aware of them. It is necessary to nominate an officer of the company to take responsibility for the maintenance of these procedures and to act as the reporting official for staff.

Chapter 4 – Lloyd's

4.1 Background

The Lloyd's broker has historically had a unique and privileged place within the insurance market. Only brokers approved by Lloyd's can enter the Room at Lloyd's and place business. Sole access to Lloyd's underwriters is of considerable value to brokers, and in the past firms and companies of brokers were content to submit to the regulatory requirements of the Committee of Lloyd's in order to obtain the privilege. The foundation for the status of the Lloyd's broker was originally an unwritten agreement between underwriting members of Lloyd's not to accept insurance business except from Lloyd's brokers. This was subsequently crystallised in the Lloyd's Act 1982, which defined a 'Lloyd's broker' as a partnership or body corporate permitted by the Council of Lloyd's to broke insurance business at Lloyd's.

Recently the Lloyd's Market Board has appointed a working group on distribution with the task of identifying how the market should obtain business in the future. It is to review:

(a) sources of business, including the role of Lloyd's brokers, other intermediaries and service companies;
(b) the principle of regulation to cover Lloyd's brokers' exclusive access to the market; and
(c) the progress and conclusions of other working groups and studies.

Although Lloyd's insists the group is not a threat to brokers, all options will be examined, including changes to the tradition of exclusive access to the market for the Lloyd's broker.

The Fisher Report of 1980 set out the terms under which companies could become Lloyd's brokers and the requirements for continued registration. This was the first time that these matters had been published; they had been developed over the years by the brokers' department at Lloyd's in the form of pre- and post-admission requirements. With the Lloyd's Act 1982 came the principle of self-regulation by means of byelaws, but it was not until July 1988 that byelaws governing the regulation of Lloyd's brokers were approved by the Council of Lloyd's.

50

Although Lloyd's brokers have to comply with special requirements, they are also subject to the overall supervision of the IBRA. Indeed, a broker cannot be registered as a Lloyd's broker unless he is already registered with the IBRC. The very high standards set by Lloyd's were recognised when the IBRA was drafted and as a result Lloyd's brokers were granted exemption from certain provisions of the Act. The reason for these exemptions is that if a broker can meet the requirements set by Lloyd's, then the requirements imposed under the IBRA have automatically been satisfied.

The exemptions available to Lloyd's brokers are as follows:

(a)   ss3(3) and 4(4) of the IBRA grant an automatic entitlement to registration or enrolment for a person or body corporate who has satisfied the Council that the Committee of Lloyd's has accepted them as a Lloyd's broker;
(b)   s11 of the IBRA imposes various accounting and solvency requirements upon brokers wishing to remain on the register or list. Part V of SI 1979 No. 408 exempts Lloyd's brokers from this section; and
(c)   part IV of SI 1979 No. 408 exempts Lloyd's brokers from the professional indemnity insurance provisions included in part II of the SI. Lloyd's brokers are not, however, exempt from part III, relating to the grants scheme.

4.2   Lloyd's brokers v non-Lloyd's IBRC brokers

There are, consequently, a number of differences between brokers registered by the IBRC and those also registered at Lloyd's. The main features are set out in Table 4.1. Detailed guidance on these matters is set out in Chapter 3 for IBRC brokers, this chapter for Lloyd's brokers and Chapter 5 for PIA brokers.

The Lloyd's Brokers Byelaw (No. 5 of 1988) makes rules for the registration of Lloyd's brokers and for the review, renewal and withdrawal of registration. It empowers the Council of Lloyd's to impose conditions and make requirements regarding:

(a)   Lloyd's brokers' financial resources;
(b)   the maintenance of professional indemnity (E & O) insurance; and
(c)   the use of IBA bank accounts.

The byelaw also makes provisions regarding accounting records, accounts, audit and annual returns.

Table 4.1

Lloyd's brokers	*Non-Lloyd's IBRC brokers*
Registration, enrolment or admission	*Registration, enrolment or admission*
(a) Principals of prospective Lloyd's broking firms must satisfy the Council and Committee of Lloyd's that they are competent and familiar with the Lloyd's market	(a) Individuals or companies wishing to be registered or enrolled must satisfy the requirements of ss3 or 4 of the IBRA regarding qualifications and experience
(b) Share capital plus non-distributable reserves will normally be in excess of £250,000	(b) No special provisions relating to the share capital of non-Lloyd's brokers
(c) Assets must exceed liabilities at three reporting levels by the margins described in this chapter	(c) Non-Lloyd's brokers must have current assets in excess of current liabilities by at least £1,000
Solvency requirements	*Solvency requirements*
(a) Both quarterly and annual returns must be made to Lloyd's in the prescribed form. The annual return includes a report made by the broker's auditors. No return is required to the IBRC	(a) An annual return must be made to the IBRC by the insurance broker. Although the return is submitted by the broker, it must be reported on by an accountant
(b) A minimum overall solvency level is required, being the greater of £250,000 and the margin for the net asset test, subject to a maximum of £2,000,000	(b) A minimum overall solvency level is required, being £1,000
(c) No fixed assets may be used in calculating working capital	(c) Certain fixed assets (except intangibles such as goodwill) may be included in working capital
(d) Capital commitments and contingencies are included in calculating solvency	(d) Commitments and contingencies are considered when assessing the broker's overall solvency requirements
(e) While there is no prohibition on a Lloyd's broker deriving any particular proportion of its business from a single source, such a situation will be taken into account by the Council in determining whether the firm is fit and proper to be a Lloyd's broker	(e) The broker should not be reliant on a few insurers. If business is placed with no more than four insurers or if at least 35 per cent of brokerage is earned from business placed with a single insurer, then the broker is required to state why it is considered that the business is not unduly dependent on any insurer
(f) If an insurance debtor is doubtful, it should be provided for in the accounts and therefore no benefit is taken in solvency	(f) Insurance debits which have been outstanding for at least nine months can only be included in the solvency return if the broker is satisfied that they are recoverable. The total amount of such debits must be disclosed

Some of the requirements of this byelaw and regulations made thereunder are considered in the following section. However, it is essential that reference is made to the byelaw and regulations themselves listed in the bibliography.

4.3 Registration

The Council is to maintain a register of Lloyd's brokers, and no person may broke insurance business at Lloyd's unless registered or the subject of an umbrella agreement. In order to be registered, an applicant must already be enrolled in the list maintained by the IBRC and must satisfy Lloyd's that it is 'fit and proper to be a Lloyd's broker'. In determining this, Lloyd's will take into account such matters as:

(a)   the character, suitability, experience and number of the directors;
(b)   the reputation, character and suitability of anyone who controls the applicant;
(c)   the adequacy of the capital of the applicant;
(d)   undue dependence upon a particular:
    (i)   insurer or insurers;
    (ii)   source or sources of business;
    (iii)   kind or description of business; or
    (iv)   class or classes of insurance business specified in Schedule 2 to the Insurance Companies Act 1982;
(e)   the existence of any arrangement which might enable the broker to influence the policy or business of a managing agent, and vice versa;
(f)   the ability and willingness of the applicant to supervise and service all of its activities and responsibilities and to account fully and properly for those activities;
(g)   the location, adequacy and suitability of staff of the applicant; and
(h)   the location of the accounting and other records of the applicant.

Registration is for either a specific or an indefinite period, although Lloyd's may make an indefinite period specific by giving a minimum two years' notice of its expiry. At any time during a period of registration Lloyd's may conduct a review to ensure that the Lloyd's broker continues to qualify for registration. Lloyd's can remove a broker from the register for technical reasons, such as ceasing to be an IBRC broker or failing to renew its registration, or because, in the Council's opinion, it is no longer fit and proper to be a Lloyd's broker.

4.3.1   The application for registration

The application form requires a considerable amount of detail concerning the company itself, its ownership and structure, its officers, organisation and business. The controllers and officers of the company must complete separate forms showing their personal details. On completion of the forms, a director has to sign a declaration on behalf of the applicant that:

(a)   all the information given is correct and complies with the instructions for completion issued to the broker with the forms;
(b)   the broker is not a managing agent or associated with one in any way;
(c)   the broker has established adequate systems and controls over its transactions and records as required by the byelaw; and
(d)   the broker has adequate working capital to continue as a going concern for 12 months from the latest accounting reference date.

The broker's auditor is required to sign a report that:

(a)   he has examined:
      (i)   the broker's systems of control over its transactions and records; and
      (ii)   its projection of working capital requirements for the 12 months following the latest accounting reference date; and
(b)   in his opinion, it was not unreasonable for the person making the statements described in paragraph 4.11(c) and (d) above to have made those statements.

The completed standard forms for the applicant, its officers and any controllers are to be accompanied by:

(a)   the latest audited accounts of the applicant and any controlling company if the applicant is already a Lloyd's broker; otherwise the past two years' audited accounts and detailed profit and loss accounts are required; and
(b)   a brief narrative summary of the applicant's business plans, covering the two years from the date of the latest audited accounts, to include projected brokerage income for each period and any material planned changes from the business profile given in the application form.

4.3.2   Ownership and structure

The Council has laid down certain conditions which applicants are required to meet prior to registration. Those relating to ownership and structure are:

(a)   the broker must be listed as a broking company under s4 of IBRA 1977 or admitted as a practising insurance broker under s11;

54

(b) the company must be incorporated in the EU and located to serve the Lloyd's market and its policyholders;

(c) the reputation and suitability of the broker's 'controllers' should be a determining factor in the registration and continuing registration of a Lloyd's broker;

(d) the broker must arrange for all controllers to give an undertaking not to interfere with the conduct of the broking business; and

(e) the broker must employ an adequate number of directors and staff with experience in the Lloyd's market, including broking in the Room, claims procedures, terms of credit, central accounting settlements and policy preparation.

The ownership of a broker is significant in determining whether the broker is fit and proper to be a Lloyd's broker and to protect the interests of both client and underwriter. The primary requirement is that a Lloyd's broker is not permitted to be associated with a managing agent. This was stipulated in the Lloyd's Act 1982 and is strengthened by the requirement prohibiting a Lloyd's broker from entering any arrangement which enables the broker to influence the policy or business of a managing agent. The requirement for an audited statement of any connections with insurance companies and members' agents is discussed in **4.5**.

Lloyd's consent is required prior to anyone becoming a 'controller' of a Lloyd's broker. A controller is defined as anyone who has the ability to control 15 per cent of the voting power of a company in general meetings. The reputation and suitability of the controller is the sole criterion considered for approval. There is in place a Code of Practice on the nature of the broker's duties to his clients, the requirement to disclose to clients any connection with an insurance company or non-Lloyd's underwriting agency when placing a client's insurance or reinsurance, and the undertaking by a controller not to interfere in the management of the Lloyd's broker's business to the detriment of the Society of Lloyd's, members of Lloyd's or policyholders. A director of an insurance company cannot also be a director of a Lloyd's broker without Lloyd's consent.

A Lloyd's broker is required to have at least three full-time directors or partners. They should be annual subscribers to Lloyd's, if they are not underwriting members, and will be subject to character and suitability assessments prior to their approval as directors.

Every Lloyd's broker has to appoint a compliance officer to be responsible for:

(a)   the broker's compliance with the Lloyd's Acts, the byelaws and Regulations made under those Acts and any conditions and requirements imposed under any byelaw and Regulation; and

(b)   ensuring that the broker pays due regard to any Codes of Practice, market circulars or other advice issued by Lloyd's.

The compliance officer should, unless the Council otherwise agrees, be a director of or partner in the Lloyd's broker, but his appointment does not relieve the other directors or partners of any of their responsibilities. Lloyd's is developing guidance notes for these officers which set out criteria relating to their appointment, their duties, including their relationships with both Lloyd's and the board of directors, and suggested formal terms of reference. Newly appointed compliance officers are interviewed by the brokers' department to ensure they have an adequate understanding of their role.

4.3.3   Level and nature of business

When determining whether the firm is fit and proper to be a Lloyd's broker, the Council will consider the nature and level of its business. There is no minimum level of brokerage or requirement relating to the number of sources of business.

There is no pre-determined minimum percentage of business that a new Lloyd's broker needs to place at Lloyd's, but the estimated volume of business that the broker expects to place at Lloyd's should include an adequate share of worthwhile business from outside sources.

4.3.4   Errors and omissions insurance

Lloyd's requires each broker to maintain errors and omissions insurance for an indemnity of six times its annual net retained brokerage (four times in respect of UK insurance excluding 'direct' motor) subject to a minimum of £3 million and a maximum of £30 million. This requirement protects the broker's clients and also subjects the broker to the scrutiny of E & O insurers (Chapter 3). The requirements are set out in the Lloyd's Brokers Professional Indemnity 'Errors & Omissions' Insurance Requirements (1990).

The Requirements set out the general terms of the cover, in relation to:

(a)   the extent of the indemnity to be afforded by the cover;
(b)   the types of liability covered;
(c)   the occurrence and reporting of claims; and
(d)   the period and level of cover.

In addition to the required levels outlined above, the uninsured excess must not exceed the level of:

(a)   25 per cent of the net tangible assets of the Lloyd's broker; and
(b)   £2.5 million.

Self-insurance is not explicitly permitted, although the Council of Lloyd's could, within its general powers to grant dispensation, allow a higher permitted deductible.

Where cover is effected on a group basis the same maximum and minimum levels of cover and excess apply, but the amounts of net retained brokerage and net tangible assets used for the calculations are the aggregates of all the broking companies in the group.

4.3.5   Financial requirements

Lloyd's must be satisfied on an ongoing basis as to the adequacy of the broker's capital. Capital (issued share capital plus non-distributable reserves excluding revaluation reserves) of less than £250,000 is unlikely to be considered sufficient. Indeed, a new Lloyd's broker is likely to be expected to have at least £750,000 of capital. Adequacy will be gauged by reference to such factors as:

(a)   the nature, type and volume of business transacted by the broker;
(b)   the level of the broker's overheads;
(c)   whether the broker is a guarantor for 'direct' motor business; and
(d)   capital requirements for overcoming any known operational problems.

In addition to the requirement for adequate capital, Lloyd's brokers have to maintain adequate solvency at various levels, properly administer insurance broking accounts (IBAs) and keep proper books and records. We shall examine each of these areas in the following paragraphs.

4.3.6   Solvency requirements

A Lloyd's broker is required to be solvent at three levels;

(a)   insurance transactions net assets (IBA);
(b)   net current assets (NCA); and
(c)   net assets (NTA)

A Lloyd's broker is required to have a surplus of IBA assets over IBA liabilities in excess of a margin based on the Lloyd's broker's turnover.

Turnover is defined as annual net retained brokerage plus other fees and charges receivable by the broker.

All levels of test have a minimum margin and are based on a sliding scale. For the IBA test the margin is calculated as follows:

Brokerage bands	%
First £1m	5.0
Next £2m	4.0
Next £2m	3.0
Next £5m	2.0
Next £21m	1.0

subject to a minimum margin of £25,000 and a maximum margin of £500,000. The total IBA assets less total IBA liabilities is required to exceed this margin.

The NCA test is designed to demonstrate the ability of the Lloyd's broker to meet its short-term liabilities. The broker should have sufficient net current assets available to meet any period of shortfall between income and expenditure. There is a margin based on the level of annual expenditure, as this represents the short-term financial exposure should the broker lose income.

Expenditure is defined as the expenditure reported in the financial statements for the immediately preceding accounting period (adjusted for long or short periods) under the normal expenditure headings and adjusted to exclude any non-recurring costs. The margin is calculated on the following percentages of expenditure:

Expenditure bands	%
First £1m	10.0
Next £2m	7.5
Next £15m	5.0

subject to a minimum margin of £50,000 and a maximum margin of £1,000,000. The IBA margin is then added to the NCA margin to give the total margin required for the test. This means that overall, current assets must exceed current liabilities by between £75,000 and £1.5 million.

For the purposes of this test, current assets are defined as those receivable within one year of the accounting reference date and current liabilities as those falling due within three years of the accounting reference date. Current liabilities additionally include contingent liabilities and capital commitments.

The objective of the NTA test is to examine the long-term financial stability of a Lloyd's broker by reference to its net tangible assets. For solvency purposes net assets are defined as those reported in the relevant financial statements adjusted to exclude goodwill and formation expenses (including those held in subsidiaries), assets lodged or loans made on behalf of Names, assets representing revaluation reserves, any loans made by the broker which are not receivable within the period stated in the loan agreement and any loans made by the broker which are subordinated to the other creditors of the borrower.

The broker's net tangible assets are required to exceed its total liabilities by the following percentages of the greater of annual net retained brokerage and expenditure (as defined below):

Brokerage/expenditure bands	%
First £1m	30.0
Next £2m	15.0
Next £28m	5.0

subject to a minimum of £250,000 and a maximum margin of £2,000,000. Examples of the calculation of these tests are given in Appendix 1.

The required margins calculated at the balance sheet date for each level of test are to be maintained at all times ('any day' solvency). However, if a broker believes that it might not be able to do so because of the expected timing of receipt of brokerage, it may ask Lloyd's to set lower requirements, subject to a minimum NCA margin of £50,000 and a minimum NTA margin of £250,000.

4.3.7 Lloyd's Brokers Security and Trust Deed

In addition to these solvency requirements, there are further restrictions under the Lloyd's Brokers Security and Trust Deed, to which all Lloyd's brokers are subject. This deed came into force in September 1989 and represents an attempt to give preferential creditor status to insurance creditors to whom the broker owes money. It requires that the realisable value of IBA assets exceeds the aggregate net amount due to insureds and insurers (details are set out in **11.5**).

The deed created a first floating charge over all the broker's insurance transaction assets in favour of Lloyd's as trustee for all the broker's insurance transaction creditors. The 1989 requirements did not include any loan or overdraft facility from a bank on an IBA account in the definition of 'insurance transactions'. This was rectified by the Lloyd's Brokers Security and Trust Deed Requirements (1993), which now include such loans and overdrafts to the extent that they are used for payments to insurers or insureds or for withdrawal of brokerage.

Any Lloyd's broker first registered after 30 June 1993 must execute the new form of deed. Existing brokers at that date may enter into a deed of variation extending the definitions in the original deed to bring it into line with the new form. The deed of variation creates a second floating charge for this purpose.

The deed, forms of board resolutions and other necessary documentation are specified by Lloyd's. The broker has to provide the Council of Lloyd's with copies of the board resolution and the registration of the floating charge. In addition, the broker is required to:

(a) inform every approved bank with which it has an IBA account, or which holds IBA assets on its behalf, of the execution of the deed;
(b) provide every such bank with a copy of the deed; and
(c) obtain from every such bank a written acknowledgement in the terms specified by Lloyd's.

The note to the broker's accounts disclosing the existence of the deed must therefore specify the total amount of insurance creditors, including any IBA overdraft which falls within the scope of the deed.

4.3.8 Quarterly solvency returns

Each registered Lloyd's broker is required to furnish to Lloyd's quarterly IBA statements in the same format as the existing Schedule 3A of the annual return, and the same accounting policies should be used for their completion. The statements must be signed by both the finance director and the compliance officer of the broker but need not be audited. The statements must be submitted no later than one month after the end of the relevant quarter.

Although it is recognised that the fourth quarter end will also be covered by the annual return, Lloyd's still requires the IBA statement to be submitted within the one month time limit. Any material difference between the IBA statement and the annual return should be referred to in a letter from the compliance officer or auditors indicating the reasons for the difference.

4.3.9 Insurance broking account requirements

All insurance brokers are required to maintain separate banking accounts, designated 'IBA', with approved banks. These accounts are required to be used exclusively for:

(a) the banking of all insurance monies received by the broker;
(b) transactions relating to the investment of monies received in short-term assets designated 'IBA';
(c) the payment to or on behalf of clients or underwriters of all monies properly due; and
(d) the payment or withdrawal of brokerage, commission, fees or allowances made by insurers.

These accounts are to be kept free from any charge, lien or encumbrance except to secure short-term IBA borrowings. They may be secured for the purposes of letters of credit issued by an approved bank for the broker's insurance broking business purposes.

The Lloyd's byelaw formalises the rules relating to the operation of IBA designated bank accounts, which were previously found in an explanatory appendix to the accountant's report to Lloyd's. The requirements have been expanded and brought into line with IBRC Rules in two important areas:

(a) on opening an IBA designated account with an approved bank the broker must inform that bank in writing, and obtain the bank's written acknowledgement, of the terms on which the account is opened; and
(b) the specific circumstances in which it is possible:
   (i)   to have an IBA overdraft or loan; and
   (ii) to grant the bank a lien, charge or other security interest over an IBA account or asset.

The definition of approved banks within the UK has been revised, while IBAs outside the UK must be held with a bank individually approved by Lloyd's. It is unlikely that Lloyd's will produce a list of approved overseas banks, since these are considered on a case-by-case basis which depends on the broker's reasons for using the bank. The list of approved IBA assets is in the process of being revised and updated to take into account developments in the capital markets.

One feature of IBA bank accounts is that brokerage may not be withdrawn from the account by the broker before that brokerage is brought into account as income under the broker's current accounting policies. This could affect those brokers who have an accounting policy to defer the recognition of brokerage over the period of servicing the insurance business and claims arising on it.

Investment income arising from IBA short-term assets need not be credited to the IBA account as it is for the benefit of the broker.

In November 1992 the Lloyd's brokers department issued a Market Bulletin on the circumstances in which Lloyd's brokers are permitted to use IBA monies to fund claims to clients. This was based on legal opinion that if a broker funded a claim to a client without the express prior agreement of the insurers concerned, such a payment was *ex gratia* and could not be settlement of 'monies due'. Thus it is not permitted to use IBA monies for this purpose.

The Lloyd's Insurance Brokers Committee (LIBC) is unhappy with this interpretation and is in discussion with Lloyd's, in particular to clarify:

(a) the definition of the insurer's 'prior agreement';
(b) whether subsequent reimbursement from the insurer to the broker would be a permitted use of IBA funds since the original claims funding would have to be from a non-IBA account; and
(c) whether passive funding is a problem, since the money has not reached the IBA in the first place.

Within the annual return to Lloyd's, the broker has to declare that IBAs have been operated in accordance with the Lloyd's Brokers Byelaw. The auditor effectively endorses this declaration. This appears to mean that he should be satisfied that no instances of unauthorised funding of claims have occurred during the period covered. It will not be clear whether this is the case until the LIBC and Lloyd's have resolved the issue. The directors may state their interpretation of these rules and possibly their inability to confirm compliance with the rules as interpreted by Lloyd's. Failing this, the auditor may wish to draw attention to the scope of his work in this matter in his covering letter to Lloyd's.

4.3.10 Books and records

All Lloyd's brokers are required to comply with the Companies Act requirements on maintenance of proper books and records. The broker should record simultaneously in the books of account the amounts due from insureds and the appropriate amount due to the insurer. In addition, the byelaw includes provisions for the broker to keep detailed records of all insurance contracts, including, for example:

(a) the identity and participation of all the insurers involved;
(b) full particulars of the terms and conditions;
(c) a copy of the policy; and
(d) the broker's slip.

The same level of detail is also required for claims and binding authorities.

The broker's records must be kept:

(a) in the case of non-business insurance within the UK, for a minimum of 15 years after the latest of:
    (i) the expiry of the policy;
    (ii) the final settlement of the latest claim; and
    (iii) the final adjustment, if applicable, of any premiums paid; and
(b) in all other cases:
    (i) with regard to the claims documentation, 15 years after the final settlement of the latest claim; and
    (ii) otherwise, 80 years after the commencement of the policy.

These requirements will increase the use of microfiche within the market. However, the need to maintain records for these long periods has been demonstrated by the asbestosis and environmental pollution claims which have been made on the market despite the effluxion of time since the risks were initially written.

4.3.11 Annual return

After a broker has been registered under Byelaw 5 of 1988, an annual return has to be submitted to Lloyd's, together with a copy of the audited accounts. The return is designed to confirm that the broker continues to comply with the requirements of the byelaw. It comprises the following schedules:

> Schedule 1 Broker's Declaration;
> Schedule 2 Auditors' Report;
> Schedule 3 Solvency Tests;
> Schedule 4 Additional Information.

In the broker's declaration, it is confirmed that:

(a) the solvency margins have been determined in accordance with the byelaws and were maintained throughout the period;
(b) the IBA accounts have been operated in accordance with the byelaw;
(c) an adequate system of control over transactions and records has been maintained;
(d) there has been no breach of the divestment provisions; and
(e) there is adequate working capital for the broker to continue as a going concern for the 12 months following the balance sheet date.

This declaration is to be signed by a director and the compliance officer of the broker.

The auditor is required to report that Schedules 1, 3, 4A and 4B of the annual return have been properly prepared in accordance with the requirements of the byelaw and that it was not unreasonable for the persons making the broker's declaration to have made the statements therein.

The additional information required within Schedule 4 includes an analysis of the profit and loss account, details of banks outside the UK used for IBA purposes, a business analysis and details of any organisational changes.

The annual return must be submitted to Lloyd's together with the broker's audited accounts within six months of the first balance sheet date after registration and thereafter within four months of the balance sheet date. The audited accounts of the ultimate holding company of a broker must be provided to Lloyd's within six months of its balance sheet date. The annual return must also be accompanied by a statement covering any interest of the broker in any other insurance business and the operation of any binding authorities by the broker as coverholder.

4.3.12   Other provisions

The byelaw has various other provisions regarding:

(a)   prior consent from Lloyd's for changes in such details as directors and the compliance officer, and notifying changes in auditors, locations and accounting dates;
(b)   giving the Council powers to:
    (i)   prescribe professional indemnity insurance;
    (ii)   provide for protection of insurance creditors;
    (iii)   establish a scheme to provide for run-off costs; and
    (iv)   prescribe fees payable by Lloyd's brokers to Lloyd's; and
(c)   agency Lloyd's brokers.

4.3.13   The auditor

Lloyd's does not maintain a register of approved auditors for brokers like the register for Lloyd's syndicates. The only stipulation is that auditors must be independent and should not, without the previous consent of Lloyd's, help maintain the accounting records.

Lloyd's has the power to arrange for a broker's auditor to execute an undertaking to provide Lloyd's with any information and explanations of which he has become aware in order to assist the Council of Lloyd's carry out its duties under the byelaw. The form of this undertaking to communicate directly with Lloyd's on clients' affairs has been encapsulated in the Lloyd's Brokers (Amendment) Byelaw (No. 8 of 1989). The Lloyd's broker, for its part, has to give a waiver of confidentiality so that the auditor can volunteer information as well as respond to a specific request from the Council to provide it. This provision of information may be with or, in exceptional circumstances, without the knowledge of the broker. Guidelines detailing the method of such communication and circumstances under which it would be appropriate have been included in the accountancy profession's Practice Note on Lloyd's. These requirements are similar to those for auditors of members of other regulatory authorities.

Lloyd's also has the power to direct a broker to submit its accounts or any other document to further examination by a person approved by Lloyd's. In such circumstances the broker must do everything in its power to ensure that the auditor and any other adviser assist the person carrying out the examination.

The auditor has responsibilities in connection with both initial registration and the annual return. There are two aspects of the registration process on which the auditor has to give an opinion to Lloyd's – the broker's systems and controls over the transactions and records, and the adequacy of its working capital.

The auditor's examination of the broker's systems and controls is likely to be wide-ranging and to cover the whole of its activities. Although concerned primarily with the systems and controls relating to broking transactions, the auditor must be satisfied that the broker has proper monitoring procedures in operation in all areas which might affect its position as a registered Lloyd's broker. The work will consist of ascertaining what systems and controls the broker has established and evaluating them to see whether they are considered adequate. It is not necessary to carry out detailed testing of the systems, but walk-through tests will be useful in many cases. Where the system is found to be inadequate or operated ineffectively, recommendations should be made to the broker immediately.

The adequacy of the system is to be measured in terms of its ability to ensure that the broker will at all times observe and comply with its obligations regarding:

(a)   financial resources;
(b)   insurance broking accounts;
(c)   the preparation and audit of accounts and other reports;
(d)   reporting breaches of solvency;

(e) the disclosure of insurance connections;
(f) professional indemnity insurance; and
(g) records and their retention.

Clearly the auditor will use the work undertaken in connection with his report on the annual accounts, although he may have to evaluate other aspects of the system especially in connection with (d), (e) and (f) above. A checklist, based on Appendix 1, should be prepared, and cross-referenced to the systems notes, to demonstrate that the requirements of the byelaw are met.

The second aspect of the application for registration with which the auditor is directly concerned is the broker's working capital requirements. The broker must prepare, and the auditor must examine, working capital projections for the 12 months following the latest accounting reference date. The broker's projections must be reviewed for reasonableness, taking into account past performance and future prospects. The actual results of the part of the 12-month period already gone must be compared with or substituted for the projections. If the date of submission of the application is substantially through the period, the broker should be encouraged to prepare projections for a further period, ideally 12 months from the date of application.

The adequacy of the projections can be assessed in absolute terms but should also be measured against solvency requirements at the net current asset level. Since the broker must meet all three levels of solvency from the date that it is registered, it is important to be satisfied that it will be able to do so before it applies for registration. A first step will therefore be to calculate solvency margins from the broker's latest audited accounts and to establish whether seasonal fluctuations in the level of business will enable the broker to request Lloyd's to apply lower margins for solvency on an 'any day' basis.

The auditor is only required to give an opinion on the cash flow for the 12 months from the last balance sheet date. The brokerage flow should be examined monthly and in currency to confirm its adequacy. Any impact of material increases or decreases in brokerage or recurring expenses should also be considered.

In the annual return, the auditor has to confirm that it was not unreasonable of the broker to make the statements, as required under 4.3.11 above. This is very similar to the requirements on initial registration and will require similar audit steps. However, it also includes the 'any day' solvency of IBA. This parallels the requirements for the IBRC return described in Chapter 3. The auditor of the Lloyd's broker will need to apply the same procedures as his IBRC counterpart. Compliance with the divestment provisions is a matter of fact and the auditor must satisfy himself that there are no undisclosed arrangements which breach these requirements.

The auditor's review of the solvency margin calculations will require him to be satisfied that they have been computed in accordance with the rules and agree with the figures included in the audited financial statements. In particular, the auditor should ensure that:

(a) fixed assets are excluded from the NCA test; and
(b) all quantifiable contingencies are included in the NTA test; and
(c) the required solvency margins are met.

4.3.14   Code of Conduct

Lloyd's has introduced a Code of Conduct, which is intended to be an explanatory statement of the principles which are expected to apply to the conduct of Lloyd's brokers. The Code is designed to give Lloyd's brokers assistance in fulfilling their duties to both insureds and insurers. Compliance with the Code is not a strict requirement for registration but the extent to which the broker does comply is a factor Lloyd's takes into account when determining whether a firm is fit and proper to be a Lloyd's broker.

4.3.15   Umbrella arrangements

There are two further areas where Lloyd's has sought to regulate brokers which are not registered as Lloyd's brokers but which have restricted authority to place risks with Lloyd's underwriters. These are 'umbrella arrangements' and agency Lloyd's brokers.

An umbrella arrangement is an arrangement between a Lloyd's broker and a non-Lloyd's broker whereby directors and staff of the non-Lloyd's broker are permitted to enter the Room at Lloyd's and place business directly with Lloyd's underwriters using the name, Lloyd's Policy Signing Office (LPSO) number or pseudonym of the Lloyd's broker. These arrangements have to be registered under Lloyd's Byelaw No. 6 of 1988, which imposes various conditions on both the Lloyd's and non-Lloyd's brokers.

The arrangement can be registered only if:

(a)   the non-Lloyd's broker is IBRC registered;
(b)   the non-Lloyd's broker is not a managing agent or associated with a managing agent;
(c)   the non-Lloyd's broker is not party to any other umbrella arrangement, unless the new arrangement is to commence after the termination of the earlier one; and
(d)   Lloyd's is satisfied that:
    (i)   the non-Lloyd's broker intends to apply for registration as a Lloyd's broker within three years of the date of registration of the umbrella arrangement; and
    (ii)   it appears likely that the non-Lloyd's broker will be able to meet the requirements for registration as a Lloyd's broker within that period.

However, if the umbrella broker is a subsidiary or a fellow subsidiary of a Lloyd's broker, it does not have to apply for registration as a full Lloyd's broker.

Both parties to the arrangement are required to give undertakings to Lloyd's. The Lloyd's broker undertakes to supervise the conduct of the non-Lloyd's broker in all aspects of the broking business carried out under the umbrella arrangement, and the non-Lloyd's broker and each of its directors or partners undertakes to submit to the jurisdiction of Lloyd's and to comply with all relevant byelaws and regulations.

As part of the umbrella arrangement there must be a written agreement between the two brokers. Lloyd's has stipulated in requirements made under the byelaw that every agreement must include terms under which:

(a)   the directors, partners, employees and agents of the non-Lloyd's broker who alone may place business at Lloyd's are identified;
(b)   only broker's slips which meet the byelaw's requirements are used by the non-Lloyd's broker for placing business at Lloyd's;
(c)   the non-Lloyd's broker undertakes not to represent itself in any way as a Lloyd's broker;
(d)   the non-Lloyd's broker agrees to comply with all reasonable directions given by the Lloyd's broker in its supervisory capacity, and in particular to provide all the necessary information to enable the Lloyd's broker to complete its annual return; and
(e)   where Lloyd's have made it a condition of registering the umbrella arrangement, one of the non-Lloyd's directors is to be nominated by the Lloyd's broker.

The application form for registration of an umbrella arrangement requires considerable information about the non-Lloyd's broker, its ownership and structure, its officers, organisation and business analysis. The form contains a declaration to be signed on behalf of both the Lloyd's and non-Lloyd's brokers, to the effect that the information given in the form and its attachments is correct and complies with the instructions for completion. The auditor of neither broker has any responsibilities in the registration process.

Registration of an umbrella arrangement is for a period of three years, during which time the non-Lloyd's broker is expected to apply for registration as a Lloyd's broker. Before the expiry of that period, however, the Lloyd's broker can apply to have the period extended, and Lloyd's may do so as it thinks fit.

The byelaws make various provisions regarding the conduct of umbrella arrangements including:

(a)   the existence of the written agreement between the two brokers;
(b)   the responsibilities of the Lloyd's broker for premiums and for servicing the business in the event of default by the non-Lloyd's broker;
(c)   the use of slips which state clearly the names of both brokers and the existence of an umbrella arrangement between them; and
(d)   the keeping of records and retention of records by the non-Lloyd's broker in accordance with the requirements of Byelaw No. 5 of 1988.

Non-Lloyd's brokers which are party to umbrella arrangements must have E & O cover which complies with Lloyd's requirements. However, as they will also be subject to IBRC Rules, they will carry E & O cover in accordance with IBRC requirements, i.e. in practice with a lower deductible than that required of Lloyd's brokers.

A Lloyd's broker must take reasonable steps to ensure that no more than 25 per cent of its total net brokerage is derived from umbrella arrangements. Lloyd's may direct a non-Lloyd's broker to reduce the amount of business placed or even deregister an arrangement if this requirement is breached.

Every Lloyd's broker, whether or not it is party to an umbrella arrangement, must submit an annual return concerning umbrella arrangements at the same time as it submits its annual return under Byelaw No. 5 of 1988. The return contains a declaration, to be signed by the Lloyd's broker's compliance officer, that:

(a) either the broker was party to umbrella arrangements during the period and:
  (i) was fully aware of its responsibilities;
  (ii) was satisfied with the conduct of the non-Lloyd's brokers involved, who complied in full with the provisions of the byelaw; and
  (iii) the information given in the return is correct; or
(b) the broker was not party to umbrella arrangements in the period.

The annual return is not subject to audit.

The information to be given in the return includes:

(a) the names of all the non-Lloyd's brokers with whom the Lloyd's broker had umbrella arrangements;
(b) the amount of brokerage earned from each separate arrangement;
(c) the percentage of the total net brokerage which the Lloyd's broker earned in total from umbrella arrangements; and
(d) confirmation that:
  (i) the non-Lloyd's brokers intend, and are still able, to register as Lloyd's brokers;
  (ii) the non-Lloyd's brokers are still registered with the IBRC; and
  (iii) there have been no changes in the written agreements with the non-Lloyd's brokers or in their shareholders, controllers, directors and partners.

The annual return must be accompanied by each non-Lloyd's broker's latest audited accounts and IBRC form 5.

An umbrella arrangement with a Lloyd's broker is a useful vehicle for a non-Lloyd's broker who wishes ultimately to become a Lloyd's broker. The costs and extent of regulation are not so onerous as those for the Lloyd's broker but give an introduction to the regulatory environment of Lloyd's.

The non-Lloyd's broker which is party to an umbrella arrangement must immediately inform the Council of Lloyd's in writing of:

(a) any change of directors or partners in the broker; and
(b) any change or proposed change of controller of the broker.

The Lloyd's broker involved in the umbrella arrangement must also inform the Council if it becomes aware of any such occurrence.

Various provisions of the byelaw do not apply to an umbrella arrangement between a Lloyd's broker and its non-Lloyd's broker subsidiary. A subsidiary is defined as being a company in which the Lloyd's broker is sole beneficial owner of more than 50 per cent of every class of voting share. In these circumstances, the registration of the arrangement is not subject to the three-year limit, as the non-Lloyd's broker is not expected to apply for registration as a Lloyd's broker, and the written agreement between the two parties is not required. The Lloyd's broker is not subject to the 25 per cent restriction on brokerage derived from umbrella arrangements with subsidiary brokers, but the amount of brokerage derived from subsidiaries will be taken into account in assessing the percentage of total brokerage derived from umbrella arrangements with non-subsidiary brokers.

4.3.16 Agency Lloyd's brokers

A wholly owned subsidiary of a Lloyd's broker or fellow subsidiary of a broker which is itself wholly owned may, as an alternative to an umbrella arrangement, apply to be registered as an agency broker under Byelaw No. 5 of 1988. This enables it to broke business at Lloyd's as the agent of the principal Lloyd's broker, even though it would not satisfy the financial resources provisions of the byelaw.

In addition to being wholly owned by either a Lloyd's broker or another company which has a wholly owned subsidiary Lloyd's broker, an agency broker must meet the following conditions:

(a)   the existence of the agency broker as a legal entity separate from the principal broker is justified;
(b)   the holding company or a wholly owned fellow subsidiary of the agency company is of appropriate financial standing and has executed an unconditional and unlimited undertaking to discharge the liabilities of the agency broker;
(c)   the principal broker's E & O insurance extends to business placed by the agency broker; and
(d)   there are satisfactory arrangements to ensure that the principal broker carries out and is responsible for the administration of the agency broker's affairs and the maintenance of its business records.

If any of the above conditions ceases to be satisfied, the agency broker will automatically be deregistered.

As, in effect, a registered Lloyd's broker, an agency broker is subject to the provisions of the byelaw. However, the provisions of the byelaw relating to financial resources, and the solvency requirements made under those provisions, do not apply to agency brokers.

An agency broker must comply with the provisions relating to IBA designated bank accounts and IBA assets, except that it may pay its insurance transactions receipts and monies received from IBA assets into an IBA account maintained by the principal broker.

Before acting as a Lloyd's broker, the agency broker must disclose to the proposer of the business and to the underwriter the identity of the principal broker and the fact that the agency broker is carrying on business as the agent of the principal broker. All the agency broker's slips, cover notes, invoices, receipts and other business documents must include a note that the agency broker acts as the agent of the principal broker.

The agency broker's annual accounts must include a note disclosing that the broker is an agency broker within the meaning of paragraph 57 of Byelaw No. 5 of 1988. The principal broker is responsible for all the acts and omissions of the agency broker, and so all such acts and omissions are deemed to be the acts and omissions of the principal broker.

This is a relatively cheap and straightforward method for groups of broking companies to pass business to Lloyd's. There are many valid commercial reasons for keeping separate entities handling different types of business, trading under long established business names or providing a means of rewarding particular business producers.

4.4   Direct dealing

For many years, direct dealing arrangements enabled Lloyd's motor syndicates to deal directly with non-Lloyd's brokers or agents. Under the Insurance Intermediaries Byelaw (No. 8 of 1990), these arrangements were rationalised and extended to all sectors of the Lloyd's market in respect of personal lines and commercial motor business. However, the non-Lloyd's intermediary has to be guaranteed by a Lloyd's broker in relation to:

(a)   the payment of all premiums due to the underwriters, except where the insured pays the underwriters directly by credit card or bank direct debit; and

(b)   the servicing of risks written by the underwriters through the non-Lloyd's broker in the event of the failure of the non-Lloyd's broker to service such risks.

In consideration for these services the Lloyd's broker receives an agreed rate of commission from the underwriters. The Lloyd's broker also has to provide an unaudited summary of business accepted under direct dealing arrangements.

4.5 Insurance connections

Every Lloyd's broker must submit to Lloyd's an audited statement of any connections with insurance companies and members' agents. The statement is not part of the annual return but must be sent at the same time. The statement and audit report will be held on a central file open to public inspection at Lloyd's.

'Connection' is defined in paragraph 37(4) of Byelaw No. 5 of 1988 in terms of control. A person is connected with a Lloyd's broker if he controls that broker, is controlled by that broker or is controlled by a person who also controls the broker. Control in this context means owning at least 15 per cent of the equity.

Where there are connections to be reported, the statement must set out the name of each insurance company and members' agent which is connected with the broker, together with the nature and extent of the connection. In respect of a connected insurance company, the percentage of the broker's net retained brokerage receivable from that company should be given, in exact terms if the proportion is 10 per cent or more or 'under 10 per cent' if that is the case. If the broker has no insurance connections to be reported, a statement to that effect must nonetheless be submitted to Lloyd's.

The statement must include a declaration signed by the compliance officer of the broker that the statement has been:

(a) properly prepared in accordance with the requirements made under Byelaw No. 5 of 1988; and
(b) approved for submission to Lloyd's by the directors of or partners in the Lloyd's broker.

Lloyd's have not presented a form of audit report, but the following may be appropriate.

REPORT OF THE AUDITORS TO THE COUNCIL OF LLOYD'S

We have examined the accounting records and systems of ABC Limited for the accounting period ended .... 19.. and carried out such tests as we considered necessary.

In our opinion the broker has established and maintained such procedures and systems as are necessary to enable it to comply with the Lloyd's Brokers (Statement of Connections with Insurance Companies and Members' Agents) Requirements.

XYZ & Co.

Date

The auditor will need to consider undertaking the following work:

(a) consider, from his knowledge of the broker's business, whether there are any insurance connections to be disclosed;

(b) review the completed statement of insurance connections and confirm that it is complete and not at variance with his knowledge of the broker's business;

(c) obtain a copy of the board minute, when available, verifying that the statement has been approved for submission to Lloyd's by the directors or partners; and

(d) confirm from his general audit work that the broker's procedures and records enable the information given in the statement to be identified completely and accurately.

Chapter 5 – The Financial Services Act 1986

5.1 Introduction

The Financial Services Act 1986 (FSA) is an extremely wide-ranging piece of legislation aimed at increasing the degree of legal protection afforded to investors. It was based on the recommendations of the Gower Report, issued in 1981 following a number of well-publicised scandals in the late 1970s. It replaces the Prevention of Fraud (Investments) Act 1958 and includes rules on insider dealing, listing of securities and offers of unlisted securities, in addition to the other matters covered by the predecessor Act. The FSA makes it a criminal offence for any person to carry on investment business in the UK without being authorised.

The FSA affects mainly those brokers within the life, pensions and unit trust markets, and those who conduct investment business as part of their overall operations. The Act defines the investments which are within its scope as the following:

(a) shares;
(b) debentures;
(c) government and public securities;
(d) instruments entitling to shares or securities;
(e) certificates representing securities;
(f) units in a collective investment scheme;
(g) long-term insurance policies;
(h) options;
(i) futures;
(j) contracts for differences;
(k) rights and interests in investments.

Thus life and pensions brokers providing advice on life assurance policies and savings schemes are implicitly included within the scope of the Act.

The Act goes on to define five categories of investment business:

(a) dealing in investments;
(b) arranging deals in investments;

(c)   managing investments;
(d)   investment advice;
(e)   establishing, operating or winding up collective investment schemes.

Of these, investment advice is arguably the hardest to interpret, and the Act gives a broad outline with its definition of investment advice as:

> 'Giving or offering or agreeing to give to persons in their capacity as investors or potential investors advice on the merits of their purchasing, selling, subscribing for or underwriting an investment, or exercising any right conferred by an investment to acquire, dispose of, underwrite or convert an investment'.

It is generally accepted that this means giving specific rather than broad-based investment advice to a person.

In this chapter, only a broad outline of the impact of the Act can be given. There are numerous books written on the subject, some of which are listed in the bibliography.

The regulatory structure is shown in Figure 5.1. As the diagram illustrates, the FSA gives regulatory power to the Treasury, which in turn has delegated those powers to the Securities and Investments Board (SIB). This body has drawn up the regulations governing investment businesses and is empowered to authorise investment businesses directly. The SIB controls a second tier of organisations comprising Self Regulating Organisations (SROs) and Recognised Professional Bodies (RPBs), which can also authorise investment businesses. Both of these types of organisation have their own detailed rulebooks, which must be at least equivalent to that of the SIB and are subject to the overriding authority of the SIB.

Several SROs have been approved by the SIB to give their members authority to carry on investment business. They are:

(a)   Securities and Futures Authority (FSA);
(b)   Investment Managers Regulatory Organisation (IMRO);
(c)   Personal Investment Authority (PIA).

Insurance brokers who transact a significant amount of life and unit trust business need to be authorised by and members of the PIA in order to conduct their business. Where the main investment business activities of an insurance broker are outside these areas, it may be more appropriate to join one of the other SROs who regulate those activities.

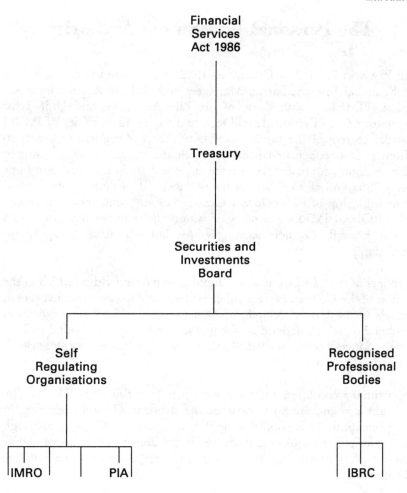

Figure 5.1

A number of professional bodies whose members carry out investment business as part of the exercise of their profession have been granted recognition by the SIB as RPBs. In 1988 the IBRC was approved by the SIB and given RPB status. This has given insurance brokers, whose income from investment business is not more than 25 per cent of total income, rising to 49 per cent once a broker is authorised from all sources who do not handle client money and whose investment business is restricted to long-term contracts and regulated collective investment schemes, an additional route to authorisation for investment business (see Chapter 4; this chapter is concerned with PIA).

5.2 The Personal Investment Authority (PIA)

The PIA was formed in December 1992 to combine the operations of the Financial Intermediaries, Managers and Brokers Regulatory Association (FIMBRA) with those of the Life Assurance and Unit Trust Regulatory Organisation (LAUTRO) and the retail activities of IMRO in order to reduce the unnecessary duplication of regulatory bodies in existence. It is concerned primarily with the regulation of investment business done with or for the private customer. Its Rules came into force in July 1994 and all members of the replaced SROs should have applied for membership of PIA before 1 October 1994. Members of FIMBRA, LAUTRO and IMRO will not gain automatic membership to the PIA on the strength of their existing status but will have to apply for membership.

Members of the PIA can be any company, firm or individual which in the opinion of the Council carries on, or is proposing to carry on, investment business in the United Kingdom. There are four different categories of membership, which depend on the investment function provided and the classes of investment handled. A summary of the different categories is set out in Table 5.1.

The primary condition for membership is to satisfy the PIA that the applicant is fit and proper to carry on the investment business specified in the application. This condition applies to a firm as a whole, although there is a further requirement for any individuals or firms appointed as member's 'appointed representatives' to meet a similar criterion (see 5.11 below).

The membership application is designed to provide information to enable the PIA to evaluate:

(a) the honesty and reputation of an applicant in dealing with regulators and clients;
(b) the solvency and financial standing of the applicant in respect of financial resource requirements of the PIA;
(c) the competence and organisation of the applicant firm to enable it to comply with the PIA Conduct of Business Rules; and
(d) whether the above three attributes apply not only to the individual applicant but to appointed representatives within an applicant firm.

The PIA's judgement on whether an applicant is fit and proper is not based solely on the information contained in the application form. Additional information may be requested and unsolicited information may be taken into account. If considered necessary, the PIA will require the applicant to arrange for an auditor to report on the applicant's accounting records and confirm that the information provided with the application form is in agreement with those records. Where an applicant is transferring from an existing SRO, the PIA will, as far as practicable, make full use of information available to existing regulators.

Table 5.1

Category 1 Unrestricted

Members of this category are permitted to:

(a)   deal as principal with investors;
(b)   deal as agents for the investors;
(c)   arrange deals for the investors;
(d)   give investment advice; and
(e)   hold client money and other client assets.

Category 2 Money-holders

Members of this category are permitted to:

(a)   deal as agents for investors;
(b)   arrange deals for the investors;
(c)   give investment advice; and
(d)   hold client money and other client assets

but are prohibited from dealing as principal with investors.

Category 3 Arrangers

Members of this category are permitted to:

(a)   arrange deals for the investors; and
(b)   give investment advice

but are prohibited from dealing as principal with investors, or as agents, and from holding or handling client money or other assets.

Category 4 Authorised apart from membership

In this category are members which do not derive their authorisation to carry on investment business in the UK from membership of the PIA, or which are also regulated or supervised by a regulator other than the PIA.

5.2.1 Code of Conduct

The PIA has its own Code of Conduct. The principle is that a member, in the conduct of his business, shall observe high standards of commercial honour and just and equitable principles of trade. A member should avoid, and endeavour to ensure that any individual associated with the member avoids, any fraudulent, manipulative or deceptive act. The individual areas covered by the Rules are:

Principles
- integrity
- skill, care and diligence
- market practice
- information about customers
- information for customers
- conflicts of interest
- customer assets
- financial resources
- internal organisation
- relations with regulators

Obligations
- keeping up to date
- independent advice
- good communications
- issuing terms of business
- keeping a record
- keeping assets safe or secure
- mandates or powers of attorney
- returning cash or cheques

Prohibitions
- inducements
- conflicts of interest
- exclusions and contradictions
- unjustifiable transaction
- dealing ahead of publication
- insider dealing
- overcharging

Dealing with clients
- seeking clients
- providing investment services
- packaged products
- other investments
- reports of transactions

5.2.2 Client agreements

Before a member can provide a service for a client, a 'terms of business' letter or a client agreement containing information including details of handling client monies, the basis of charges and the protection afforded to the client against losses or errors and omissions has to be prepared. This agreement is likely to be in standard form and tailored according to the circumstances of a particular client.

5.2.3 Advertisements

Any advertisements made by a member must show that the firm is bound by PIA Rules by including the name of the member and the statement that the member is regulated by the Personal Investment Authority. Copies of any advertisements issued should be retained, together with details of which member's employee approved and checked compliance of the advert. Similarly, if the advertisement will become out of date after a certain event or period of time, that date should also be noted.

As a general rule, each member will be required to include the statement 'Regulated by the Personal Investment Authority' on all business letters, business cards, contract notes and other documents. The Rules also specify the required contents of advertisements containing either an offer, or an invitation to offer, to enter an investment agreement such as a life insurance contract or a personal equity plan.

5.2.4 Record-keeping

Members must maintain at an office or offices of the firm, for at least seven years, all such records as may be necessary to demonstrate compliance with all aspects of PIA Rules. Clients should be permitted to inspect any record kept which relates exclusively to a transaction effected with or for that client.

When receiving instructions from clients, the member must record:

(a) the date instructions were received and, if applicable, the time;
(b) the date those instructions were carried out or entrusted to a third party to carry out; and
(c) sufficient information to show that the transaction was suitable and advantageous to the client (or that no other transaction/product was more advantageous) if the investment advice was given by or on behalf of the member.

The member must keep copies of all communications sent to the client, including contract notes relating to sales and purchases, reports and valuations as set out in Table 5 Rule 5 of the PIA Rulebook.

5.2.5 Client's assets

Documents of title belonging to a member's client but held by the member must be held securely and only passed on:

(a) to the client; or
(b) in accordance with his directions.

The Rules on documents of title apply only to investments falling within paragraphs 1 to 6 of Schedule 1 to the FSA 1986. They do not therefore apply to life assurance policies. The owner's name must be identifiable on all client assets and details of individual client's assets should be summarised in a clients' asset register. A periodic statement of assets held for safekeeping is required to be sent to the client.

There are strict Rules for handling clients' money. They require that clients' money must at all times be separated from the member's money. Client money is 'money held or received in respect of an investment business client and not immediately due to the firm itself'. Any business receiving cheques from clients made payable to the business, where the cheques are wholly or in part payable to a third party in respect of investment business, handles clients' money. If the cheques are received by the investment business but they are made payable to a third party (say an insurance company) and the investment business simply passes them on to that third party, that is not handling clients' money. Clients' money must be held in designated client accounts, which must be in the name of the member and include the words 'client account' in the title.

The IBRC (Accounts and Business Requirements) Rules Approval Order 1979 provides that:

> 'Practising insurance brokers and enrolled bodies corporate shall without delay pay or cause to be paid into the Insurance Broking Account and into no other account all moneys paid to or received by them from all sources and which relate to insurance transactions of any kind in connection with their insurance broking business, including brokerage.
>
> Practising insurance brokers and enrolled bodies corporate shall use the Insurance Broking Account and no other account for payment to any insured or an insurance company of all monies due under insurance transactions of any kind in connection with their insurance broking business.'

This requirement would appear to give rise to a conflict between the PIA Rules and the IBRC Rules for brokers who are regulated by both bodies. In this situation the IBRC Practice Note 2 stipulates that mixed money (i.e. clients' money and money relating to insurance transactions) should be paid into an account designated 'client account (Insurance Broking Account)'.

5.2.6 Accounting records

The accounting records rules are similar to the requirements of the Companies Act 1985 but modified for an investment business. The requirements are set out in Rule 5 of the PIA Rules. There is no specific guidance within the PIA Rules as to the actual required content of the accounting records and the following is given as guidance only:

(a) daily entries of all sums of money received or expended, the matters to which they relate, and the persons from or to whom the payments were received or paid;

(b) a record of all items of income and expenditure, explaining their nature;

(c) a record of all assets and liabilities, including any commitments or contingent liabilities;

(d) for an unincorporated sole trader only, sufficient records of all assets and liabilities arising from personal and non-investment business activities to demonstrate solvency at all times; and

(e) for Category 1 and 2 members who handle client money, the transaction details required by the SIB's Financial Services (Clients' Money) Regulations 1991.

Information must be kept in such a way as to show compliance with the requirements of the PIA Rulebook and there must be procedures and controls in place to ensure that accounting entries are made promptly and accurately and, where appropriate, records are brought up to date at regular and frequent intervals. These records must be able to show at any time with reasonable accuracy the financial position of the member at that time, and provide the information required to prepare the reports and financial statements required by the PIA. These records must be kept in English and must be capable of being reproduced on paper. A member must also take reasonable steps to protect records against loss, unauthorised access, alteration or destruction.

Members must be able to produce their accounting records promptly at their place of business. Where records are retained away from business premises, the PIA must be informed of this in writing and provided with the address and telephone number of the place at which they are kept.

These records must be retained for six years. A member's client must be allowed to see all correspondence and records relating to any business relevant solely to him.

5.2.7 Financial reporting

All members are required to provide the PIA with financial information at the frequency and within the time limits specified in the rules applicable to each category of member. Members subject to the liquid capital or adjusted capital requirements (see Table 5.2) are required to submit audited financial statements within four months of the annual accounting reference date. This applies to both incorporated and unincorporated businesses. Members subject to the liquid capital requirements are also required to submit monthly unaudited financial statements within three weeks of each monthly accounting reference date, while members subject to the adjusted capital requirements must prepare quarterly financial statements although these only have to be submitted to the PIA in certain circumstances. Annual financial statements consist of:

(a) balance sheet;
(b) profit and loss account;
(c) notes to the balance sheet and profit and loss account;
(d) statement of financial resources;
(e) liquid capital or adjusted capital calculation;
(f) discount rates for investments;
(g) sole trader's statement of solvency (if applicable); and
(h) a reconciliation of the amounts in the annual financial statements with those in the monthly/quarterly accounts.

Detailed requirements and formats can be found in the PIA Rules.

The amount at which the items are required to be included in the financial statements must be determined in accordance with the rules laid down by the Companies Act and accounting standards.

For unincorporated businesses, only the items relating to investment business are to be included in the accounts of a sole proprietor (if a sole proprietor has more than one business, separate accounts are required for the investment business). Tax liabilities representing income tax on:

(a) the whole of the profits up to the accounting reference date; or
(b) the greater of the year of assessment basis or cessation basis

will be liabilities for the purpose of the financial resources calculations.

As regards incorporated members where the member has subsidiaries, the financial statements are to be unconsolidated.

The PIA has prescribed the form and content for the annual financial statements in the adopted Rules of FIMBRA, Appendix 4. The formats are based on the Companies Act 1985 Schedule 4 formats but require some additional disclosures.

One particularly important area of detailed categorisation is commission income, and where a firm deals in life assurance policies it should be noted that commission has to be split between:

(a)   commission on indemnity terms;
(b)   renewal commission; and
(c)   other.

Commission is received on indemnity terms where the broker is liable to repay all or part of commission received from the insurance company should the client break the contract within, say, three years (the bulk of the first year's premium on an insurance policy is effectively to cover the commission).

As the PIA formats are more detailed than the Companies Act formats, incorporated members cannot simply attach a statement of financial resources to their statutory financial statements in order to satisfy PIA requirements. Incorporated members will also need to produce additional statutory financial statements for filing with the Registrar of Companies.

The annual financial statements must state that they have been approved by the directors or partners and be signed by two directors or partners. In the case of a sole proprietor the financial statements must contain a statement that at the balance sheet date the total assets of the proprietor exceeded his total liabilities regardless of whether the assets and liabilities have arisen in the course of his investment business.

5.2.8   Questionnaires

Category 2 and 3 members of the PIA are required to submit an annual questionnaire within two months of the end of their accounting reference date as well as any other returns required by the PIA. The questionnaire must be signed by two directors or two partners. It seeks to ascertain compliance with the rules and to collect relevant information on a firm's financial position which the financial statements would not reveal.

5.2.9 Special reporting matters

All members must inform the PIA, as soon as practicable and at least within five working business days, if any of the following circumstances have arisen or are likely to arise:

(a)   a breach of the member's financial resources requirements;
(b)   legal action being instituted by a creditor against the member;
(c)   inability, through a failure in computerised or other accounting systems, to comply or demonstrate compliance with the Rules;
(d)   inability to submit a financial return as required by the Rules;
(e)   for Category 1 and 2 members, the likelihood that the auditors' report on the annual financial statements will be qualified;
(f)   the office of an auditor becoming vacant;
(g)   fraudulent or other dishonest activities on the part of partners, directors, appointed representatives or employees;
(h)   legal proceedings or investigations instituted against the member;
(i)   inaccurate information supplied to the PIA;
(j)   refusal or cancellation of indemnity cover;
(k)   an emergency which makes it impracticable for the member to comply with a Rule; the PIA must be informed of the emergency, the Rule affected, and the steps being taken as a consequence; and
(l)   a material breach of any requirement or prohibition in the Rule-book in relation to the conduct of its investment staff.

5.2.10 Financial resource requirements

The PIA requires its members to meet two financial resource tests. These tests are as follows:

(a)   All firms will be required to demonstrate that they maintain a minimum capital share base of £10,000 'own funds'.

For an incorporated entity 'own funds' include initial capital, other reserves and audited profit less any intangible assets and material current year losses.

For an unincorporated entity 'own funds' include current and capital accounts less any intangible assets and material current year losses.

(b)   Minimum financial resource requirements as set out in Table 5.2.

5.2.11 Auditors

In addition to the audit report to the members of a corporate body, an auditors' report, addressed to the PIA should be prepared for the following PIA members:

Table 5.2

Category	Mininum financial resource requirements
1	Liquid capital equal to the higher of: • 13/52 of relevant annual expenditure; or • £10,000; or • £400 per salesperson/adviser
2 With 1–25 salespersons/advisers	Adjusted capital equal to the higher of: • 4/52 of relevant annual expenditure; or • £2,500; or • £400 per salesperson/adviser; and Adjusted net current assets of £1
2 With discretionary portfolio management or with 26+ salespersons/advisers	Adjusted capital equal to the higher of: • 8/52 of relevant annual expenditure; or • £2,500; or • £400 per salesperson/adviser; and Adjusted net current assets of £1
3 With 26+ salespersons/advisers	Adjusted capital equal to the higher of: • 4/52 of relevant annual expenditure; or • £2,500; or • £400 per salesperson/adviser; and Adjusted net current assets of £1
2 or 3 Network member	Adjusted capital equal to the higher of: • 13/52 of relevant annual expenditure; or • £2,500; or • £400 per salesperson/adviser; and Adjusted net current assets of £1

Full details of these requirements can be found in the adopted FIMBRA Rules 19–21. Certain kinds of business may require compliance with special financial resource requirements and these, for example, need to be checked against the original rules.

(a)   all members of Categories 1 and 2;
(b)   members of Category 3 with more than 26 investment staff or proposing to carry on discretionary portfolio management; or
(c)   members of Category 4 prudentially regulated by the PIA or bound by Clients' Money Regulations or PIA Rules for custody of client's assets.

The auditor appointed must be eligible to act under the Rules of the PIA and the PIA must be informed in writing of the name, address and qualifications of the auditor within five business days of the appointment.

An auditor has the right of access at all times to the accounting and other records of the member and the right to obtain from the officers, controllers and managers such information as he requires.

In addition, the member must permit and require the auditor to provide the PIA with any information and opinions which are relevant to the functions of the PIA. Further guidance on reporting directly to the PIA can be found later in this chapter.

5.2.12   Audit reports

The auditors' report to the PIA on the member's financial statements must state that:

(a)   the member's financial statements have been audited in accordance with auditing standards;
(b)   the auditor has obtained all the information and explanations which to the best of his knowledge and belief are necessary for the purpose of the audit.

In addition it must state whether in the auditors' opinion:

(a)   the annual financial statements have been prepared in accordance with PIA Rules;
(b)   the statement of financial resources has been prepared and calculated in accordance with PIA Rules;
(c)   the financial statements give a true and fair view of the state of affairs of the business at the balance sheet date and the profit or loss for the period;
(d)   where the member is required to reconcile the financial statements it has submitted to the PIA with its annual financial statements, that the reconciliation has been properly prepared;
(e)   proper accounting records have been maintained throughout the year;

(f)   the balance sheet and profit and loss are in agreement with the member's accounting records and returns;

(g)   as at the date at which the balance sheet was prepared, the member had financial resources of at least the minimum required to comply with the financial resources requirement to which it was subject;

(h)   where applicable, the member has maintained throughout the year systems to enable it to comply with the Rules and regulations relating to client money and other client assets;

(i)   where applicable, the member was in compliance with the relevant Clients' Money Regulations as at three specified dates, being the member's accounting reference date and two other dates chosen by the auditor;

(j)   where applicable, the member has not committed any breaches of the Clients' Money Regulations, other than trivial breaches which have been remedied; and

(k)   where applicable, the member has carried out reconciliations required by PIA Rules (including reconciliations of client money and other client assets) and there are no outstanding unexplained differences which require adjustment.

If appropriate, the auditor must confirm that nothing has come to his attention to indicate that the member held client money or other client assets during the financial year.

5.2.13 Second audit

The PIA may appoint a second auditor to re-examine any accounts or other information reported on by the member's auditor, or to examine any other specified information. The member is required to assist the second auditor and to take all reasonable steps to obtain his auditor's assistance for the second auditor. The expenses of any second audit are borne by the member.

5.2.14 Audit approach

The requirements for the auditor to report on the adequacy of the member's systems with respect to clients' assets, including clients' money, and on the statement of financial resources must be considered at the planning stage of the audit. The work should be carried out in accordance with APB Practice Note 1, *Investment Business.*

In order to form an opinion on the systems controlling clients' assets, a detailed record of the systems should be prepared to identify the internal controls the member has instituted to ensure adherence to the Rules. Compliance testing should assure the auditor that the controls are operating effectively. The auditor must also be satisfied that the member has clients' assets held in safe custody on their behalf.

In addition to the items set out in the Auditing Guidcline *Engagement Letters*, the engagement letter to PIA members should state:

(a) the period for which the auditor is appointed;
(b) the duty to provide the member with written comments on its internal controls and management information, or with a statement that he has no such comments to make;
(c) the duty to carry out any investigations he considers necessary to form an opinion on the matters required to be included in his report under (d) below;
(d) a duty to submit to the PIA a report on the annual financial statements within four months of the accounting reference date;
(e) a duty to provide additional information or verification as requested by the PIA;
(f) a duty to report to the PIA any circumstances in which he has reasonable cause to believe that the matter is likely to be of material significance for determining whether a person is fit and proper to carry on investment business, or whether action should be taken in order to protect investors from significant risk of loss;
(g) a duty to assist any other auditor appointed by the PIA; and
(h) a duty to notify both the member and the PIA, and to resign his office, if he becomes ineligible to act or disqualified from acting as auditor.

Where a PIA member is part of a group for whom the auditor acts, a separate letter of engagement should be prepared for the PIA member. This letter should be referred to in the group letter of engagement.

The following additional planning procedures should be followed for all PIA members:

(a) obtain details of bank accounts, ensure proper designation for client accounts and inspect acknowledgements from the bank;
(b) review returns and questionnaires submitted to the PIA during the period to identify any problem areas;
(c) review previous management letters and, if applicable, any reports of the compliance officer to identify problem areas;
(d) ensure availability of PIA Rulebook and FSA 1986; and
(e) ensure audit staff are familiar with PIA Rules, s109 FSA, SAS 620 and APB Practice Note 5 (described later in this chapter).

The statement of financial resources should be audited by agreeing all items included in the statement as set out in the adopted FIMBRA Rules, parts 19–21, to the audited balance sheet, profit and loss account and related notes. All calculations of admissible amounts should be checked by reference to the relevant rules as stated within the Rules.

Under PIA Rule 7.4.2, an auditor has a duty to provide the member with written comments on its internal controls and management information, or with a statement that he has no such comments to make. Within ten business days of receiving this report to management the member must send a copy to the PIA, together with a statement setting out details of recommendations to be implemented or reasons why recommendations are not to be implemented as per adopted FIMBRA Rule 25.2.

5.2.15 Auditors' duty to report direct to the PIA

Under Statement of Auditing Standards 620, *The Auditor's Right and Duty to Report to the Regulators in the Financial Sector* (SAS 620), and FSA 1986, s109 auditors of PIA members have the statutory duty in certain circumstances to bring information to the attention of the PIA without the member's prior knowledge or consent. These instances occur when during the course of his ordinary audit work the auditor becomes aware of information that is relevant or of material significance to the PIA.

This duty normally arises when an apparent breach of PIA requirements comes to the auditor's attention. These breaches can be divided into the following main categories:

(a) a breach in the financial requirements of the member;
(b) a breach by the member of the Conduct of Business Rules;
(c) an indication that the directors are not fit and proper to act as such.

On determining whether a breach should be reported directly to the PIA the auditor would normally discuss the breach with the member's directors and obtain their knowledge and agreement before making a report to the PIA. A copy of this report would be sent to the directors as well as to the PIA. When the auditor concludes that the breach does not give rise to a statutory duty to report directly to the PIA, he may advise the directors to report the breach themselves. Any matter casting doubt on the integrity of the directors must be reported without informing the directors in advance.

When determining whether the breach gives rise to a duty to report to the PIA, the auditor will consider the following:

(a) whether a minor breach indicates a general lack of compliance with PIA requirements:

(b) whether the breach has already been reported to the PIA and corrected by the directors;

(c) whether the breach still exists, or the directors have taken corrective action, or the breach has recurred; and

(d) whether a report to the PIA is necessary immediately to protect the interests and assets of the member's clients.

Detailed guidance on special factors to be considered in the application of SAS 620 to audits of investment businesses is given in Practice Note 5 *The Auditor's Right and Duty to Report to SIB and Other Regulators of Investment Businesses*. The Practice Note is issued by the Auditing Practices Board.

However, in certain circumstances the auditor would report directly to the PIA without consultation with directors. These instances would occur where the breach related to the fit and proper criteria concerning directors, where there was no indication that the directors had reported a breach brought to their attention by the auditor to the PIA, or where prompt action is necessary to protect clients interests.

Under both SAS 620 and s109 FSA 1986 an auditor is entitled to communicate directly to the PIA without contravening the duty of confidentiality owed to a member if the information and opinions are made in good faith.

PART III

Financial management

Chapter 6 – In the high street

6.1 Introduction

The variety of insurance broking operations brings with it a variety of management structures and styles. However, basic structures tend to follow the size of operation, and there is a clear distinction between the provincial or high street broker and a London, Lloyd's or international broker. We shall look at the former in this chapter and at the larger London-based organisation in the next.

6.2 Management structure

High street brokers are generally concerned with life and pensions, and personal and commercial lines business. Some, like many London brokers, may handle particular types of business requiring specialist expertise. For the purposes of this chapter, a general broker has been assumed, with significant involvement of the owners.

Such a broker will typically have the structure shown in Figure 6.1. The principals will often handle life and pensions and commercial lines business themselves, since this is the most profitable. They will obviously play a significant role in business management but with increased regulation the importance of this role is enhanced, since proper systems and controls are essential to any broking operation, however small. Personal lines business and office management will generally be the direct responsibility of senior staff. The larger personal risks should certainly be overseen by a partner or principal.

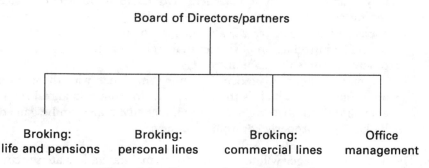

Figure 6.1 Structure of a high street broker

Claims processing is an area in which many high street brokers are involved. They prefer that clients deal only with them, both when placing business and making claims, rather than having too much direct contact with the insurer. Where the business handles claims, this will generally be the responsibility of the person who placed the business.

Office management is critical, and competent administration will help the smooth running and successful growth of the business. Maintaining renewal diaries, ensuring that the computer systems and data are kept up to date, processing debit notes and other documentation promptly, and cash and credit control are all matters requiring discipline and administrative skill. The office manager will have these responsibilities, together with basic bookkeeping. Financial management in its broadest sense, however, embraces more than maintaining books of account, and the principals will need to be involved if this aspect of the business is to be properly controlled.

6.3   Financial management

There are a number of reasons why insurance brokers need good financial management.

(a)   To comply with the regulations of the IBRC or Lloyd's (see Part II).

(b)   To comply with the Companies Act 1985. It is a legal obligation for company directors to know at any time whether or not their company is solvent and it is illegal for them to carry on trading if the company is insolvent. They must also maintain proper accounting books and records. If the broking business is not a limited company, bankruptcy law may influence its owners to ensure proper financial control and to protect their own interests.

(c)   To comply with Inland Revenue regulations. The Inland Revenue requires all businesses to submit accounts in order that an annual assessment to tax can be made. The Revenue has wide powers to levy amounts which it considers reasonable if no accounts are submitted. These estimates can often be well in excess of the correct figures but are payable in the absence of other information. The introduction of Pay and File reinforces the importance of timely accounts production.

(d)   To gain a competitive edge. It is not compliance with these rules and regulations which is the best reason for sound financial management. A competitive edge and market advantage can be gained by having a properly controlled business.

The financial manager will therefore need to maintain adequate systems and controls to ensure compliance with the regulatory requirements.

Financial information will have to be available on a timely basis so that management can monitor performance and maintain solvency. Annual financial statements must be prepared to meet regulatory, legal and fiscal requirements and to avoid estimated assessments.

In order to meet these obligations, the financial manager will be involved in the business plan (see **6.6** below) and its conversion into financial targets, budgets and forecasts. The recording and processing systems will be developed to provide timely information and to manage assets effectively.

6.4   Letters of engagement

Letters of engagement are an increasingly common feature of any broker's business and often provide the first stage in a new client relationship, especially where remuneration is fee-based rather than by means of brokerage. It is important that the letter sets out clearly the respective obligations and rights of the client and broker, and the price to be paid for the service provided. Each letter will contain some common clauses but it will need tailoring to the particular circumstances of the relationship. Drafting may well benefit from legal advice, especially the standard paragraphs.

The letter should cover the following matters:

(a)   the extent and duration of the appointment;
(b)   the basis of remuneration, whether by way of fees or commissions;
(c)   the services offered by the broker and the extent to which the client wishes to take a 'cradle-to-grave' package or specialised advice;
(d)   the settlement of accounts;
(e)   any obligations for vetting security of markets used;
(f)   responsibility for claims negotiation and collection; and
(g)   termination of the relationship, including running off business, transfer of documentation and settlement of termination fees.

6.5   Recording and processing

An essential feature of any broking business, irrespective of the sophistication of its management information, is the adequacy of its recording, accounting and processing procedures. BIIBA, in a booklet on manual accounting procedures, now out of print, suggested that the objectives of an accounting system were to:

(a)   collect what is due;
(b)   pay what is payable;

(c)   know one's brokerage earnings;

(d)   record expenditure;

(e)   prepare budgets based on past expenditure and on expected changes in that expenditure; and

(f)   have such records that periodic financial results can be prepared.

In order to achieve these objectives, BIIBA indicated that the following records were required:

(a)   a detailed record of cash received;

(b)   a detailed record of cash paid, including 'household' expenditure;

(c)   a detailed record of premiums and returned premiums;

(d)   a record to show at any time the balance on insurance company accounts; and

(e)   a system which will identify a true list of debtors and creditors for the balance sheet.

This guidance remains valid.

Often, prior to the IBRC Rules, insurance brokers did not have good accounting systems. However, the relaxed attitude of the market towards settlements and the relationships between brokers and underwriters has been changing in recent years, with a consequent requirement for systems to be improved. Insurers now require earlier settlements as they seek to maximise their own investment income, and they are cutting brokerage rates at the same time. Clients demand greater service and often require renewals to be rebroked. This places pressure on the broker to ensure that his system is working as efficiently as possible. If the business is high volume and low premium, such as motor or personal lines, the speed of throughput is crucial to the success of the operation. Direct sales techniques used by insurers increase the pressure on traditional brokers handling this type of business.

The objective of a good system is to provide information which is accurate and complete, meaningful and economic. The system should also enable the broker to control events and limit his dependence on information from either the client or the underwriter. The broker will have the following particular objectives for the system:

(a)   early identification and invoicing of renewals;

(b)   a clear policy on settlement;

(c)   a clear policy on funding;

(d)   regular reconciliations with underwriters; and

(e)   a full listing of all outstanding client premiums on a strict ageing basis.

Cash flow is essential to an insurance broker, and clients must therefore be invoiced promptly. Renewals should be rebroked as a matter of course and renewal notices should include a statement that this has been done, even if it is still placed with the same underwriter. This will help to pre-empt clients requesting the service at a later stage.

Provided clients are invoiced and reminded at an early date, the settlement date should not be later than the risk date. The client should be warned that if premiums are not paid by the risk date the policy will lapse. This will help avoid funding premiums. Brokers should avoid funding either the market or the client for premiums or claims. In the majority of cases such funding will cost the broker money either through lost investment income or bad debts.

It is important for brokers to maintain independent records of amounts due to or from underwriters and that these are regularly reconciled with statements received. Payment policy will vary according to the individual broker. Insurance companies are encouraging payment of premiums direct from the insured on an instalment basis, with the insurance broker's account being credited with commission. While this affects the broker's cash flow position, a higher proportion of business is often retained with the existing insurer as a result. However, there is less opportunity for rebroking at renewal. Proper records of these instalments must be kept by the broker to ensure no lapse of cover or default of premiums.

An efficient recording and processing system generates a wealth of information concerning clients and underwriters. Much of it emanates from the original source document, the proposal form or slip, and the design and completion of this form is therefore important in creating a business database. The proposal form will typically include the following details:

(a) Name of insured;
(b) Address;
(c) Business;
(d) Type of insurance;
(e) Details of risk;
(f) Underwriting company; and
(g) Method of payment.

Invoice details, including premium and brokerage, will be shown in the broker's accounting records. The brokerage rate is only disclosed to the policyholder on request, although this situation is changing for regulated business.

This information will be used to maintain the insurance ledgers. In the larger broker it may be useful to analyse information by branch or type of risk so that the underlying components of the profitability of the business can be examined for management control purposes. A master file containing the above details for all the broker's clients will be most useful if it is held in a flexible form, such as a computer database. Measurement of performance often consists of applying different criteria to a selection of basic information. A well-managed computer database speeds up this process. For instance, in order to measure actual performance against budgets drawn up in accordance with the business plan, it should be possible to split brokerage by:

(a) type of business (motor, fire, property, etc.);
(b) location; and
(c) salesman or source of introduction.

This information can be used to test the validity of the assumptions and estimates made in setting budgets. Trading accounts allocating brokerage and costs between life and general business can be drawn up to identify the sources of profit. A computer system will expedite the collation of this information both for financial management and for the production of mailing lists, quotation systems for most domestic business and word processing, among other areas. The advantages of information technology for the broker are discussed in Part V.

The accounting system of recording and processing is designed to provide information both for management purposes and to help prepare the annual financial statements in accordance with the Companies Act 1985. These statements are also the basis for the annual IBRC and PIA returns and for the submission of taxation computations to the Inland Revenue. The accounts formats illustrated in Appendix 4 include only the basic information required to be submitted for compliance purposes, and further detail is necessary for 'true and fair', Lloyd's and IBRC requirements. The need for compliance can conflict with the need for management information, particularly in the four areas of presentation, economy, speed and accuracy which are discussed in the following paragraphs.

Compliance regulations on presentation embodied in both the Companies Act and the IBRA represent a compromise between political, public and commercial interests. They have been designed to apply to all broking companies, regardless of size and specialisation, and for the protection of the client or shareholder who does not play a role in the management of the business, rather than for the use of the business itself. By definition, compliance reporting deals in past events and in

100

historical data; it is usually carried out after the end of the accounting period to which it relates. By contrast, management accounting should be dynamic. It will make use of historical information but as a means of preparing forecasts and budgets for the future and measuring performance.

The increasing size and complexity of the annual financial statements makes it more difficult to isolate key indicators and trends in the figures. This skill often belongs to the trained professional analyst. Management information, on the other hand, should be presented briefly and economically, without sacrificing quality, and in a manner which avoids confusion.

The filing requirements for the financial statements of insurance broking companies are as follows:

(a) the Companies Act requires audited financial statements to be filed within ten months of the end of the financial year for a private company;

(b) the IBRA requires audited financial statements and other returns to be filed within six months of the end of the financial year; and

(c) the PIA and Lloyd's require audited financial statements and other returns within four months of the end of the financial year.

The need for timely management information is much more urgent, especially in view of such developments as:

(a) changes in brokerage structure and fees;

(b) the scarcity of underwriting capacity in certain specialist fields (e.g. product liability); and

(c) changes in the broker's role, such as responsibility for risk management.

Compliance information has to be audited by outside firms, which adds to the time involved in producing the necessary reports. Insurance brokers' accounting systems and staff should produce internal management information soon after the end of an accounting period.

The accuracy of the information generated will depend on the quality of the system and the people who operate it. The requirement to produce the key information quickly overrides the need for making small adjustments to the figures. The annual financial statements are therefore unsatisfactory for management control purposes in these four critical areas of presentation, economy, speed and accuracy.

The form in which management accounts are presented needs to be readily understood by all users. It is critical in a high street broking business that the principals, who are usually not accountants, should be able to understand and use the figures, and they should therefore actively contribute to the shape and form of the information which they receive. It is important for management and owners to establish their business objectives so that management information can be presented in a form that enables the achievement of those objectives to be monitored.

6.6 Business plan

The business plan sets out the management objectives and gives shape and structure to an organisation. It may cover a period of up to ten years and take the form of an outline memorandum. The objectives identified in the plan are translated into detailed financial form by the preparation of annual budgets and cash flow forecasts, which provide the link between strategic objectives and day-to-day tactics.

The budget also provides a realistic target for performance. Those ultimately responsible for the business must play the main role in the preparation of the budget. Their knowledge of the particular business, its employees, clients and markets, and their perception of how it fits into the insurance industry will determine what the budget contains. The budget should be prepared in the same format as the management accounts but will be based on many underlying perceptions, estimates and assumptions as to how the business will behave in the next 12 months. It may be necessary to budget during the year as circumstances change.

Cash flow forecasts target liquidity in the same way as budgets target profit performance. One key contributor to profit performance is investment income, which can only be maximised if workable predictions of cash flow are made. These predictions should be based on the knowledge and experience of the principals, who have a key role to play even if they are not accountants. Specific predictions have to be made about how quickly debts will be collected when creditors will be paid, when capital expenditure will be incurred and the timing of new sources of finance.

The assumptions on which the plan, budgets and forecasts are based will derive from management's perception of a variety of internal and external influences, such as:

(a) changes in the business environment;
(b) changes in personnel;
(c) changes in market;
(d) changes in technology;

(e)   changes in brokerage rates;
(f)   identification of different objectives;
(g)   increased competition;
(h)   tax changes; and
(i)   changes in interest rates and, if applicable, exchange rates.

The financial services industry is in the midst of change, with major advances in information technology, greater freedom in currency markets and increasing legislation, all demanding a response from the individual business. The financial effects of this response need to be assessed, and the assumptions and estimates made in preparing the annual plan changed if necessary. Estimates and assumptions need to be tested against actual results to determine whether right decisions have been made and, if not, to assist in the correction of those decisions. The nature of this process is quite different from meeting the compliance regulations – it is dynamic rather than static and needs to be regularly updated if it is to be useful.

6.7   Management accounts

When the projected financial consequences of the business plan have been embodied in the budget, actual results can be monitored. Standard formats for budgets and cash flow forecasts make computer production of the reports easier, and comparisons between products and divisions simpler. The management reporting package should be brief and include a profit and loss account, summary of key information, including IBA solvency reports, and cash flow statement. A trial balance sheet should be included in the reporting package but only as a memorandum. It will not usually need detailed consideration.

Ideally, management reports should be prepared on a four-weekly basis, making 13 reporting periods in a year, in preference to monthly reports of uneven length. The reports should be completed within two weeks of the end of the reporting period if they are to be useful in decision-making.

6.8   Profit and loss account

The profit and loss account should be arranged to report the actual compared with budget results for both the reporting period and the year to date, together with variances.

A suggested format is set out below. A report in identical format should be used for the year-to-date figures against the budget, and the year-to-date variances.

MONTHLY MANAGEMENT PROFIT AND LOSS ACCOUNT FORMAT

ABC Brokers Ltd

Reporting date 7 March 199X

Year ending 31 December 199X
Reporting period 2
29 January–25 February
Division: Personal lines

	Actual £	Budget £	Variance £
Brokerage and/or fee income			
Direct costs	———	———	———
Gross profit			
Add:			
Investment income	———	———	———
Less:			
Fixed overheads:			
Administrative salaries			
Administrative overheads			
Costs of premises			
Depreciation	———	———	———
Operating profit before tax	═══	═══	═══

The same format can be used to report results for different divisions or different locations. A broker with an office in Norwich specialising in commercial risks and pensions, and an office in Ipswich writing life business and personal lines, can use this format to generate profit and loss accounts for four profit centres:

Norwich	Commercial lines
Norwich	Pension
Ipswich	Life business
Ipswich	Personal lines

The format of the report is straightforward but it highlights important control points, such as gross profit, brokerage and direct costs, which are discussed in the following paragraphs.

Gross profit is calculated by deducting the direct costs of earning brokerage from the brokerage itself. Direct costs are essential, unavoidable costs which are incurred in generating income. Although it may be possible to influence the ratio of one cost to another, without them there can be no income and hence gross profit effectively makes up the real income of any business. An ability to influence and increase gross profit is one of the most important advantages a broker can have.

The calculation of the brokerage figure or fee income should normally be straightforward and a product of a reliable recording and processing system. For management accounting purposes, this figure could usefully be shown gross, that is, before any payments to other intermediaries, split commissions or policy costs. Each particular item of income and expenditure is subject to different influences on its behaviour and 'netting' figures may cause management to draw incorrect conclusions. Complications in assessing income may arise, notably from life and pensions business where substantial initial commissions are paid which may be returnable if the policy lapses within its first three years. Provisions based on experience should be set up to ensure commission is not regarded as income until it is earned.

Direct costs are the sum of all costs incurred in earning the brokerage. They may be fixed and accrue with time, or variable and change with the level of activity. Examples of direct costs are brokerage paid away, split commissions, and commission, salaries and expenses of salesmen or representatives.

Overheads are usually largely fixed, in the short term at least, and include:

(a) salaries for directors and staff, other than those regarded as direct costs;
(b) rent and rates;
(c) heat and light;
(d) post, telephones, telex and fax;
(e) computer leasing charges; and
(f) depreciation.

Service costs, such as electricity, will vary with usage, but they tend to stay reasonably constant as long as the business operates from the same premises. Individually, these costs are not usually significant in terms of their effect on the profitability of a business, and they are therefore grouped in the profit and loss format.

The most difficult expense to allocate is the salaries and employment costs of the brokers or sales executives themselves. Overhead staff – secretaries, claims and clerical personnel – are a fixed cost, but management will fulfil both selling and administrative functions, and sales teams may have responsibilities for liaison with insurance companies and underwriters which do not directly relate to the selling function.

One method of controlling and allocating salary costs properly is to develop a time recording system. Employment costs, which should include all benefits, can then be allocated between the fixed and variable categories according to the ratio shown by the time summary. Hours worked should be analysed between administrative work, development of new products, and dealing and negotiating directly with customers, both potential and existing. Time spent with clients can be analysed between new and renewal business and claims. Time with underwriters should be charged to new product development or the particular client involved. Allocation to individual clients probably depends on the size of their account and will not be appropriate for a small business. The time analysis should be compared with a budget.

Identifying costs and income as suggested provides a means of judging the effectiveness of management in generating gross profit. Brokerage and direct costs are the variable elements in the profit and loss account to which successful brokers pay the greatest attention. Once a cost has been identified as fixed, there is little that management can do about it, at least in the short term.

All variances must be analysed to ensure that management understands how they have arisen. Explanations should be verified and discussed with the management team. Appropriate action should be taken to correct deficiencies or enhance benefits and, if necessary, assumptions made in the budgeting process should be amended. In the latter case a new budget may have to be prepared for the remainder of the year.

6.9 Key analysis

Further analysis of performance is important for adequate management control. The budget will have been built up from detailed assumptions relating to brokerage, and these figures should be monitored and subjected to critical analysis. For each division of the business the following statistics should be produced:

(a) number of policies written;
(b) number of new policies written;
(c) average premium (per policy);
(d) average brokerage (per policy);
(e) lapse rate; and
(f) renewal rate.

These statistics can be reported by individual, division or company. The larger and more diverse the business, the greater the level of analysis required. After allowing for lapses and adjustments, brokerage is determined by the number of policies written multiplied by the average premium multiplied by the average brokerage rate.

Estimates will be made of direct costs such as:

(a) average commission/brokerage paid away;
(b) average policy processing fee; and
(c) claims servicing costs.

Unless the business employs a sales staff paid on a commission basis, none of the above figures is likely to be significant. If a time recording system is used for staff responsible for producing new business, direct costs can be budgeted and monitored by recording information on hours worked and salary rate per hour. If this method is not used, the most practical alternative is to classify staff by function (i.e. either broking or administrative) and charge their salaries to direct costs or salaries as appropriate.

A number of statistics produced are 'average' figures and may therefore be criticised on the grounds that they are imprecise. If averages reveal significant variances from budget, these should be investigated by means of more detailed reports and analyses. Again, the information should be used to stimulate management decisions.

The full report could take the following format:

ABC Brokers Ltd

Reporting date 7 March 199X

Year ended 31 December 199X
Reporting period 2
29 January–25 February
Division: Personal lines

	Actual	*Budget*	*Variance*
Broking statistics:			
Number of policies written			
Number of new policies written			
Average premium (per policy)			
Average brokerage (per policy)			
Lapse rate			
Renewal rate			
Direct costs:			
Average commission (per policy)			
Average policy processing fee			
Claims servicing costs			
Direct selling – hours worked			
Salary rate per hour			
Collections/payments:			
Debtors payment period			
Creditors payment period			

107

6.10 Cash flow forecasts

The format of the cash flow forecast should be designed to give management a clear overview of business performance in cash terms. Profit is very much a judgemental figure determined after applying accounting policies to items such as depreciation and claims servicing, which can retrospectively be seen to have been flawed. Cash performance is more clearly understood by non-accountants and is not so susceptible to creative accounting or management.

The assumptions made in estimating brokerage earnings should also be applied to cash flow. As brokers act as collecting and paying agents on behalf of their clients, substantial fluctuations in liquidity occur. If brokerage rates average 20 per cent and, say, £200,000 is earned in one year, then £1,000,000 of premium will pass through the IBA bank account. Interest at 5 per cent for one month generates approximately £4,000 of investment income. This situation does not apply to life and pensions or other business where premiums are paid direct to the underwriter.

It is not only commercial considerations but also IBRC and PIA solvency requirements which should stimulate brokers to pay careful attention to their cash flow. The principal estimates which need to be made in predicting cash flow, in addition to those already made to predict brokerage, are the debtor and creditor payment periods. The flow of cash should be predicted and monitored so that investment decisions can be made without risking current account shortages, delays in paying creditors or non-compliance with regulations. A useful base date for calculating debtor and creditor payment periods is the risk inception date. This is not susceptible to management manipulation.

The format set out below will help monitor the performance of the business from a balance sheet view. The monthly report of cash flow should be complemented by an annual, month-by-month, forecast in similar format, which is updated on a month-by-month basis for actual results.

MONTHLY MANAGEMENT CASH FLOW FORECAST

ABC Brokers Ltd

Reporting date 7 March 199X

Year ended 31 December 199X
Reporting period 2
29 January–25 February
Division: Personal lines

	Actual £	*Budget* £	*Variance* £
Total debtors			
Total creditors			
Net current assets			
Profit/(loss) before tax			
Adjustment for non-cash items:			
Depreciation			
Other			
Cash profit/(loss)			
Increase/(decrease) in net current assets			
Funds introduced			
Sales/(purchases) of fixed assets			
Cash/bank movement for the month			
Closing balance/overdraft			

The cash flow format attributes movements in cash and bank balances to:

(a) movements in net current assets, i.e. the movement in the relationship between debtors and creditors, which is usually the most important factor in cash flow movements;

(b) profits, adjusted for non-cash items such as depreciation and movements in provisions for liabilities and charges; and

(c) capital movements such as sales or purchases of fixed assets or changes in the financing of the business.

This format complements the format of the profit and loss account by examining primarily the management of debtors, creditors and cash and bank balances. Cash flow performance is achieved by managing the assets and liabilities of the business – creating the assets in the first instance is achieved by managing the profit and loss account. Levels of capital expenditure in insurance brokers are lower than in many other businesses, although investment in computers, other information technology equipment or companies pregnant with goodwill, may be significant.

The financial manager's responsibilities in respect of different categories of asset and liability are set out in Table 6.1.

Variances between actual and budgeted cash flow require detailed appraisal. Management action may be necessary to correct shortfalls in other areas by more efficient use of the liquid assets of the business.

Table 6.1

Balance sheet category	*Financial manager's responsibility*
Investments	Choice of investment – type of security, duration and interest rate. IBRC regulations
Bank and cash balances	Maintaining appropriate levels of bank and cash balances; complying with IBRC restrictions on designated IBA accounts; keeping clients' and insurer's monies separate from the private expenses account
Debtors	Controls over renewal notices and debit notes; collection policy, bad debts and funding
Creditors	Controls over settlement with underwriters and clients

We have seen that both budgets and cash flow forecasts depend on making a number of estimates of business performance. Often estimated figures need to be changed because of changing circumstances; hence the need for reporting to be dynamic rather than static. This can be aided by setting up computer models for budgets and cash flow forecasts which can be readily adapted for these changes.

In a high street broker, the role of the financial or accounting manager is vital. Developments in information technology – networking, for example – still have a major role to play in improving the quality of the business quotation, recording and processing function in broking companies. It is the strength of that function which enables financial managers to add to their compliance function an effective contribution to the commercial development of the company.

Chapter 7 – London and international

7.1 Organisation

The financial management of an international insurance broking group, a company acting mainly in the London market, or a Lloyd's broker, is similar to the high street or provincial broker, only on a larger scale. Consequently, aspects of internal control, for example, take a higher profile since the requirements to comply with the regulatory authorities are the same whatever the size of company.

A major insurance broking group may operate through a non-trading holding company with a number of associate or subsidiary companies. These will often be organised to deal with broking in particular areas of activity, such as:

(a) classes of insurance, for example aviation, property or reinsurance;
(b) industries, for example agriculture or nuclear power; or
(c) geographical, such as UK, North America or Europe.

Other group companies will handle specialised internal services.

The organisation chart might be as shown in Figure 7.1.

In certain instances, a subsidiary company may be created to enable the group to give senior personnel director status. Other subsidiaries may be involved in providing underwriting facilities to their clients in the company market. A broking group may not, of course, act as a managing agent at Lloyd's. Corporate underwriting activities will again be through a separate subsidiary. The individual subsidiaries will not act in isolation and will generally share common facilities and management services, and work for the common good of the group as a whole.

Within this complex environment, good financial management is essential to the success of the business. In this chapter we shall consider some of the critical areas where a contribution can be made to the profitability of the group. These are:

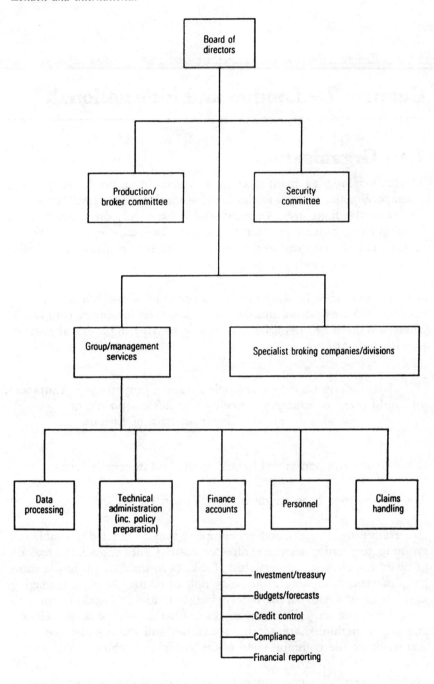

Figure 7.1 Typical major broking group – organisation chart

(a)   working capital control;
(b)   business processing standards;
(c)   treasury function; and
(d)   the security committee.

Financial management encompasses the following:

(a)   the recording of economic transactions both internal (profit and loss account) and external (the balance sheet), which includes the current status of relationships with the providers of capital, clients, the insurance market and the Inland Revenue;
(b)   compliance with statutory requirements, which include the 1985 Companies Act, the particular requirements of the IBRC and Lloyd's, the proper provisioning and payment of taxes (PAYE, corporation tax and value added tax) and the requirements of the financial services legislation; and
(c)   provision of management information.

A major contribution which financial management can make towards the profit goal is the control of working capital, which requires that premium debts are quickly converted into cash in order to pay insurers and that claim debts are speedily collected in order to pay the client. The application of commercial logic may require a broker to fund premiums or claims, but both decisions depend on the economic marshalling of cash. Cash funds generate investment income, which can be an important element of an insurance broker's profit, but they may also require the management of foreign exchange exposure and control over bad debt exposure. The latter two items can have a very significant effect on an international broker's profit and loss account.

It is likely that competition between major brokers will revolve increasingly around the ability of brokers to process information in an accurate and timely fashion, and to deliver funds in the correct medium and as early as possible. Implementation of the London Insurance Market Network (see Chapter 12) will accelerate this trend and business will be lost or won by the contribution offered by the financial and business processing functions.

7.2   Working capital control

Working capital is a well-known accounting concept and for most organisations includes debtors, creditors, cash, stocks and work in progress. Funds are required to finance working capital – usually stocks and work in progress, as well as credit allowed to clients. Insurance brokers are probably unique in that:

(a) there is no stock or work in progress – even underwriters carry stocks in the form of claim and premium reserves; and

(b) it is usual for the broker to owe more to creditors (i.e. the market) than is owed by debtors (clients), thus generating surplus working capital which can be invested as a contribution towards profit.

The working capital cycle commences with a premium due from the client, which is normally paid to the market only after receipt. A broker will attempt to collect claims from the insurer before paying his client but all brokers, to a greater or lesser extent, fund claims to clients as a part of their customer service. The elements of working capital are constantly changing as debtors are converted to cash and payments to creditors subsequently reduce cash. The working capital fund is the lifeblood of any insurance broker and it is usual to find at least 80 per cent of the finance function's staff devoted to the recording and control of working capital.

7.2.1 The measurement of working capital

A net creditor ratio (i.e. the ratio of creditors to debtors) of one implies that debtors and creditors are in balance, but it is common for an insurance broker to generate a ratio greater than one, which produces investable funds. A ratio of less than one suggests that more is due from clients than is due to the market or, more probably, more is due from the market than is due to the client (i.e. funded claims). This can only be financed by borrowing from the bank (or from shareholders) but there is no divine right which allows the broker to have a ratio greater than one. Recent history has produced examples of brokers who have failed to control their working capital and have subsequently gone out of business.

It is not uncommon for a significant proportion of an insurance broker's pre-tax profit to be made up of investment income. Current discussions about terms of trade may reduce those earnings, or convert investment income to additional brokerage, but there can be little argument that control of working capital will always form a major part of the finance function's contribution towards the profit goal.

During the 1960s it was the norm for brokers to account with under-writers (the market) on a cash basis. Indeed, personal ledgers were often only maintained on a memorandum basis. This gradually changed, and during the 'soft market' of the 1970s, brokers paid balances due to the market irrespective of whether the client had paid. This practice applied particularly to business written in sterling and US dollars, other currencies usually being treated in a more conservative fashion. It was, and still is, usual for brokers to offset balances arising on different contracts and different clients. If both insured and insurer pay on time, offset is a cheap and efficient method of transmission, although it is not a method that US and European underwriters and brokers favour or often understand. Towards the end of the 1970s some markets refused to pay, usually because the company was in financial difficulty.

A typical situation is shown below:

Market (underwriter)	Dr £	Cr £
Client A net premiums	100	
Client B net claims		70
Balance		30
	100	100

This assumes that the broker places a contract from client A and a contract from client B with the same underwriter. At the end of an accounting period, client A owes net premiums for the underwriting year of £100 and client B is owed £70 of net claims for the underwriting year. It is tempting for the broker to offset the two contracts and settle a net £30 to the underwriter. If this is done, the broker appears to be in a position to settle the net claims of £70 to client B. Let us assume that, after paying out client B, the underwriter goes into liquidation and client A is still unable to pay, perhaps due to exchange control restrictions. As long as client A is unable to settle, the position is that the broker has funded net claims to client B on behalf of an underwriter who has not settled, in the belief that the offset against net premiums due from client A will be realised.

There is little legal authority on funding. In the above example the broker has voluntarily paid client B before recovering the money from the underwriter. It is not clear who can recover it from the insurer; it is probably client B, but he already has his money and has no incentive to sue. The broker may not be able to force client B to sue, especially if the latter does not know that the broker has funded the claim. Brokers should consult with their legal advisers before embarking on funding.

The circumstances outlined above have forced brokers to reconsider funding. Although funding will always be an intrinsic part of the broker's role, it must be carefully controlled and only exercised on behalf of good clients and underwriters. The current maxim is 'pay as paid'. The non-responding underwriter has forced brokers to segregate that part of the client's business placed with such an underwriter and account for it separately. Offset is under attack and there is a move towards a form of contract-by-contract accounting. Brokers' personal ledger systems must cater for both contract-by-contract and offset accounting, with rigorous control of funding and segregation of any business placed with non-responding underwriters.

The implications for brokers of FRS 5 are discussed in Chapter 11. This standard requires insurance debtors and creditors to be shown gross of offset in the financial statements. Offset will become less common as the industry adjusts to these requirements.

All these matters form part of the London insurance market terms of trade. Current terms of trade have reduced the period of credit allowed to the broker and impose premium warranties to encourage compliance. Essentially the client warrants payment of premium by a fixed date; otherwise cover will be cancelled. There will be a further squeeze on working capital in the future, which means that the successful broker will be the one that controls his working capital.

It is essential that clients and underwriters (a single entity may be both client and underwriter) understand their financial relationship with the broker. It is in the broker's best interest to conclude an accounting agreement with each entity. The following matters might form the basis of the agreement:

(a) who will render statements to whom and at what intervals;
(b) terms of credit for inwards and outwards business;
(c) method of settlement, including currency rules;
(d) special procedures for premium warranties and cash calls;
(e) procedures for non-responding underwriters, particularly liquidations, and defaulting clients; and
(f) treatment of exchange differences.

7.3 Communication

Like most functions which service the production areas, the finance team of an insurance broker can have difficulty in communicating with broking divisions. It is necessary for broking divisions to understand the importance of accurately processing documentation, be aware of what happens to that documentation within the finance function, and appreciate the impact on divisional profit. This can best be achieved by establishing a commonality of interest between finance and broking divisions which is reinforced by regular liaison meetings and the attendance of senior finance executives at divisional management meetings.

Training is an important ingredient of a successful finance function. This will lead to an understanding of the insurance industry and how the particular broker operates, as well as a thorough familiarity with the broker's own systems and procedures. Those staff controlling individual ledger accounts must understand where they fit into the overall working of the division and the company, as well as appreciating the impact on profit that their actions have.

It is often said that insurance broking is a 'people business' and this also applies to financial matters. Control of ledgers can only be exercised by understanding the other person's viewpoint. It is necessary to have regular communication with finance personnel in other UK companies and, provided that the size of the account warrants it, it is even more important to visit overseas companies. If a company is dealing with a foreign language company, it may pay to recruit ledger keepers who are proficient in the language, as well as in accounting skills. An understanding of government and foreign exchange restrictions is a self-evident requirement, but it is also helpful for the broker to understand the business ethics of the country concerned.

7.4 Business processing standards

It is axiomatic that working capital control, and particularly the quality of the debtors and creditors ledgers, is only as good as the input to the accounting system. In the main, the input is generated by business divisions and includes debit notes (premiums), credit notes (claims) and treaty balances (a mixture of premiums and claims). Business processing standards in insurance broking are not as efficient as they might be, as illustrated by the long delay which often arises between the inception of a risk and issue of a debit note. There are many reasons for late debiting, which include the complexity of the risk, the number of parties within the business chain, the variety of currencies and the particular problems when dealing with another country, such as different procedures and exchange control regulations. However, there are two primary reasons for late processing:

(a) a broker does not have to build up work flow controls from purchase records, through stocks and work in progress, to sales, and often seeks to record the progress of a risk some way downstream; and

(b) there are many different functions and persons involved in recording and processing a risk and often technicians are ignorant of the end product.

This has been tolerated in broking offices partly because emphasis has traditionally been placed on generation of 'paper brokerage'. Reputations have been built on how much brokerage has been credited to the company or division compared with last year or budget, rather than the total profit contribution. This attitude is changing as management recognises the significance of total profit contribution. There are two further reasons why business processing standards are important:

(a) Slipshod processing has produced a number of very substantial errors and omissions claims (see also Chapter 3). The cost of E & O insurance will, for most brokers, absorb several points of broker-age income, and brokers who cannot demonstrate that they are processing in accordance with a set of standards will find it difficult to obtain any sort of reasonable cover.

(b) Business is lost or gained through, in part, the broker's processing ability. The financial manager has a key role to play in demonstrat-ing to business processing technicians the impact of their work on the company's profit and loss account, and in introducing effective work flow controls.

Accounting manuals are found in most large organisations, and these will typically specify the way in which transactions are to be recorded and presented over all branches, divisions and companies within the group. Perhaps less well known is the business procedures manual, which specifies the way in which business is to be processed.

Such a manual might include the following:

(a) how to deal with incoming enquiries with particular reference to proposal forms and valuations;
(b) how information should be submitted to insurers;
(c) approval of insurers;
(d) responses to clients, including minimum periods for the production of cover notes and debit notes;
(e) standards for checking client closings and premium collection;
(f) standards for despatch of outward closing advices and payments to the market;
(g) checking and issue of policies;
(h) renewal procedures – keeping a register;
(i) claims procedures – acknowledgement of notification, work in progress checks, 'repudiations', claims collection and payment, recording claims statistics;
(j) procedures for facility management, including those potentially difficult cases where a broker operates a binding authority with power to commit the underwriter – it is essential that the facility is operated within the terms of the agreement;
(k) procedures for the immediate recording of cancellation notices and advice to all parties; and
(l) standards for file documentation and retention of records.

118

7.5 Internal audit and the audit committee

Accounting and business procedures manuals require some reinforcement. Management must be certain that the required standards are in operation throughout the group. Internal audit has been used in companies with a large number of autonomous branches or divisions, and has been confined to accounting matters. This function can also be used to ensure that business processing standards are applied across companies within a group and within divisions of the same company.

The selection of members of the internal audit team usually poses difficulties. It needs to be financially based but must include members of the trading divisions. Ideally, the team should contain a nucleus of permanent members supplemented by individuals on assignment from other duties. In this way, it is possible to present membership of the internal audit team as a vital part of career progression. The reporting line is also important as there must be an independent right of access to the highest management. This is probably best achieved by appointing an audit committee.

This committee, in accordance with Cadbury recommendations, should comprise a minimum of three non-executive members of the board. A majority of those should be independent of the company. The head of internal audit and the finance director would normally attend meetings. The external audit partner will also attend at least one meeting per year.

Responsibilities of the audit committee will include consideration of:

(a) accounting policies and the audit plan; and
(b) the interim financial information and annual financial statements,

in addition to its review of internal control, including internal audit.

7.6 Client profitability analysis

In the past a combination of favourable exchange rates, improved investment income and a less competitive environment enabled brokers to achieve good profit growth.

The current financial climate is very different, and many brokers are reporting falling profits. It is essential that the sources of broking profit are identified so that alternative strategies can be developed to improve contributions. Increasing computerisation in the broking network is likely to increase costs in the short term, but also provides information to enable management to identify profitable areas.

One method of analysing profitability is by client. Obviously, some clients may provide only a small amount of business and strategic decisions have to be made on the basis of the class of business being broked, the geographical area covered or other criteria. Brokers should, however, consider the profitability of their major clients. This is becoming a significant issue as more clients require a fee rather than a brokerage-based charge for work done. Fees, of course, are generally lower than brokerage rates and have to be justified by reference to the completion of the work done for the client.

The following information is needed to assess client profitability, and the most effective way of collecting it is from the computer system:

(a) analysis of brokerage by client, but consider discounts and commission-sharing arrangements;
(b) analysis of expenses by client, to include the broking and all support functions:
    (i) acquisition and broking – form of timesheeting, probably most difficult to assess;
    (ii) administration, processing and closing – relate to number of accounts, policies, lines, adjustments;
    (iii) data processing and financial services – relate to the number of items or other volume data; and
(c) the resulting broking profit can be expressed as a percentage of broking income. This should be compared with the required company average that covers unallocated central costs and a certain contribution to company profitability.

Once obtained and collated, these figures should be interpreted against pre-set criteria. Where business from particular clients falls below these standards, it must be decided what action will be taken:

(a) to increase the brokerage level from that client;
(b) to alter processing and marketing methods to minimise costs;
(c) to retain certain unprofitable business where it is related to profitable business elsewhere in the organisation; or
(d) consider ceasing business.

This analysis also provides a basis for judging new business and should encourage producers and other staff obtaining new business to consider its profitability before accepting it. Since overhead costs in the short term are fixed, increasing the volume of business to make maximum use of existing facilities increases profitability disproportionally to the increase in costs. This may be another reason for accepting business which is less profitable.

7.7 Claims servicing

Many brokers are taking a close look at the costs of servicing future claims. Generally, brokers have recognised income immediately a transaction is placed, either at inception or debit note date. Similarly, costs are expensed as incurred. This practice can be deemed imprudent. No provision is made to meet claims servicing and run-off costs which will arise in later accounting periods. This is in contrast to other parts of the insurance industry, where deferral of income to meet future expense is common practice.

Reasons for this practice are:

(a) a desire to maximise brokerage in any one year;
(b) the danger that reserves for unearned brokerage or other similar provisions may be regarded as taxable income;
(c) the fact that such provisions would strain balance sheets by increasing insurance liabilities; and
(d) perceived difficulties in matching income with expense.

However, the current practice means that many brokers have to rely on increasing brokerage each year to pay for the claims servicing and run-off costs of previous years. There is a distortion of the true underlying profitability of the business by failing to match expense with income.

In the current market, many wholesale and reinsurance brokers are questioning the validity of the assumptions underlying these accounting practices. Very material accounts can be lost or gained and broker teams may transfer to competitors, taking business with them. These events may leave the placing broker servicing claims on the run-off, but receiving no further income, or the acquiring broker having to accept significant front-end costs servicing old business, for which he received no income, in order to protect his future brokerage flows. Clearly, these costs can have a major impact on profitability.

Unless the broker or client has specified or implied the services to be provided, there appears to be no general legal duty for the broker to deal with the claims. However, market practice and a desire to provide a first-class service dictate that the broker will service claims, certainly in respect of business he has placed. For the reinsurance or treaty broker, this can involve considerable expense long after the business was placed. Where a client transfers business to another broker, the original placing broker will not be obliged to service late claims.

The stage the broker has reached in his life cycle will influence these decisions. Is it an operation just starting out, trying to generate business in a period of dramatic growth with high brokerage but low staff levels? Has it reached a plateau in terms of attracting new business? Is it a very diverse broker offering a full range of services across market and national boundaries? Perhaps it is now in decline, with significant accounts of business producers having departed.

The type of business written will have an effect on the total and timing of

121

claims servicing costs. For short-tail business the cost of settling and processing claims arising on policies can be limited within a short period after the period of insurance (usually less than one year). Deferral of brokerage income or claims service provisioning for short-term business is not so relevant since the costs of providing the service are incurred close to the period in which income is credited. The costs of servicing claims are unlikely to change significantly year on year unless the volume or mix of business changes, and so there is no significant timing difference between crediting income and charging expenditure.

Long-tail business is, by its very nature, more complex, and gives rise to claims being made a significant time after the period to which the insurance relates. This leads to a mismatch between the timing of revenue and costs.

A further influence on these management issues will arise if the broker has a Stock Exchange quotation. The adoption of an accounting policy which makes provision for claims servicing costs or defers brokerage income will have an impact on the amount of distributable profits available and on key investment figures such as earnings per share and P/E ratios.

Chapter 10 contains discussion on the accounting principles relating to claims servicing provisions. However, the London market broker must take account of these issues in his management decision-making even if he does not include an accrual in his annual financial statements. It is, therefore, necessary to consider the basis on which such provisions should be calculated.

The following factors must be considered when formulating the provision:

(a) volume of claims serviced in each year;
(b) nature of insurance placed and impact on timing of claims;
(c) historical claims servicing costs;
(d) future cost inflation;
(e) future income accruing on funds retained; and
(f) whether the service provided is continuous or one-off.

The volume of future claims could be assessed by setting up a triangulation showing the period over which claims have been made in relation to the date the business was placed. 'Claims' can be identified as the date of a claims event (advice, notification and so on). Depending on the systems available, it may be possible to monitor this activity by type of business or even by insured if major accounts are involved.

Costs associated with claims servicing will usually include a proportion of:

(a) salaries of personnel handling claims activity;
(b) computer costs; and
(c) premises costs.

Finally, the average cost of processing each claim is calculated and the likelihood of such an event is established from the triangulations. At this stage it will be appropriate to consider cost inflation. It is often assumed, however, that inflation will be covered by future investment income earned by the additional funds retained in the business as a result of setting up the claims servicing provision. The taxation implications of these provisions are set out in Chapter 14.

7.8 Credit control and the security committee

As with any business, control over the creditworthiness of the customers of a broker must be established before business is accepted. However, unique to the London broker is the need to assess the creditworthiness of the insurer too. Recent failures of high-profile insurers have increased the client's expectations of brokers.

Only the marine broker is responsible for defaulting security (s53 Marine Insurance Act 1906); other brokers are only acting as middlemen between two principals. The insured, however, expects the broker to place business with sound insurers. Indeed, the broker who places business with insurers who do not settle claims promptly will soon lose credibility in the market. Alternatively, the broker himself may have to write off bad debts where he has funded transactions.

Many brokers have established a security committee to vet insurers before business is placed with them. The financial manager should have an important role to play in making an assessment of the potential underwriter from financial statements, Department of Trade and Industry returns and other published information. The key broking departments should also be represented at a senior level to help with commercial considerations and market gossip.

A senior director, preferably either the deputy chairman or chief executive, should take the chair, and the group may include an external member who can contribute to discussions from a broad knowledge of the insurance industry.

Such a committee should:

(a) be well disciplined and have a senior chairman, regular attendance, a proper agenda and a timetable;

(b)   have maximum contribution from members in terms of market awareness and financial implications; and

(c)   be aware of the broker's current position in terms of throughput of business and debt problems with a particular insurance company.

Most brokers' security committees produce a clearly defined list of those companies, agencies and pools with which they are prepared to place business. The list is available to all broking staff, and placing business with security outside the list is a serious offence which may lead to instant dismissal.

A full list of approved insurers is the preferred procedure, rather than a graded list where an insurer is coded by strength of security or the type of business for which it may be used. A client is not going to be pleased to find a broker has given his insurers a low grade and is proved correct when the insurers go into liquidation. Black lists of insurers which cannot be used carry an obvious potential legal liability. With an approved list, an insurer does not know whether he has been positively rejected or never considered. Any list is, however, strictly confidential and ought to provide the broker with a commercial edge over his rivals.

The security committee often operates on a modest budget with a small full-time secretariat. In smaller brokers, or where security is not highly rated in terms of management objectives, the financial department may provide the back-up resource, maintaining the approved list, fielding requests for new security and compiling information on existing security.

Assessment of new insurers will generally be based initially on financial information. This should be measured against established criteria covering the type of business written, reinsurance protection maintained and with whom, an appraisal of the parentage of the insurer, together with its asset backing and management. If reinsurance is placed with major companies this provides more confidence than a list of lesser known reinsurers. First, it suggests that the well-known companies are prepared to share in the risks written by the insurer and second, collection against reinsurance should be easier.

Financial information is usually out of date, and care must be taken in judgements made on a six-month-old balance sheet. The financial analysis should include ratio comparisons of reserving, assets, underwriting results and solvency margins over several years. It will also involve comparisons with other insurers and the sector norm.

Changes in personnel, such as underwriters or directors, may also be warning signs. Developments in capital, management and company ethos will be important. Market knowledge should include details of litigation, relationships with other insurers or reinsurers and other underwriters' views of the risk written.

Foreign companies, underwriting agencies and pools require special care. The nature of the regulatory authority controlling the insurer, exchange control regulations, the country of origin's economic status and the terms of any management agreement all have to be considered. Where a pool is concerned, it is important to consider the criteria used by the agents for assessing members of the pool.

Once a list of approved insurers is established, it is important to reappraise the list at least annually. Market intelligence or other matters may cause reassessment in a shorter period.

Monitoring the use of the approved list should be a function of the broker's accounting system. It should be capable of rejecting non-approved security early in the transaction cycle and must work quickly.

Any security committee must know the limits of its responsibility and should take a consistent view in approving security. It should not be influenced in any way by the commercial implications of a decision. If the latter are important, they should be considered at main board level, and only the directors acting together should overturn a security committee decision on commercial grounds.

Although there are organisations which supply information on insurance security, there is no centralised system. There would be great benefit from the major brokers grouping together, involving others who might wish to participate, and forming a central resource unit, thus enabling all brokers to draw on a mass of information. This would eliminate much duplicated effort, ensure up-to-date information was available and give considerable muscle to the central unit. The unit would be able to use its power to obtain information and could take the drudgery from acquiring, analysing and accumulating vast quantities of paperwork for individual broking companies. However, the decision on whether or not to use a particular insurer is the responsibility of the broker in the light of information supplied. Such decisions could then give due weight to commercial considerations.

7.9 Treasury

The treasury function may be carried out by a separate department or it may form part of the responsibility of a clerk. In the largest broking groups there will be a department comprising the treasurer, a small number of dealers operating from a dealing room, and administrative and secretarial support. In many medium-sized brokers the function is performed in the finance department or by the finance director.

In essence, treasury management is dealing with cash receipts and payments. It involves managing bank accounts to ensure that there are no idle funds, and assessing settlement procedures to benefit cash flow. It is therefore closely linked with working capital control. The credit risk assessment of investment vehicles and the electronic transmission of funds also fall within the treasurer's responsibilities.

Monitoring and negotiating bank charges, and researching new investment products and changes in the tax regime are an essential part of this function. However, the most important responsibilities are the investment of surplus funds and the management of foreign exchange exposure. The objective of the latter may be to ensure that the broker neither suffers nor benefits from the volatility of foreign exchange. Fluctuating exchange rates can have a significant effect on many London brokers because much of their brokerage is earned in US dollars although their costs are in sterling.

The treasury function is often centralised to provide economies of scale and avoid duplication of effort. If decentralisation is adopted, the team in each location will still need to work within centrally determined parameters. Reasons for decentralisation are the geographical problems of time zones influencing financial markets, although information technology is minimising this aspect, and the effect of different regulatory authorities both in finance and insurance.

Three examples of how a treasury function can contribute to the operating success of a broker are set out in the following paragraphs. It does not fall within the purpose of this book to give more than an introduction to this function, and therefore details of types of transactions and other matters are not covered.

7.9.1 Example 1 – cost of banking services

Corporate banking services are diverse and the cost is often negotiable. The larger and more important a company is as a customer of the bank, the stronger the negotiating position of the treasurer. Apart from negotiating specific prices for specific services, the treasurer should also try to monitor those areas where a company could modestly rearrange the way it does business and reduce its costs. There are a number of ways funds can be sent from one entity to another, for example – cash, cheque or draft and electronic funds transfer in its widest sense. In the UK this

126

would take in such services as BACS (Bankers Automated Clearing System) and CHAPS (Clearing House Automated Payment System).

The advantages of electronic banking over, say, cheques, in addition to cost, are that payment:

(a)   is certain and cannot be recalled;
(b)   is for a specific value and date; and
(c)   reduces the need for paper systems.

Each method of transmitting money has a different cost structure, and it is the treasurer's responsibility to try to arrange the corporation's affairs to minimise this cost, while weighing the advantages and disadvantages of the alternatives. An international Lloyd's broker with a large, geo-graphically dispersed client base involves the company in a multiplicity of methods of collection and payment, and of differing banking systems.

Lloyd's brokers still continue to receive a large number of payments by cheque even though their total value has diminished in recent years. The US dollar remains the principal currency of payment and the following comments concentrate on this, although much is relevant to other currencies too.

Outside the main clearing bank systems, the treasurer will probably investigate the benefits and practicality of negotiating cheques rather than sending them for collection. Negotiation involves a bank agreeing to give value on cheques after a predetermined time, irrespective of how long it actually takes to collect the funds.

Certainty of value is a useful tool for the treasurer. In the US the method most usually adopted to achieve this is the 'lock box'. This aims to accelerate cheque collections by concentrating them in the US, usually New York. The alternative is to collect these payments through a London current account. A US lock box probably has a time advantage of close to a week over the alternative method, however, when mailing, bank clearing time and holidays are considered. The logic for a lock box system is to ensure that cheques are collected in the most efficient manner possible. Consideration must always be given to the client making payment, who may not appreciate losing value so immediately, and the treasurer will need to weigh both the pros and cons of any proposed system before implementation.

This example has concentrated on the collection of cash but the argu-ments stand equally for making payments. If a company has movements of US$100m a year and the treasurer can get value on these funds four days earlier than previously, he will be increasing the company's financial resources significantly. If he has managed to do this and reduce the cost of the company's banking services at the same time, he would appear to have fulfilled the aim of corporate treasury management of optimising the financial resource.

7.9.2 Example 2 – foreign exchange exposure management

Traded options give the holder the right to buy or sell currency at a predetermined rate. Options are traded in lots and sterling lots on an exchange like the Philadelphia exchange are traded in a lot size of £31,250. The nearer the exercise price is to the present spot rate, the dearer the option will be and vice versa. There are also counterparty to counterparty options which may well, if the size of the deal is large, be more appropriate.

Assume that in May a company anticipated earning US$5m of brokerage by the year end. The spot rate was 1.50 and the expectation was that sterling could go to 1.60 versus the dollar. The company desires an option to sell $5,000,000 by the year end.

The number of contract's required is determined by the following formula:

$$\text{Contracts required} = \frac{\$5,000,000}{\text{option rate} \times £31,250}$$

$$\begin{aligned}
\text{therefore @ } \$1.60 &= 100 \text{ contracts} \\
\text{@ } \$1.55 &= 103 \text{ contracts (approx)} \\
\text{@ } \$1.50 &= 107 \text{ contracts (approx)} \\
\text{@ } £1.45 &= 110 \text{ contracts (approx)}
\end{aligned}$$

The cost of this strategy, therefore is:

Contract month	Premium per contract	No. of contracts	Cost* $	% of principal
Dec 1.60 call	1.23	100	$38,438	0.77
Dec 1.55 call	2.29	103	$73,709	1.48
Dec 1.50 call	4.08	107	$136,425	2.72
Dec 1.45 call	6.65	110	$228,593	4.59

* Cost = number of contracts × 31,250 × premium.

Option costs are determined by a number of factors, but primarily by the spot rate, historic volatility and interest rates.

The large increases in cost for the $1.50 and $1.45 options reflect the immediate profitability at that time of the contracts. Options are akin to catastrophe insurance premiums and are used to limit exposure. In the example, a $1.60 option purchase protects against a major move through $1.60 while retaining the right to do nothing. Accordingly, if the rate dropped to, say, $1.30 the option would be written off. If the rate rose to £1.70 the option would be sold in the market, the profit offsetting the loss from having to sell in the spot market at $1.70. Accordingly, the purchase of December 1.60 calls protects the company from a major strengthening in sterling, while at the same time leaving it free to participate in any sterling weakness.

In addition to the premium payable for the option there would also be investment house brokerage fees. These are negotiable, but could be around $3.00 per contract per trade. On this basis, the brokerage fees in the example above of 100 contracts would be $300.00. There would be further fees to pay on any sale of the same magnitude.

7.9.3 Example 3 – surplus funds investment

Corporate policy may dictate that the treasurer buys a negotiable instrument, such as a trade bill, bank certificate of deposit or Government security. This gives flexibility to respond to changed market conditions and, potentially, an increase in the return by generating tax-free capital gains.

An interest rate future is a tradeable instrument entitling the holder to a rate of interest determined today for some time in the future. There are interest rate futures along the yield curve – three months sterling, a short gilt future and a long 20-year gilt future. This enables a strategy to be put in place for most projects.

Assume in August the broker borrowed £500,000 three-month money from a bank at a rate of 10 per cent which is due to be rolled over at the end of October. There are concerns that rates will have risen by then.

This risk could be hedged by using a three-month sterling interest rate futures contract. This contract is for a three-month deposit facility of £500,000 commencing in March, June, September or December. At any particular time, contracts for all these different months are being dealt on the market. In this case, the December contract would be selected because the September contract will have already matured before roll-over is due.

The contract is priced by deducting the interest rate to be paid on the deposit from 100. On 1 August the interest rate is 10.00 per cent and the price of the contract is accordingly 90.00. The price of the contract changes up or down in minimum movements of 0.01 known as 'ticks' and the value of each tick is £12.50. A hundred tick movements, therefore, is valued at £1,250. The value of ticks is derived from the following formula:

$$\begin{matrix} 0.01\% \text{ p.a.} \\ \text{of interest} \end{matrix} \times \begin{matrix} \text{the face value of the} \\ \text{contract, i.e. } £500,000 \end{matrix} \times \begin{matrix} \text{one quarter} \\ \text{of a year} \end{matrix} = £12.50$$

Because of the concern that the interest rate will rise and hence that the price of the contract will fall, one December contract is sold at a price of £90.00.

By October, when the borrowing is rolled over, the interest rate has risen to 11 per cent. The result of the hedge is shown below.

Cash market	*Forward market*
1 August	
It is planned to roll over the £500,000 three-month borrowing in October. Current rate on loan is 10%	Sale of one December (£500,000) three-month sterling interest rate futures contract at a price of 90.00 (rate = 10%)
End October	
Roll over the borrowing at the new rate of 11% (rate = 11%)	Purchase December futures contract at the new price of 89.00
Extra cost: 1% on £500,000 for one quarter = £1,250	Gain: 100 ticks at £12.50 = £1,250

This hedge worked out perfectly; the gain on futures was exactly equal to the extra interest paid. The borrower thus achieved a net borrowing cost of 10 per cent per annum. In practice, such perfect matching will not be achieved. Futures prices may not move exactly in line with cash market rates. If interest rates had fallen, the hedger's loss on his futures position would have been matched by lower interest payments, so that his net borrowing cost would still be 10 per cent per annum.

PART IV

Accounting and auditing

Chapter 8 – Basic accounting and document flow

8.1 Introduction

This chapter introduces the basic accounting entries and flow of documentation that result from the processing of insurance transactions by brokers. Because of the diverse broking market-place, with its specialisations and variations in size, it is difficult to specify the flow of documentation. For the purposes of this section, a medium-sized London market broker has been assumed. However, larger or smaller brokers can break into or extend the flow lines as required. Several flow lines are included, where appropriate, to illustrate differences in flow from varying types of business.

8.2 Premiums – risk borne by one underwriter

Documents produced	Process
(i) Proposal:	The proposal is completed and signed by the insured.
(ii) Slip*:	The slip is prepared by the broker who takes it to the market for subscription.
(iii) Cover note:	This constitutes an interim document evidencing the grant of insurance cover prior to the finalisation of a policy document.
(iv) Policy:	Based on the information included in the proposal, the policy is prepared by the underwriter.
(v) Debit note:	A debit note is prepared by the broker where the client settles to the broker and by the underwriter where the client settles directly to the underwriter, who then accounts to the broker for his brokerage.

* Optional

8.3 Premiums – risk borne by more than one underwriter

If a risk is borne by more than one underwriter it may be split between several insurance companies, a number of syndicates at Lloyd's, insurance agencies or pools, or a combination of any of these.

133

Documents produced	*Process*
(i) Proposal:	The insurance proposal is completed and signed by the insured.
(ii) Slip:	A slip is prepared by the broker. The slip is presented to underwriters, who initial it to indicate their proportion.
(iii) Cover note:	When the risk is totally covered, a cover note may be prepared by the broker and sent to the insured. This constitutes an interim document evidencing the granting of insurance cover prior to the finalisation of a policy document.
(iv) PAN:	Where the risk has been underwritten by Lloyd's syndicates, or ILU/LIRMA companies, a premium advice note (PAN) is prepared by the broker for submission to the Lloyd's Policy Signing Office (LPSO) or other central accounting bureaux (see **8.8**).
(v) Accounting documents:	Bureau raises underwriters' advice cards, tabulations and broker's daily settlements. These documents initiate the underwriters' accounting entries and provide confirmation of the premium amounts due from the insured to the broker. Increasingly information is given in magnetic form and transactions occur by electronic transfer. The slip is numbered by Lloyd's and returned to the broker.
(vi) Policy:	The broker prepares the policy document, which is submitted to the Underwriters/LPSO, who sign and number the policy.
(vii) Debit note:	The broker sends the policy document with the debit note raised to the insured.

Where part of the risk is written by overseas insurance companies, the broker is responsible for preparing a closing, which details the name of the underwriters and the proportion of the risk they agreed to accept. When agreement has been received from each underwriter, the policy can be prepared.

8.4 Premiums – insurance broker has binding authority

Documents produced	*Process*
(i) Slip/contract:	Where the broker has a binding authority, the underwriter has delegated the power to underwrite risks (within predetermined limits) to the broker.

	Risks written on this basis are usually done by means of a contract but may be evidenced only by a slip.
(ii) Proposal:	The proposal is completed and signed by the insured and submitted to the cover holder (broker).
(iii) Cover note:	The cover note giving interim confirmation of cover is prepared by the broker.
(iv) Policy:	The policy is prepared by the broker.
(v) Debit note:	The debit note is sent to the client. In many cases the policy is only issued after receipt of the premium, and the policy itself acts as a formal receipt so no debit note is required.

8.5 Renewals

Where a risk is renewed in a subsequent period and the conditions remain largely unchanged, it is often not necessary to issue a new policy document to the insured or to require a new proposal. Any minor amendments to the policy conditions or details are made by way of an endorsement and the current cover would then be evidenced by the renewal receipt. The insurance broker's records should therefore include a diary system which will enable the broker to control and monitor all renewals.

8.6 Claims

When the insured suffers a loss or injury covered by the insurance, a claim is made against the insurers. Claims are notified by the insured direct to the insurers or to the broker. In the latter case the broker will inform the underwriter of the loss and negotiate a settlement on behalf of the insured. The broker occasionally receives additional remuneration for this service by the receipt of claims collecting commission retained from the monies collected from the insurers.

8.7 Reinsurance

In order to protect himself against large claims or an accumulation of claims, an insurer (the reinsured or cedant) may choose to reinsure (cede) certain risks to another insurer (the reinsurer). When reinsuring a reinsurance risk the original reinsurer becomes the retrocedant, and the reinsurers are commonly known as retrocessionaires. There are two main methods by which reinsurance is arranged, facultative and treaty. The document flow varies for the two types of reinsurance.

Under facultative reinsurance, every risk which is offered is individually described by the broker, usually on a slip. This method of reinsurance is similar to that where the original risk is accepted by a number of

135

insurers. Cover notes, policy and debit notes are produced by the broker and underwriters in similar way to that described in **8.3**.

A treaty is a written agreement between the ceding company and the reinsurer providing for the cession of all business falling within certain limits defined by the treaty. Under the treaty, the ceding company is obliged to include all such defined risks and the reinsurer is obliged to accept every such risk allocated to it. Originally, reinsurers were supplied with details of business placed on the treaty by means of lists known as 'bordereaux'. These lists detailed each risk ceded, and it was possible for the broker and the cedant to check that all risks were within the limits of the treaty. These 'open lists' have now been largely replaced by 'blind' treaties where only a summary of the premiums due to the reinsurers and claims due from the reinsurer are sent to the broker on a regular (quarterly) basis.

The simplified document flow arising from the processing of treaty reinsurance is outlined below. Two flow lines are detailed, showing the flow resulting from the preparation of a cover note and the processing of the resulting reinsured's statements.

Document produced	*Process*
(a) *Preparation of cover note*	
(i) Proposal:	The insurance proposal is completed by or on behalf of the ceding company.
(ii) Slip:	A slip is prepared by the broker detailing the terms of the treaty agreement.
	The broker presents the slip to underwriters.
(iii) Cover note/policy:	The cover note and policy document are produced. Policy wording may be generated entirely by the placing broker or follow the wording of another party to the contract, such as another order on the same reinsurance placed with a different lead broker or direct insurer.
(iv) Document:	The policy and slip are signed by the underwriters or at central accounting bureaux where applicable.
(b) *Processing of treaties*	
(i) PAN:	A premium advice note is used for placements with Lloyd's, ILU and LIRMA, particularly for 'excess of loss' business.
(ii) Treaty statement:	Treaty statements, particularly for proportional business, are prepared by the ceding company

136

and sent to the broker on a regular basis.

On the basis of the information contained on the reinsured's statements, the broker calculates the brokerage due on the premium ceded and the amount due to the reinsurers.

(iii) Debit notes/credit notes

The broker prepares debit/credit notes which:

- initiate the accounting entries in the books of account relating to the reinsurance transaction; and
- are sent to the reinsurers to inform them of the net premiums/claims due to/from them. Depending on the type of treaty, deposit premiums may also be payable in advance.

More complex accounting relating to treaties is discussed in paragraphs 8.33 to 8.35.

8.8 Central accounting bureaux

Net premiums due to and claims settlements due from Lloyd's syndicates are accounted for centrally by LCA. There are similar arrangements for insurance companies which are members of the Institute of London Underwriters (ILU) and/or the London Insurance and Reinsurance Market Association (LIRMA). These arrangements allow the broker to settle net amounts due to the underwriter involved and so reduce the number of settlements.

8.9 Basic accounting systems

The previous paragraphs illustrate and discuss the flow of documentation which is generally produced when processing insurance transactions. The broker should therefore have an accounting system which will enable him to record and deal with the documents being raised and handled in the course of his business. The following paragraphs discuss the minimum accounting records which need to be maintained in order to comply with the relevant legislation and meet the basic business requirements of a broker.

The office and accounting procedures should enable:

(a) appropriate policy decisions based on current information to be made by management;
(b) a register of technical and statistical data to be maintained so that the broker can offer advice to clients and monitor their needs;

(c) accurate and complete accounting information to be recorded in respect of policies arranged; and

(d) policies to be renewed on a timely basis.

BIIBA recommendations for basic accounting systems are discussed in Chapter 6.

All incorporated insurance brokers are regulated by the Companies Act 1985 and therefore have to comply with the relevant sections of the Act with respect to accounting records. Unincorporated insurance broking businesses must also maintain accounting records that disclose with reasonable accuracy, at any time, the financial position of the company so that the directors may prepare a balance sheet and profit and loss account to 'true and fair' standards similar to those required of a company under the Companies Act.

In addition to the Companies Act requirements, as discussed in Part II, all insurance broking businesses enrolled under the IBRA must comply with that Act and, *inter alia*, with the IBRC Accounts and Business Requirements. These include comprehensive sections detailing the minimum accounting systems that the broker should implement. The additional requirements over the Companies Act are in respect of matching items on the personal ledger accounts and the ageing of debit items on the ledger.

The requirement to match items on clients' and insurers' personal ledger accounts means that cash received from an insured for a particular policy must be identified with the debit entry raised on processing a debit note. This procedure is easily executed if an insured pays the correct monies for particular premiums. However, because of the nature of insurance, some insureds pay for several premiums at one time and deduct any claims monies they believe to be due. One cheque received may, therefore, relate to several items on the broker's personal ledger account with that client, and all items to which the monies relate will need to be identified and matched against the receipt. This system can be executed by labelling items with a certain prefix in a manual system, and by flagging the items in a computer system and will result in the identification of individual 'open' items making up personal ledger balances.

It is a requirement of the IBRC that old debits can be easily identified from the accounting records. The IBRC requires all debits over nine months old to be reported. The accounting records must therefore be such that a broker can easily identify:

(a)   individual open items within an account; and

(b)   the age of a particular item.

Accounting records must be maintained to comply with IBRC Rules and regulations, and, in so doing, the records should be adequate to ensure compliance with the Companies Act in regard to brokerage, debtors and creditors. Specific accounting systems will be developed by each broker to meet the particular needs of the business. The Lloyd's regulations are similar to those of the IBRC.

8.10   Basic accounting entries

The timing and simplicity of the ledger postings depends on the type of business and how the brokerage is to be accounted for in the books of the broker. There are three main ways of accounting for brokerage received on insurance premiums. Income is recognised on:

(a)   a cash paid basis;

(b)   a cash received basis; or

(c)   a debit note or inception date basis.

Brokerage may be withdrawn from the IBA bank account as soon as it is recognised in the broker's books, subject to IBRC or Lloyd's solvency rules.

8.10.1   Cash paid basis

Some brokers, mainly the smaller ones, bring their brokerage into account only when they pay premiums to the underwriter. Under this system, it is not necessary, although it may be desirable, to set up the debtor for the premium due from the client. The entries are:

Debit   Client

Credit   Underwriter (or premiums suspense – see **8.17**)
  with the gross premium due (optional)

Credit   Client

Debit   Insurance broking bank account

          OR (if no client's ledger):

Credit   Underwriter (or premiums suspense)

Debit   Insurance broking bank account
  with the cash received

Credit   Insurance broking bank account
Debit   Underwriter (or premiums suspense)
  with the net premium due to the insurer

Debit   Underwriter (or premiums suspense)
Credit   Brokerage (profit and loss account)
  with the brokerage retained

Many smaller brokers do not set up a debtors' or clients' ledger because of the large number of lapses on renewal. This can lead to an artificially high level of debtors who will never pay, and where the money may never actually become due, because small insurances are on a 'no cash, no cover' basis. Such brokers usually have a register or file of renewals due and/or invited, with a follow-up system to ensure lapses are not unintentional on the part of clients.

It is inappropriate to take account of brokerage on the cash paid basis because, once the client has paid the premium, the brokerage has been received and is unlikely to be returned. The question of whether it is appropriate to take all the brokerage to the credit of the profit and loss account at this point is dealt with in Chapter 10.

8.10.2   Cash received basis

Accounting for income on a cash received basis usually assumes that the debit note will be entered into the accounting records when the cash is received from the insured. Pro forma debit notes or 'invitations to renew' may be raised at an earlier stage. The following entries are initiated by the receipt of cash:

Debit   Insurance broking bank account
Credit   Underwriter's personal account
Credit   Brokerage (profit and loss account)

The settlement to the respective underwriter(s) is accounted for by the following entries in the books of account:

Debit   Underwriter's personal account
Credit   Insurance broking bank account

This basis is commonly used for smaller insurances arranged on a 'no cash, no cover' basis and for treaty and binding authority business, including binders where the broker acts as intermediary between the underwriter and the cover holder, when the cash arrives with the notification from the cedant, insured or cover holder of the quantum of business. Strictly speaking, the brokerage on such business may be due when the treaty period concerned terminates (e.g. quarterly) or when the broker or cover holder 'writes' the business on behalf of the underwriter concerned. It is also prevalent in cases (typically for life assurance) where the client settles direct with the underwriter, who periodically pays the broker his commission.

8.10.3 Debit note basis

For most brokers with larger business, cover is arranged between the client and the insurer before the issue of documentation and there is little likelihood of non-renewal. In such cases it is generally accepted accounting practice to recognise the brokerage when the debit note is raised (see Chapter 10 for further discussion of accounting policies) and accordingly the accounting entries are:

On raising the debit note:

Debit   Client's personal account
Credit Underwriter's personal account
Credit Brokerage

On receipt of the premium from the insured:

Debit   Insurance broking bank account
Credit Client's personal account

On payment of the net premium to the insurer:

Debit   Underwriter's personal account
Credit Insurance broking bank account

Many brokers will not process the debit note or take the brokerage to credit until on or after the inception date of the relevant policy. This avoids some of the risks of distorting the broker's results by accounting for brokerage twice on successive annual renewals, within a 12-month period ('double counting').

8.11 Additional and return premiums (APs and RPs)

If the terms of the insurance cover change during the life of the policy, or if the original terms state that a deposit premium is to be followed by adjustments on declarations, an additional premium or return premium may be charged or refunded to the insured. APs and RPs are usually recognised when raised rather than being related back to the original debit note. This accounting policy should be disclosed, and may be unacceptable when the incidence of APs and RPs is very substantial in relation to the initial brokerage. The nature of a particular broker's business may be such that a large number of APs and RPs are processed shortly after the accounting date and, where these are material to the financial statements, appropriate accruals or provisions should be set up.

The bookkeeping entries are identical to those used under the debit note or cash basis, but in reverse for RPs. However, in some circumstances brokerage may not be returnable because the main services for which it is paid have already been rendered by the broker to his client.

8.12 Claims

Where the underwriter accepts a claim it may be settled by:

(a) the underwriter making a direct payment to the insured;
(b) the broker raising a credit note to the client and offsetting the amount against premiums and other amounts due;
(c) cash via the broker; or
(d) cash via a loss adjuster.

The broker may receive claims collecting commission or a fee for handling the claims. This is most common in marine business. Otherwise, the broker meets any costs of servicing claims from brokerage or from interest earned on claims funds in transit from underwriter to insured.

If monies are settled directly by the underwriter to the client there will be no accounting entries in the broker's books, only a note in his file if he is kept informed. Where the broker raises a credit note the entry will be:

Debit   Underwriter's personal account
Credit   Client's personal account

If the underwriter settles to the broker the accounting entries will be:

Debit   Insurance broking bank account (cash)
Credit   Client's personal account or underwriter's personal account if a credit note has already been raised
Credit   Commission if claims collecting commission is receivable

8.13 Facultative reinsurance

The accounting entries for facultative reinsurance are similar to those for direct insurance. The ceding company is the debtor for the premium due and the respective credits are brokerage and the reinsurer's personal account.

8.14 Treaty reinsurance

There are two main types of treaty: proportional and non-proportional. A proportional treaty is one in which premiums and claims are divided between the ceding company and the reinsurer in previously agreed proportions. Examples of proportional treaties are quota share treaties and surplus treaties.

The accounting entries which deal with both premiums and claims are usually dealt with quarterly. For example, the following figures might arise on a 20 per cent share treaty:

	100% £	20% ceded £	
Premiums	10,000	2,000	
Less:			
Overriding commission retained by cedant to contribute to cost of managing the business, say 5%		100	
		1,900	A
Brokerage (10%)		(200)	B
Claims	(3,750)	(750)	C
Net due		950	D

The cedant would be debited with A–C, the reinsurer credited with D and the broker credited with B.

The most usual form of non-proportional reinsurance is 'excess of loss', where the crediting company decides the maximum loss arising from any one event it is prepared to bear and then reinsures losses in excess of that amount up to an upper limit or on an unlimited basis. The reinsurance premium is usually calculated in one of three ways, each of which will be accounted for in different ways in the books of the broker:

(a) as an agreed sum of money or premium in full;
(b) as an agreed percentage of the ceding company's premium income. This is usually estimated at the beginning of the period of risk and is adjusted by way of APs and RPs as necessary; or
(c) under the 'burning cost' method. Under this method, the premium payable is dependent to some extent on the level of claims. The entries in the books of the broker initially account for a minimum and deposit premium and subsequent entries will depend on any further premium being payable.

143

The accounting principles for non-proportional treaties are similar to those for direct business except that premiums and claims are sometimes dealt with on the same document.

8.15 Instalment premiums

Premiums are sometimes settled on an instalment basis. Essentially this requires the premium to be paid in equal instalments throughout the period of the policy. The accounting entries will depend, to a large extent, on the terms of the instalment payment scheme.

Where debit notes are raised, it is normal for only one such document to be produced when the policy is initiated. This accounts for all premiums due under the policy and for the brokerage at this date. The client is then given the option to settle the premium in instalments. Where the business is on a cash basis, it is more normal to account for the brokerage pro rata to the cash received although, strictly speaking, the broker is entitled to his brokerage as soon as the policy is in place.

8.16 Deferred premiums

Deferred premiums differ from instalment premiums in that the insurance cover will cease if the deferred premiums are not paid. Thus, if there is one policy and the insured is given the option to pay by instalments, then it is an instalment premium. Where there are separate policies or periods of insurance cover for each part of the premium, even though they are arranged at the same time, deferred premiums result. The accounting entries for deferred premiums follow the normal pattern, although memorandum accounts of premiums and brokerage not yet due may be kept.

The settlement to the underwriter will depend on the terms agreed with him. In some cases, the brokerage is deducted in full from the first payment; in others it will be spread pro rata over each payment.

8.17 Suspense accounts

As part of a broker's system for controlling his cash flow, suspense accounts are often used, both for premiums and claims. Where debit and credit notes initiate entries, it can be financially risky to credit the active account of the underwriter (for a premium) or the client (for a claim). This may lead to the payment of the creditor before the debtor has paid, thus giving the broker exposure to bad debts in regard to the premium or claim. One method of avoiding this inadvertent funding is to establish suspense accounts whereby the credit entry is passed to a premium or claims suspense until the debtor has paid. The entries for premiums would be:

On raising of debit note:

Debit   Client's personal account
Credit   Brokerage
Credit   Premium suspense

On receipt of cash from client:

(a) Debit   Insurance broking bank account
     Credit   Client's personal account

(b) Debit   Premium suspense
     Credit   Underwriter's personal account

The entries for claims suspense would be similar. The suspense accounts can be 'block' accounts dealing with all premiums and claims in the course of collection, or split over all the underwriters and clients concerned so that each underwriter would have a current and a suspense account. This latter course is recommended as it will enable greater credit control to be exercised.

8.18   Volume of transactions

Because insurance broking is a service industry, transactions do not reflect movements of tangible goods that can be physically verified. Raising debit notes gives rise, sooner or later, to the receipt of brokerage in an essentially 'in-house' activity. Careful controls need to be in place to ensure that all insurances placed give rise to debit notes, and that all debit notes reflect insurances arranged. The scope for falsifying accounts is considerable in an ill-controlled environment.

In addition, there is a large volume of transactions and documents, many of them giving rise to very little income to the broker. The accounting function needs to process this activity and, most importantly, to match cash received and paid against the technical items (i.e. claims or premiums) to which it relates. If this matching is not kept up to date and under control, a large number of unallocated items can arise on personal accounts.

The audit implications of these control points are considered in Chapter 9. However, such controls should be well established before the auditors visit the broker.

Chapter 9 – Audit approach

9.1 Introduction

The auditors, whether acting under companies legislation or in accordance with the requirements of the regulatory authorities, are expected to complete their work in accordance with auditing standards. The main procedures they must follow are to:

(a) plan the audit work so that an effective audit is performed in an efficient and timely manner;

(b) obtain an overall understanding of the accounting and internal control systems of the broker sufficient to plan and develop an effective audit approach. The auditors should use professional judgement to assess audit risk and to design audit procedures to ensure that risk is reduced to an acceptably low level;

(c) document matters which are important to providing evidence to support the audit opinion and evidence that the audit was carried out in accordance with statements of auditing standards;

(d) obtain sufficient and appropriate audit evidence to be able to draw reasonable conclusions on which to base the audit opinion; and

(e) carry out such a review of the financial statements and solvency returns as is sufficient, in conjunction with the conclusions drawn from the other audit evidence obtained, to give them a reasonable basis for their opinion on the financial statements.

The standards detailed above form part of the 'Revision of Auditing Standards and Guidelines' project. At the time of writing these are still in draft form.

The auditors have to satisfy themselves that the financial statements comply with the Companies Act 1985. They must report if proper accounting records have not been kept or the financial statements are not in agreement with them. Similarly, if they have not received all the explanations and information they require, they must say so in their report.

Insurance brokers, whether sole traders, partnerships or incorporated bodies, are subject to IBRA, Corporation of Lloyd's or FSA Rules.

IBRA, Lloyd's and PIA Rules for certain members require a 'true and fair' audit opinion so that, with the exception of certain disclosure items, a similar audit approach is appropriate whether or not the broker is incorporated with limited liability. This means that members of these bodies cannot take advantage of the CA85 exemption from audit of small companies.

Under PIA Rules the 'true and fair' requirement relates to all members of Categories 1 and 2, members of Category 3 with more than 26 investment staff or proposing to carry on discretionary portfolio management, and members of Category 4 prudentially regulated by the PIA or bound by CMR Regulations or PIA Rules for custody of clients' assets.

Only those aspects peculiar to insurance brokers are dealt with in this chapter. It should be appreciated that the accounting entries in a broker's books reflect market practice and not always the legal form of a transaction. Clearly a broker cannot successfully sue an underwriter for settlement of a claim on behalf of his client, if the underwriter has already paid the insured. This may be obvious, but sometimes the broker will be unaware of such settlement and show the underwriter as a debtor and the insured as a creditor in his books. The same situation applies in respect of a premium due from a client, except that the broker may sue for his brokerage if he has performed the necessary services. The treatment and disclosure of insurance debtors and creditors within the financial statements of a broker are discussed in Chapter 11, where the implications of FRS 5 *Reporting the Substance of Transactions* are considered.

A broker's books should reflect the practical situation – how he expects the accounting to take place. If debts are not collected, the auditor needs to be on his guard to ensure that the debtors and creditors have not settled direct, leaving the broker with invalid debtor and creditor items.

9.2 Audit approach and planning

Limited liability insurance broking companies are subject to the same financial reporting and auditing requirements as other companies under companies' legislation. Both corporate and unincorporated insurance brokers will also be subject to IBRA, Lloyd's or PIA Rules. The IBRC, under authority given by the IBRA, requires insurance brokers to comply with the IBRC Accounts and Business Requirements Rules 1979 as amended. Lloyd's brokers must comply with the Lloyd's Brokers byelaws. The IBRC requires an accountant's report, while the PIA and Lloyd's require a special audit report. These are usually given by the insurance broker's auditors to the regulatory authority.

The scope of these reports extends the auditors' responsibility to confirm compliance with specific rules relating to:

(a) daily transaction accounting;
(b) valuation of assets and liabilities; and
(c) solvency.

Letters of engagement and audit planning documentation must recognise the scope of the auditors' work. It is usually most efficient to collect evidence in connection with the regulatory reports at the same time as completing the Companies Act audit.

The auditors will need to ensure that they understand the business in which their client operates. They will make an initial assessment of:

(a) the nature of the insurance broking industry and the market in which the broker operates, including changes in regulation, 'hard' or 'soft' markets, competition either by specialism or geography and central accounting arrangements;
(b) the structure of the broker, its attitude to internal controls and the nature of management information, changes in types of business broked, the organisation and control systems to assist with regulatory requirements;
(c) the present business strategy, management's attitude to risk and management ability;
(d) the accounting policies adopted and comparisons with those customary in the market; and
(e) the audit history with the client.

An initial assessment of the risks associated with the business should be made. Many risk areas have been identified in earlier chapters but some of the main points are summarised for convenience below:

(a) (traditionally) weak accounting, arising from the variety of business, the volume of transactions handled, the frequency of net settlements, foreign currency settlement and the reconciliation of central accounting balances, although with the aid of computers the position is improving;
(b) delays in processing business and accounting for transactions;
(c) income recognition, e.g. double and nil debiting, timely processing of debit notes, deferred brokerage, returned brokerage on cancelled debit notes;
(d) debtors and creditors, e.g. lack of control arising from poor accounting procedures and funding;
(e) IBA regulations relating to cash and Lloyd's trust funds;
(f) bordereaux, especially if binding authorities are involved;

148

(g) foreign exchange exposure and accounting, including forward contracts and options;

(h) expense recognition, including claims servicing costs; and

(i) the application of VAT rules (see Chapter 13).

With this information the auditors can plan the audit strategy, identify the areas of audit risk and prepare the work programme. Where the auditors wish to make use of computer interrogation software, the impact on the audit approach should be considered at the planning stage.

In the following paragraphs a comprehensive list of audit techniques is given. The auditor should consider which of these procedures is appropriate in order for him to form his opinion and report to regulators. Clearly, materiality and risk will help in coming to that judgement. Additional work may be undertaken to meet client expectation or add value to the assignment.

9.3 Analytical review

An important part of this work will be completion of analytical review procedures, applying business judgement to financial information. These procedures will include:

(a) comparison with similar brokers;

(b) calculating the insurance debtor/insurance creditor/IBA cash ratio;

(c) identifying main classes of business and brokerage contributions, and making comparisons of monthly analyses of brokerage by class of business with previous periods by means of charts or graphs;

(d) reviewing brokerage rates for each class of business;

(e) identifying significant clients and the number of debit notes issued during the period;

(f) reviewing substantial variances in brokerage by client from previous years and enquiring into reasons;

(g) reviewing the ratio of expenses to brokerage with previous year and enquiring into changes;

(h) reviewing renewal dates from billing diaries and graphs of brokerage to determine emphasis to be given to double and nil debiting tests; and

(i) considering the ratio of investment income earned to investment funds held and enquiring into unexpected results.

Graphical representation of the brokerage flow by month, sub-analysed by class of business, currency or customer, is an invaluable tool for identifying changes in the broker's business and possible errors in accounting for transactions. An analysis of the expense ratio, identifying

149

separately the main expense items such as directors' remuneration, staff, premises, travel and entertaining, administration, E & O insurance, depreciation, differences on exchange and interest costs, allows for comparison year on year and with ratios derived from similar brokers.

Explanations should be obtained where the review procedures give results which are materially different from those expected. Even where the results are similar to previous years or periods, they should still be discussed with management to ensure that this is not the result of one or more significantly changed factors which happen to cancel each other out.

Larger brokers will prepare annual budgets and longer period forecasts. The auditors should compare actual performance against budget either by currency or by using predetermined notional exchange rates.

9.4 Internal control

The management of the enterprise is responsible for deciding the nature and extent of the internal control system. In determining this, the size and type of organisation will be important. In a small director-controlled company, for example, where the directors are closely involved in all aspects of the financial affairs, there will be less need for a rigid system and built-in checks than in a large company with many staff and a large volume of transactions. However, the regulatory environment will necessitate some formal controls even in the smallest broking business.

Basic segregation of duties should provide for the following:

The person responsible for the:	*should not be the same person who is responsible for the:*
nominal ledger	cash book
nominal ledger	insurance ledgers
control accounts	insurance ledgers
cash book	opening of post, recording receipts, making payments; insurance ledgers
signing of cheques	cash book
broking of business	authorising payment of claims
raising debit and credit notes	insurance ledgers
amendment of programs and inputting of ledger and data files	cash transactions

150

Typical aspects of a broker's system of internal control which the auditors may wish to evaluate are as follows:

(a) Client instructions are controlled and recorded in order to ensure that they are executed promptly and cover is only arranged in accordance with those instructions for good credit risks or on a 'no cash, no cover' basis, is authorised and is placed with sound security.

(b) Insurances arranged are controlled and recorded to ensure that premiums and the related brokerage of all business give rise to debit notes, accounting entries and the receipt of premiums.

(c) The validity of debit notes and adjustments is checked and authorised before being entered in the accounting records.

(d) Valid insurance transactions, and only those transactions, are completely and accurately entered in the accounting records.

(e) Claims notified are controlled and recorded to ensure that proper recoveries are promptly initiated from insurers and payments made to the insured.

(f) Insurance transactions are controlled to ensure compliance with IBRC and Lloyd's IBA and solvency requirements.

(g) Ledgers are maintained on an open item system and controlled to ensure that any funding is identified and recorded and that cash is regularly and promptly matched.

Whether or not the system of internal control is to be relied on to produce complete and accurate accounting records, it will be necessary to record the key elements of such a system at an early stage of the audit. The aim here is to provide a comprehensive and permanent record which will facilitate the evaluation of the system. Only those elements of the system which assist in improving the effectiveness of the audit should be included. The two most common means of maintaining such records are flowcharting and detailed, step-by-step notes. In either case it is essential to ensure each year that the record is updated for any changes in the system which may arise from changes in the client's staff or from deliberate or inadvertent procedural changes. These changes may be the direct or indirect consequence of audit recommendations. The auditor should enquire as to the reason for the change as this may indicate areas of audit concern.

9.5 Audit objectives

Having made their initial appraisal of the broker's business, results for the period and internal control, the auditors will need to complete further audit tests to satisfy themselves on the following points:

151

(a) All brokerage earned by the insurance broker is properly attributable to the broker, is accurately recorded and fully disclosed (occurrence, completeness, propriety, measurement and disclosure).
(b) Insurance debtors represent assets that exist. They are complete, properly attributable to the broker, accurately valued and fully disclosed (existence, completeness, ownership, valuation and disclosure).
(c) Insurance creditors represent liabilities that exist. They are complete, properly owned by the broker, accurately valued and fully disclosed (existence, completeness, ownership, valuation and disclosure).
(d) All receipts and payments relating to insurance business are paid into or out of an IBA maintained with a recognised bank (compliance with regulatory requirement).

Detailed objectives from which audit tests can be derived are as follows:

(a) All cover arranged is debited to the client.
(b) Proper cover is arranged in accordance with clients' instructions and with authorised security for all brokerage recorded.
(c) Cover is not arranged for bad credit risks.
(d) Proper recoveries are initiated from underwriters for all claims notified to the broker.
(e) Claims paid or credited to the insured are properly authorised.
(f) All cash receipts and payments are recorded.
(g) All deposited cash receipts are recorded.
(h) All debit notes and credit notes are recorded.
(i) All debit notes and credit notes are accurate and correctly classified.
(j) Overdue debts are identified and proper provision made.
(k) Brokerage is recorded in the correct period.
(l) Cash receipts are recorded in the correct period.
(m) All credit entries to debtor accounts are valid, authorised and correct.
(n) The lists of insurance debtor and creditor balances have been properly extracted from the client and underwriter ledgers.
(o) Insurance balances are properly described and classified and fairly stated in the financial statements.
(p) All recorded insurance cash receipts and payments are deposited in and made out of IBA designated accounts.
(q) Transactions in foreign currency are translated at the correct rate.
(r) All premiums paid to underwriters have been received from clients or funding of premiums paid has been properly authorised.
(s) All claims paid to clients have been received from underwriters or funding of claims paid has been properly authorised.

There are no specific detailed objectives in connection with money laundering. The auditor's obligation is to be aware of the laundering possibilities and to remain alert at all times to identify possible transactions.

9.6 Detailed audit steps

Set out below are examples of substantive audit work which can be undertaken in addition to analytical review and scrutinies of books of prime entry, ledger accounts and other records. The auditors will need to select their work in accordance with their assessment of the audit risk associated with each account item. It is unlikely that all the following steps will be applied in every situation.

9.6.1 Brokerage and other income

(a) Where income is accounted for on a debit note basis, for new business select client instructions and, for renewals, select items from the debit note register or renewals listing, and for each item check:
- the cover arranged appears to be in accordance with the instructions;
- the debit note is correctly raised, particularly regarding date, amount, agreement with policy, completion of debit note prior to original being sent to client, and brokerage rate;
- that debit notes are processed in accordance with the period of cover, i.e. nil or double debiting has not occurred within the same accounting period on repeat business; and
- the signing of the slip.

(b) Test:
- the numerical sequence of debit notes, enquiring into the reason for missing numbers, particularly just before the period end;
- the percentage and calculations of brokerage by reference to slips and other independent evidence;
- exchange rates used; and
- postings to debtors, creditors and brokerage accounts.

(c) For income accounted for on a cash received basis, test:
- that anticipated brokerage is received;
- the completeness of statements received from underwriters; and
- that cash receipts are not manipulated around the period end.

(d) For business done on a fee basis, test:
- that fees issued are for business actually completed; and
- the completeness of fees issued.

153

(e)   For other income included as brokerage, check management information and agreements and establish completeness of inclusion of income.

(f)   Select commission payable agreements or, where these are not available, items from the commission account and check:
- to debit notes; or
- where commission is not paid direct, to payments made; and
- authorisation.

9.6.2 Claims

Select claims advised to the broker and check:

(a)   with correspondence;
(b)   that they are promptly notified to the insurer;
(c)   that they are properly recorded in claims registers;
(d)   that the broker has evidence of the claim having been accepted by the underwriter before credit is given to client; and
(e)   where claims are funded by the broker, subsequent realisation is effected.

9.6.3 Binding authorities

(a)   Select items from binding authorities and check that:
- they are within the terms of the authority both individually and overall;
- income is computed and received in accordance with the authority and that no secret commissions arise; and
- a policy has been issued.

(b)   Check that bordereaux are submitted to the underwriter on time and in accordance with the terms of the authority. If submissions are delayed, establish and verify the cause.

(c)   Check that there has been no double counting of claims or premiums on bordereaux.

(d)   Select claims arising under binding authority business and check that:
- they are properly supported by evidence of loss;
- those in excess of any stated limit are referred to the underwriter before settlement; and
- they relate to policies actually in effect at the date of the claim.

(e)   Select accounts rendered and check that they include all business done in the binder in the relevant period.

(f) Review control over policy documents and check that for each document used a premium arises.

9.6.4 Insurance debtors and creditors

(a) Complete:
- overall ledger and balance scrutinies;
- confirmation, by circularisation of debtors, of unsettled transactions on the debtors ledger or, for direct business only, balances.

(b) Select individual balances (including credit balances on the debtors' ledger and debtor balances on the credit ledger possibly caused by unprocessed items) and:
- identify, reconcile and agree items and balances with third parties;
- check and review the age analysis of debits. This is also necessary for reporting to the IBRC;
- match old debit balances (according to the type of business) with corresponding unsettled credit balances to ensure that no funding losses arise;
- review correspondence with clients, underwriters and lawyers; and
- check and review post-dated cash receipts and payments.

(c) Review suspense accounts, such as claims suspense accounts, which may include unidentified, collected or funded claims

(d) Ensure that business has been closed to underwriters promptly. Note that Lloyd's brokers should comply with Lloyd's Terms of Trade and Terms of Credit Regulations.

9.6.5 IBA transactions

(a) Vouch cash book receipts to copy paying-in slips, checking for:
- stamp and initial of bank;
- any alterations;
- deposits made late; and
- daily banking.

(b) Identify all bank accounts used for insurance business transactions during the accounting period and confirm that:
- they are properly designated 'IBA' and appropriate trust funds;
- they are with banks approved by the regulatory authorities;
- if not current accounts, they are subject to less than one month's notice of withdrawal; and
- they are free of any lien or charge, except as permitted by Lloyd's or IBRC Rules.

(c) Ensure that the insurance broker has received for each IBA account the bank's acknowledgement that the account has been set up in accordance with Lloyd's or IBRC Rules, and obtain confirmation directly from the bank that the terms of the acknowledgement existed throughout the period under review.

(d) Check cash receipt items relating to all types of business from client's and underwriter's ledgers to the IBA cash book. Include receipts of brokerage and commission direct from underwriters and recorded in general ledger, and any other brokers' or agents' ledgers.

(e) Check from the general ledger or investment files that transactions relating to the purchase and sale of short-term assets are processed through IBA bank accounts.

(f) Ensure that payments from IBA accounts are settlements to clients or underwriters, or the withdrawal of brokerage, fees and commissions. Check that such withdrawals do not take place before the brokerage, fees and commissions are credited in the books of account.

(g) Scrutinise the IBA accounts for any payments other than transfers between IBA accounts, for IBA short-term assets, to underwriters and clients, and withdrawals of brokerage, fees and commissions.

(h) Scrutinise non-IBA cash books to ensure that they include no insurance business transactions.

9.6.6 PIA members

For appropriate PIA members where a special audit opinion is required, further detailed verification is necessary as follows:

(a) Documents of title and certificates evidencing title to investments are registered in accordance with Rule 23.4.3 of the adopted FIMBRA Rules.

(b) Documents of title and certificates are adequately safeguarded.

(c) Arrangements with eligible custodians are in compliance with Rule 23.5.1 of the adopted FIMBRA Rules.

(d) A record of investments, documents of title and certificates evidencing title are properly maintained in accordance with Rule 23.3.3 of the adopted FIMBRA Rules.

(e) A reconciliation of the total of the investments and other assets held on behalf of clients (whether on the member's premises or with third-party custodians) with the record of individual holdings in respect of each client is carried out every six months in accordance with Rule 23.4.1 of the adopted FIMBRA Rules.

(f) The reconciliation in accordance with Rule 23.4.1 of the adopted FIMBRA Rule is agreed to a physical inspection of documents held by the client plus statements from custodians in accordance with Rule 23.4.3 of the adopted FIMBRA Rules.

(g) Client bank accounts are properly opened and maintained at authorised institutions in accordance with Rule 3.1 of the Financial Services (Clients' Money) Regulations.

(h) Client money held or received by the member in cash is paid forthwith into a client bank account or to the client concerned.

(i) No money is paid into a client bank account other than money required to be so treated by Rule 3.2 of the Financial Services (Clients' Money) Regulations.

(j) Amounts deposited or withdrawn from client bank accounts are completely and accurately entered in the accounting records.

(k) Interest which the member is liable to pay clients is correctly calculated, credited to the client account and recorded.

(l) A reconciliation of the total balances on client bank accounts with the total of the corresponding credit balances in respect of clients is carried out in accordance with Rule 4.07 of the Financial Services (Clients' Money) Regulations.

(m) A reconciliation of the balance of each client bank account set out in the statement issued by the bank with the balance of that account as recorded by the member is carried out in accordance with Rule 4.07 of the Financial Services (Clients' Money) Regulations.

(n) Proper accounting records, appropriate for the type of business carried on, have been maintained.

(o) The annual financial statements, including the statement of financial resources, have been prepared and calculated in accordance with Appendix 4 and Rules 20 and 21 of the adopted FIMBRA Rules and the resources at the balance sheet date are at least the minimum to comply with the Rules.

9.6.7 Audit completion procedures

Normal audit completion procedures will be extended to include the solvency and other audit returns. It is essential that the auditors are satisfied the broker has complied with the requirements of its regulatory authority before signing their report on the statutory company accounts. A failure to comply might result in the authority suspending the broker and thus prejudice the continued going concern of the business.

Chapter 10 – Profit and loss account

10.1 Introduction

As already discussed in Chapters 3, 4 and 5, insurance brokers' financial statements must comply with IBRC Accounts Rules, Lloyd's brokers byelaws or PIA Accounts Rules. They should also comply with applicable accounting standards – statements of standard accounting practice (SSAPs), financial reporting standards (FRSs) and pronouncements from the Urgent Issue Task Force (UITF) and, if the broker is a limited company, they must also comply with CA 1985. The regulatory authorities' rules for unincorporated businesses also require them to comply, so far as is practicable, with CA 1985. The Stock Exchange Listing Rules will be applicable to publicly quoted companies.

There are two main formats prescribed by the CA 1985 Schedule 4 for the profit and loss account, and each format can be displayed either vertically or horizontally. Format 1 categorises expenditure into functions, format 2 into types of expenditure.

The formats do not prescribe any headings or subheadings but require the following to be disclosed on the face of the profit and loss account:

(a) the profit or loss on ordinary activities before taxation;
(b) any amount transferred between the profit and loss account and other reserves; and
(c) the amount of any dividends paid and proposed.

In addition FRS 3 *Reporting Financial Performance* requires the following to be disclosed separately on the face of the profit and loss account after operating profit and before interest:

(a) profits or losses on the sale or termination of an operation;
(b) costs of a fundamental reorganisation or restructuring; and
(c) profits or losses on the disposal of fixed assets.

These need only be shown if material and disclosure should include any provisions in respect of the items.

158

Having adopted a particular format for the profit and loss account, the same format must be used in subsequent years unless, in the opinion of the directors, there are special reasons for adopting one of the alternative prescribed forms. It could be that a change in market conditions (e.g. revised terms of credit leading to a change in the way the broker's remuneration is determined) might provide the basis for such an argument. The fact of and reasons for any change must be disclosed. Included in Appendix 4 is a pro forma profit and loss account under format 2. This sets out items which will generally be found in a broker's accounts. It is not intended to be a comprehensive layout showing everything required to be included in financial statements.

There are also two formats prescribed for the balance sheet in CA 1985. Format 1 constitutes a vertical format and format 2 a horizontal format. The vertical format shows headings and subheadings in a continuous list whereas the second format displays assets separately from liabilities. Few companies have adopted format 2. Included in Appendix 4 is a pro forma format 1 balance sheet.

The debate within the industry over the application of FRS 5 *Reporting the Substance of Transactions* to brokers' financial statements (see Chapter 11) has led to a call to produce a statement of recommended practice (SORP). This would determine the appropriate accounting policies and disclosure to be adopted by brokers. A SORP would be 'franked' by the Accounting Standards Board (ASB) and carry the same authority as an FRS. We understand BIIBA has initiated the development of such a document. In the meantime, brokers and their auditors have some flexibility over the accounting policies to be used.

10.2 Accounting principles

CA 1985 sets out five accounting principles derived from the EC Fourth Directive. In the absence of comment to the contrary, these are assumed to be applied by companies in the preparation of financial statements. The majority of the principles are embodied in applicable accounting standards and consist of the following:

(a) the company is a going concern, capable of continuing in business;
(b) accounting policies are applied on a consistent basis;
(c) the bases used must be prudent, recognising only realised profits and providing for all liabilities and losses that have arisen or are likely to arise;
(d) all income relating to the period, and all expenses incurred in earning that income, must be included, regardless of the date of payment or receipt (the accruals concept); and

159

(e) in determining the aggregate amount to be included in the account in respect of any item, the amount of each individual asset or liability must be accrued separately.

In addition to the five principles described, amounts representing assets or income must not be set off against amounts representing liabilities or expenditure.

These principles apply to all companies. However, their application to the insurance broking industry is not straightforward, and in this chapter the implications for the profit and loss account will be considered, together with the audit approach. In Chapter 11, particular considerations for the assets and liabilities disclosed in the balance sheet are outlined. The overall audit approach to insurance brokers is discussed in Chapter 9, which includes examples of detailed audit steps.

10.3 Turnover

Turnover is defined in CA 1985 as 'the amount derived from provision of services that fall within the company's ordinary activities'. An insurance broker derives income from the following main sources: brokerage, fees and commissions earned on insurance policies arranged, claims collection commission, fees for risk management services, and investment income. To comply with the strict definition of turnover given in the Act, it is necessary to consider whether these sources of income derive from the ordinary activities of the broker.

Brokerage earned derives directly from the ordinary activities of broking and therefore constitutes turnover. The classification of investment income is, however, not as simple. Investment income arises from two main sources:

(a) the broker's own resources (i.e. shareholders' funds not required for fixed assets as working capital); and
(b) IBA monies invested by the broker before being paid on to the respective parties (e.g. premiums collected from the insured before they are paid to the insurers).

If the premium is paid promptly by the insured, the broker may have several months in which to derive income from the funds. Investment income arising in this way may form part of the bargaining process for fixing brokerage rates between the underwriter and the broker, and may therefore be thought of as part of the ordinary activities of the Lloyd's broker. However, other brokers may consider such earnings arise from a subsidiary activity of the broker, that of investing funds.

The majority of brokers do not consider investment income to be turnover because it is not derived from the 'provision of services'. This income is therefore described in the profit and loss account as 'other operating income' and constitutes part of operating profit. Some brokers take the opposite view and disclose their investment earnings as part of turnover. The latter approach is not to be favoured.

Brokers often do not distinguish between investment income earned on funds 'in transit' between insured and insurer, and that earned on own funds retained in the business for solvency or other commercial reasons. Such disclosure would give emphasis to the debate on whether income earned on funds in transit strictly belongs to the broker. There is no reason why 'other operating income' should not be analysed into its various sources in a note to the accounts.

CA 1985 requires the amount of turnover to be disclosed either on the face of the profit and loss account or by way of a note to the financial statements. The Act also requires turnover to be analysed over classes of business and geographical markets if, in the opinion of the directors, the classes of business or geographical markets differ substantially from one another. In the case of insurance brokers, it is often the case that there is only one principal activity and the market is taken to be 'Lloyd's' or 'London market'. It may be considered, however, that this does not address the source of the business, in other words where the insureds operate, but rather the destination of the business. For many brokers, brokerage is actually negotiated with and received from the insurer (see Chapter 2).

Every effort should be made to clarify the basis of the disclosure in the notes to the accounts. Thus the broker may analyse by clients' operating base, currency in which business is received or destination of business, depending on the most appropriate description to give readers a true and fair view and comply with the spirit of the Act.

Where a broker services different sorts of insurance (e.g. reinsurance, treaty, direct) or earns fees from different sources (e.g., placing insurance, collecting claims or risk management), the turnover should be analysed accordingly. If investment income is included in turnover, it is usually disclosed by way of analysis. This may not be strictly necessary since it is argued that it arises from one activity with the brokerage.

10.4 Continuing and discontinuing operations

Items shown between turnover and operating profit or loss must be analysed between continuing operations, acquisitions and discontinued operations, either in a note to the accounts or on the face of the profit and loss account. The acceptable formats are shown in Appendix 4. Where all activities are from continuing operations and there have been no acquisitions, the company can state that its turnover and expenses all relate to continuing operations and omit the disclosures as shown in the appendix.

10.5   Accounting policies for brokerage

The accounting policy followed by the broker in determining the turn-over of the company must be stated in a note to the financial statements. A considerable variety of policies for recognition of brokerage is currently in use. The main ones are discussed in the following paragraphs. They are:

(a)   the date of issue of the debit note;
(b)   the date cash is received;
(c)   when underwriter is paid;
(d)   when declarations are received;
(e)   by allocation evenly over the term of the policy; or
(f)   by spreading income over the likely period during which the policy is expected to require servicing.

As it is necessary to attempt to match income with the costs incurred in earning it, the policy relating to expenses is also relevant. This may be either:

(a)   expenses are written off as incurred; or
(b)   expenses are written off as incurred and provision is made for future costs expected to be incurred in relation to brokerage already credited to the profit and loss account.

Within the London market, the generally accepted practice for recognising brokerage as income is the date when the debit note is issued to the insured. This method is both practical and appropriate, since debit notes are usually issued close to the policy inception date. They should not predate inception. The introduction of inception date allocation for the 1995 year of account at Lloyd's will make this practice even more appropriate. Brokers carry out most of their work relating to any complex insurance policy in the course of determining and arranging the cover required, seeking insurers to accept the risk and generating the relevant documentation. This is mainly done prior to policy inception, and therefore to recognise income at the end of this process closely matches the labour costs incurred in arranging the policy. It would not be appropriate to take credit before the policy is placed, as either the

162

client or the underwriter may withdraw at any time up to that date. It follows from this policy that alterations (either additional or return premiums, APs or RPs) giving rise to brokerage adjustments are reflected as they are put through the books and no accrual is taken for anticipated adjustments.

This practice is acceptable where the incidence of APs and RPs is immaterial in relation to premiums billed and related brokerage. However, large APs and RPs may arise from the nature of the business broked, changes in insurance cover or business cancellation. For example, they may arise from:

(a) income related to events coming to fruition after the financial year end, such as credit insurance in respect of a client's turnover, where premiums may be provisional with a final adjusting or return premium once the client's turnover for the year has been finalised; or

(b) policy cancellation either wholly or in part, causing time on risk or other negotiated adjustments with underwriters and clients.

Where the nature of a particular broker's business may give rise to significant APs and RPs each year end, their effect must be assessed both year on year and on the balance sheet.

Many brokers have considered ongoing servicing costs which are incurred after the brokerage is earned to be too small to be considered or too difficult to measure with sufficient accuracy to accrue costs within their financial statements. Generally, therefore, expenses are written off as incurred where this policy is adopted.

The cash received basis is the most commonly adopted policy for life and pensions business, where the premiums are usually paid directly by the insured to the underwriter, who will subsequently send a commission account, with a cheque, to the broker. It is also used for personal lines business conducted on a 'no cash, no cover' basis and in respect of profit commissions. In both these cases it is appropriate, since the receipt of the cash is the earliest time the broker can be confident that the insurance contract will be completed. It is unlikely that there will be significant servicing costs arising after this type of business is placed, as most claims will be dealt with directly between the insurer and the insured without the need for significant assistance by the broker. It is therefore appropriate to write off costs as incurred in such cases.

Some brokers, mainly the smaller ones, have adopted a policy of taking credit for brokerage when the underwriter is paid. This practice is justified on the basis that the underwriter gives the brokerage and, until there is an accounting transaction between the broker (or the client) and the underwriter, there can be no earnings. The policy also has the effect of delaying for as long as possible taking credit for income, and thus potentially defers profits.

This practice is not acceptable from an accounting viewpoint for a number of reasons:

(a) the underwriter has committed himself to the transaction on the signing of the slip or other document confirming cover;

(b) in practice, once a client has paid or, for a more complicated case, once the insurance has been arranged, it is very rare for the insured to drop out, other than for insolvency reasons. Accounting policies should reflect normal business patterns, not be manipulated to deal with every case on the basis that a few may not be completed; and

(c) it is likely that the payment pattern of premiums to underwriters is not sufficiently consistent to give a 'true and fair' annual turnover.

It is appropriate for a broker to take credit for his brokerage on the basis of declarations received in the following instances:

(a) Where he deals with treaty reinsurances and he receives a periodic statement from the ceding company setting out premiums, claims and so on for passing, after deduction of brokerage, to the reinsurer. In such instances cash may not immediately pass depending on the terms of the treaty and whether there are other offsetting transactions between the broker and the ceding company.

(b) Where he operates a binding authority on behalf of an underwriter and third parties are authorised to accept business under the binder and to report premiums, claims and so on periodically. Again, cash may not necessarily flow instantly, especially if claims exceed net premiums.

In general terms, this basis is similar to a cash basis. It allows brokerage to be accounted for at the earliest opportunity the broker can quantify it.

Some brokers defer a proportion of their brokerage on the basis that it represents remuneration for arranging, placing and subsequently servicing the business. The deferral attempts to quantify the proportion unearned, usually on the basis of the proportion of expenses expected to be incurred at a later date. If a policy of deferral of income to fund future claims servicing costs is adopted, the requirements set out in **10.7** must be met. This proportion is arrived at by projecting current costs and assumes that the profit percentage is the same for each element of the service. This assumption may not be valid and may not be acceptable to the Inland Revenue for tax purposes. It may be appropriate to account for brokerage over the life of a policy, possibly in monthly rests. This is so where a policy life is not 12 months, or where a proportion of premium is repayable if the policy is cancelled before the expiry date.

Where deferred and instalment premiums are a significant aspect of the broker's business, a suitable accounting policy should be identified and disclosed. There are two particular methods of accounting for these items:

(a) where the broker raises a debit note and closes the full premium for a one-year risk to the underwriter, but the client pays the broker by instalments, the broker thus funding the balance of the premium; or

(b) where the broker closes a periodic (usually quarterly) premium to the underwriter and the client pays the broker by corresponding instalments.

In the first case, the broker's income should be recognised when the debit note is raised. Where quarterly closings are effected, as in the second case, the auditor should check that debit notes are raised quarterly and dealt with in compliance with the accounting policy.

In some circumstances, for example where a long-term contract is being insured, premium instalments may neither be of equal amounts nor determinable in advance. In such cases, the auditor should consider all the circumstances of the business being broked, as well as the terms of the policy, when planning his audit work or carrying out analytical review.

10.6   Fees and commissions

Brokers may agree a fixed fee for arranging the insurance requirements of certain clients and refund any brokerage in excess of that amount. The arrangement is usually for the clients to be debited with the full premium due under their policies and then to receive a rebate of excess brokerage. These arrangements can be identified from agreements and by comparing brokerage accounted for against premium handled. Where such arrangements exist, either:

(a) provision should be made against excess brokerage refundable; or

(b) credit should be taken for fees at the debit note date if the full brokerage is held in suspense rather than being credited to the profit and loss account immediately.

Brokers may commonly receive commission for:

(a) claims servicing and collection;
(b) bureau introductions; and
(c) long-term agreements when business is lost to other brokers.

These commissions are usually accounted for on a cash received basis. Where receipts arise irregularly, the management should consider the need for an accounting adjustment or appropriate disclosure.

A broker may also receive contingent commissions, repayable on the basis of some future event, such as cancellation, or reduced profits to underwriters. The auditor should ensure such items are identified and accounted for appropriately.

Brokers often pay commission to third parties, such as other brokers, for introducing business to them. This expense, some of which is frequently identified on the 'accounts copy' debit note, particularly with reinsurance business emanating from other brokers, should be accounted for on an accruals basis. This may be difficult where the rate of commission is variable, dependent on the aggregate brokerage for a period not yet completed. The auditor must be satisfied as to the propriety, nature and reason for payment, as it may provide an opportunity to divert income to a related party. Other commissions are paid away after premium collection, often to the broker's employees. The auditor should consider such arrangements and confirm their completeness. Commission payable to directors and staff in this way forms part of their remuneration and should be disclosed as such in the financial statements, as well as being subject to PAYE and NIC.

10.7 Expenses

The accounting policies must reflect the accruals concept, which includes matching income with costs incurred and to be incurred in earning that income. Any departures from this principle are only permitted if it appears to the directors of the company that there are special reasons for so doing. They must, however, give particulars of the departure, the reasons for it and its effect.

It is very difficult, in practical terms, to identify all the costs which arise from any particular item of business. Typically costs will be as follows:

(a) The cost of obtaining the business – this may well be incurred substantially before the business is placed or incepts, and many such costs may lead to no business at all.
(b) Where the broker holds a binding authority, costs of negotiating its terms will fall in advance of any business written under it.

(c) The cost of placing the business – this may be substantial but in most cases it occurs within a short period prior to the recognition of the income.

(d) The cost of processing in the technical and accounts department, including credit control and ledger reconciliations – this may be spread over a considerable period.

(e) The costs of dealing with APs, RPs and subsequent transactions on reinsurances which may give rise to little or negative brokerage; the broker is, however, committed to such costs.

(f) The costs of dealing with any claims that may arise – some types of business claims' negotiations and processing give rise to substantial costs over a long period.

(g) The interest cost or benefit arising from the timing of receipts and payments of premiums and claim monies.

The prudence principle requires that costs incurred should not be carried forward except where subsequent income is assured, but few brokers actually analyse their costs in such a way as to enable a judgement to be made. A large part of these costs are incurred indirectly in any case. The allocation of both income and expenses to a particular accounting period is thus an inexact science. It is essential to combine consistency with prudence while having as much regard as possible to the accruals and matching concepts.

Traditionally, most London market brokers took the view that the debit note, or inception date, basis of taking account of brokerage, combined with the identification of expenditure on an actual incurred basis, was the most appropriate and practical method. This recognised that, while some expenses were still to be incurred in respect of brokerage included in the accounts, others already incurred related to brokerage to come in later periods. Moreover, in practical terms, it was usually true that such a broker's business could be sold, with the run-off, for a positive sum. This argument, however, conflicts with the going concern principle.

The increased mobility of individual broking executives, who may take major clients with them to their new employers, and the loss of substantial accounts to competitors have caused many London brokers to reconsider this expense policy. They consider it appropriate to recognise that they may well have significant future costs in providing service to clients in settlement of claims. This is the case with complex, large, reinsurance business, particularly where a number of underwriters are involved with a policy or where it is a Lloyd's policy and the client has no direct access to the underwriter. Where the broker deals with long-tail business he may be incurring costs many years after taking credit for the brokerage, and if the growth of business does not substantially exceed that of a few years previously, he may find that the costs of

167

handling claims exceed his current brokerage. For this reason he should provide for such costs against the brokerage as earned. More detailed commercial considerations are set out in Chapter 7. He may, of course, consider that he has no obligation to service claims, where on-going business has gone to a competitor.

The taxation implications of providing for future claims handling costs are set out in Chapter 14. Where such a provision is set up, the broker must meet certain requirements for accounts, audit and tax purposes:

(a)   It is necessary to demonstrate that a liability to service claims exists, either by reference to agreements with clients or by reference to established market practice (e.g. Lloyd's syndicates may only be approached through Lloyd's brokers, or in the case of policies with many different underwriters subscribing to them).

(b)   Future costs likely to be incurred must be computed on a reasonable statistical basis. This means in practice that the costs of handling the business of prior years in any year must be identified and projections made to calculate the liability. It is likely to be necessary, in demonstrating a 'reasonable statistical base', for different classes of business to be dealt with separately. Projections are based on the number of policies processed and the number of claims handled.

(c)   Any income that will arise in respect of the policies concerned must be taken into account. Examples are future brokerage where policies such as treaties give rise to periodic declarations. It is not considered appropriate either to discount the future costs or to provide for inflation if such factors cancel each other out.

Set out below is a basis for computing the provision required to service claims on business where the brokerage has already been taken.

A broking company started business in 1990.

Year of debiting	Total number of policies	Number of claims handled year by year				
		1990	1991	1992	1993	1994
1990	100	5	15	5	3	1
1991	120		5	20	6	6
1992	150			10	20	12
1993	200				10	30
1994	250					15
Total		5	20	35	39	64
% relating to prior years	–		75%	71%	77%	77%

From this it might be assumed that say 75 per cent of the claims servicing costs in any year relate to prior years. However, it would not be possible on that basis alone to project future costs on a year by year basis as follows.

Year of debiting	*Number of policies giving rise to claims expressed as a percentage of total policies issued*					
	Year 1	*Year 2*	*Year 3*	*Year 4*	*Year 5*	
1990	5	15	5	3	1	
1991	4	17	5	5	1	⎫ Projected
1992	7	15	8	4	1	⎬ total 'below
1993	5	15	6	4	1	⎟ the line'
1994	6	15	6	4	1	⎭ + 34
						Total
Average	6	15	6	4	1	32

So 6/32 of claims costs may be expected to be incurred in year 1, 15/32 in year 2, and so on. This still does not give us sufficient information to compute the future costs as the percentages need to be weighted by reference to the number of policies sold:

Year of debiting	*No. of policies*	*1995*		*1996*		*1997*		*1998*		
		%	*No.*	%	*No.*	%	*No.*	%	*No.*	
1990	100	–	–	–	–	–	–	–	–	
1991	120	1	1	–	–	–	–	–	–	
1992	159	4	6	1	2	–	–	–	–	
1993	200	6	12	4	8	1	2	–	–	
1994	250	15	38	6	15	4	10	1	3	
			57		25		12		3	*Total* 97

In 1994, 64 claims were dealt with. In 1995 and subsequent years 97 can be expected, so 97/64 (roughly 150 per cent) of the cost of handling claims in 1994, including broking, technical administration and accounting costs, should be provided at the end of that year for future costs.

10.8   The audit of brokerage

The auditor should assess the accounting policy for turnover and consider its appropriateness based on his knowledge of the broker's business and processing procedures. The auditor should ensure by testing insurance transactions that brokerage is recognised in accordance with the accounting policy. It is also necessary to verify that documents giving rise to brokerage reflect the insurance contracts placed.

The audit programme should contain tests to determine whether premiums and the related brokerage are received for all insurance cover arranged, and to ascertain whether the processing has been complete and accurate, dealing only with authorised entries, and with all of them.

For income recognised on a cash received basis, the emphasis of the work should be directed towards ensuring that documentation is processed for all insurance receipts. These tests will generally be designed to check the numerical sequence of the policy documents or cover notes raised on the receipt of cash. Particular attention should be paid to the control over cash and cheques received.

The following procedures in the broker's office will enable the auditor to reduce his test samples:

(a) A letter of engagement will establish the terms and conditions of the relationship with a client (see Chapter 6).
(b) A risk register should be maintained, preferably for each class of business, identifying each enquiry.
(c) It should be cross-referenced to debit notes raised for all policies subsequently arranged.
(d) The absence of a debit note number should be explained and the explanation regularly reviewed by a responsible official.
(e) Debit notes should be pre-numbered, with a copy filed in numerical order, and those that have lapsed as a result of non-payment should be regularly reviewed and notified to the underwriter where appropriate.
(f) Debit notes where the cash has been received should be cross-referenced to the cash book and underwriters' accounts.
(g) The allocation of cash received between brokerage and premium due to the underwriter should be regularly reviewed.

The auditor should:

(a) consider whether there are sufficient internal controls to enable him to rely on the system;
(b) check a sample of the transactions, including those that have not given rise to valid policies; and
(c) scrutinise the records to identify unusual items.

Audit work should confirm whether all transactions entered into are properly documented. In practice, all business dealt with other than on a cash received basis will be covered. Internal procedures should enable the auditor to appraise the system and set his level of tests and scrutinies accordingly. The tests should be designed to ascertain whether debit notes raised are in accordance with the client instructions and the insurance policy. The existence of evidence that the debit note has been checked for accuracy and validity before being processed will enable the level of testing in this area to be reduced.

The auditor should review the nominal ledger entries arising from insurance transactions to check accuracy of processing. A creditor for money due to the insurer should be posted to the underwriters' ledger control and a credit for the brokerage entered in the nominal ledger for all debit notes processed for cash received business. For other business, the auditor should satisfy himself that client, brokerage and underwriter ledger entries have been properly processed for all debit notes.

One of the problems of recognising brokerage as income at the point when the debit note is issued is that it is relatively easy to manipulate the level of income by either advancing or delaying the processing of debit notes around the year end. In assessing whether a 'true and fair' amount of income has been recognised in any one year, the auditor should particularly consider those insurance policies that have been renewed on a regular basis. He should verify for each such policy that brokerage is recognised in respect of only 12 months each year (i.e. ensure that nil and double debiting does not occur).

This is explained by reference to the following example:

> If the broker's accounting year ends 31 December and a policy year ends 31 January then double debiting occurs in 1994 if the debit note for an annual premium is issued on 31 January 1994 in respect of the policy year 1994/95 and on 30 December 1994 for the policy year 1995/96. Similarly, nil debiting occurs in 1995 if for the same policy the debit note for 1996/97 is not issued until after 31 December 1995.

To assess whether there is nil or double debiting the auditor should review policies with a renewal date just before or just after the accounting reference date and ensure that debit notes are issued on a consistent basis. If nil or double debiting has occurred the auditor should consider whether there is a material distortion of the results of the broker and whether an adjustment should be made to brokerage recognised during the year.

The impact of double or nil debiting can be significant because the adjustment for related expenses is likely to be relatively small; indeed it will be nil unless provision for servicing costs is made. For example:

(a) *Consistent basis*

	1992 £'000	1993 £'000	1994 £'000
Brokerage	1,000	1,200	1,400
Overheads	850	1,000	1,150
Interest received	50	70	90
Pre-tax profit	200	270	340

(b) *Double debiting occurs to the extent of £200,000 in 1992 and nil debiting occurs in 1993*

	1992 £'000	1993 £'000	1994 £'000
Brokerage	1,200	1,000	1,400
Overheads	850	1,000	1,150
Interest received	50	70	90
Pre-tax profit	400	70	340

Particular care should be taken when considering the acquisition of a broker to ensure that the figures are not artificially inflated. If the above broker had been purchased on the basis of £1,200,000 recurring annual brokerage in 1991, the purchaser might well feel aggrieved. Even if provision for servicing costs is made, no account will be taken of the costs of producing and placing the additional renewal which will normally be incurred on a year-by-year basis.

One way of reducing the risk of double debiting is to ensure that no brokerage is processed prior to the policy inception date. A report should then be produced covering at least the first two months of the new accounting period, setting out the brokerage earned on all policies incepting before the previous balance sheet date. It may be appropriate in exceptional circumstances to accrue such brokerage in the previous accounts in order to avoid distortion and to give a true and fair view. If material, such an accrual should be disclosed if it is a departure from normal accounting policy. Similarly, disclosure should be made of any exceptional income arising from double debiting so that the accounts are not misleading.

Some brokers deliberately fix their accounting reference dates away from their main renewal season in order to reduce the risk of double and nil debiting, and also the cost of controlling it.

10.9 Binding authorities

A binding authority is a contract under which an underwriter gives authority to a broker to grant insurance cover on the underwriter's behalf within agreed limits. Binding authorities operate mainly in the non-marine, aviation and motor markets, and a substantial amount of smaller personal lines business is transacted under such 'covers'.

Under binding authorities, the broker ('cover holder') is remunerated in three distinct ways:

(a)   he is paid a commission at a flat rate to remunerate him for administering the business on behalf of the underwriter, i.e. accepting business, issuing policies, settling claims and rendering accounts;
(b)   to encourage him to write profitable business and to deal firmly with any fraudulent or overstated claims, he will be paid a profit commission calculated on the profit of each year's business after claims have been settled; and
(c)   he is permitted to pay brokerage to any broker, including himself, who introduces business.

Where a broker issues insurance policies under a binding authority the auditor should carry out tests to satisfy himself of the following:

(a)   Individually and overall, the policies issued are within the terms of the binder and therefore fall within the authority given by the underwriter for the broker to underwrite the risks. If risks fall outside the terms and conditions of the binder, the broker will be liable for any claims due on the policy issued and is contravening the law as he is underwriting without government authority.
(b)   Income is recognised in the books of account for all policies issued and no commissions are paid away which cannot be substantiated to commission agreements.
(c)   A liability is recorded for premiums due to the underwriter on all insurance policies issued under the binder and the accounting procedures laid down by the contract are adhered to.
(d)   A policy is issued for each risk as recorded in the books of account.
(e)   Claims are covered by a valid policy, held at the time of the loss, and all claims can be substantiated by evidence of a loss.

10.10 Pools

Pools are broadly similar to binding authorities, except that the broker enters into an agreement with a number of underwriters who, subject to predefined limits, agree to allow him to accept on their behalf a certain percentage or amount of any risk falling within those limits and classes of business defined in the agreement. When placing the business on behalf of the client, the broker allocates a proportion of the risk to the pool. The remuneration methods and audit tests for pools are similar to those applicable to binding authorities.

10.11 Claims

The audit risk associated with claims is not as large as that associated with premiums, because the broker rarely recognises income for claims servicing and is often not involved in the settlement of monies due to the insured, the insurer frequently settling directly with the insured. However, brokers may be liable if they deal negligently with claims, so the auditor should confirm that for a sample of claims:

(a) they can be substantiated with relevant documentation as evidence of the loss;
(b) the claim was promptly notified to the underwriter and was accepted by the underwriter before credit was given to the client – late notification may lead to an underwriter denying liability, giving rise to an E & O claim against the broker;
(c) the claim was accurately recorded in the claims register and the respective accounting entries made in the books of account;
(d) funded claims were authorised by responsible officials and any monies funded will be recovered from underwriters; and
(e) any income due, e.g., claims collecting commission, is properly recorded and accounted for.

10.12 Reinsurance

The audit tests for facultative reinsurance will be similar to those for general insurance. In respect of treaty reinsurance, the auditor will need to gain comfort in additional areas. This will include tests to cover the administration of such policies.

(a) Verification that the reinsurance statements are received from the reinsured on a timely and regular basis, and that income is not distorted by processing statements for a greater or lesser period than the accounting period.
(b) Testing that the risks ceded and included on the statements are

174

prima facie within the terms of the treaty. This is becoming increasingly difficult to test since treaty statements are often submitted blind. These blind statements include only a summarised statement without any details of the policies issued or risks covered.

10.13 Foreign currency

The provision of insurance services to world-wide clients and the placement of risks in the international market has led to the need for brokers to settle monies in more than one currency. Large intermediaries and Lloyd's brokers deal in pure currencies (sterling and US and Canadian dollars) and 'convertible' currencies.

Pure currencies are those where the insurance transactions, including brokerage, are recorded in the broker's accounting records in the currency concerned. The payment or receipt of pure currency will not give rise to exchange differences in the books at that point since the settlement to the underwriter will be in the same currency as the premium received from the insured. This leaves the brokerage (and any interest on deposits) recorded in the nominal ledger in currency. For the purposes of translating this into sterling the normal method is to reflect the income at the average rate of exchange ruling, usually on a monthly basis.

Exchange differences will arise either when the currency brokerage is converted into sterling in order to pay sterling expenses, or on the production of a balance sheet when all currency assets and liabilities will need to be translated into sterling at the current rate. Such exchange differences should be recognised separately in the profit and loss account and disclosed if material. It should be noted that while differences may not be material viewed in isolation, an exchange gain in one year and an exchange loss in the next can combine to produce a significant amount when considering year on year profits.

Convertible currency transactions are normally recorded in the broker's books, and reported to and settled with the underwriter, in sterling, with a memorandum of the currency amounts involved. Statements are, however, sent to the client and settlement is effected between client and broker in the original foreign currency. Thus if the exchange rate used for the initial recording of the transaction is different from that achieved when the client settles, an exchange difference will immediately arise:

		Fr. francs	*Sterling equivalent*
1 January	Client debited, exchange rate 10f = £1	10,000	1,000
28 February	Client pays, exchange rate 11f = £1	(10,000)	(909)
	Exchange loss		91

In practice, when this occurs the broker will put through an adjustment to the underwriter so that he will take his proportion of the gain or loss. For example, if in the above case the brokerage was 10 per cent the underwriter will be charged £91 less £9.10 as a return premium. Brokers normally operate a *de minimis limit*, so that if the amount to be charged or credited to an individual underwriter is less than a certain figure, no entries are raised. This is on the basis that it is fairly costly in terms of time for the broker and the underwriter to put through small adjustments, which in any event will tend to even out over time.

As with pure currency balances, current assets and liabilities at the balance sheet date will need to be translated at the closing rate. If, however, a significant difference arises consideration needs to be given to the quantum that will be passed on to the underwriter.

10.14 Realised/unrealised profits

Exchange differences arising on settled transactions will already have been reflected in cash flows and are therefore realised. Similarly, it is reasonably certain that exchange gains or losses on unsettled short-term monetary items will soon be reflected in cash flows. A short-term monetary item is one which falls due within one year of the balance sheet date. In accordance with the prudence concept contained in SSAP 2, the ultimate cash realisation of exchange gains on short-term monetary items can be assessed with reasonable certainty, and as such they will be realised profits as defined by the CA 1985. SSAP 20 on foreign currency states that it is normally appropriate, because of the cash flow effects, to recognise such gains and losses as part of the profit or loss for the year.

Schedule 4, CA 1985, states that only profits realised at the balance sheet date shall be included in the profit and loss account. Taking exchange gains and losses arising on settled transactions and on unsettled short-term monetary transactions to the profit and loss account will comply with this statutory requirement. However, exchange gains on unsettled long-term monetary transactions are unrealised profits. Schedule 4 permits departure from the accounting principle only to include realised profits in the profit and loss account if it appears to the directors there are special reasons for doing so, provided certain disclosures are made. SSAP 20 states that the need to show a true and fair view of the results by including both gains and losses on long-term monetary items in the profit and loss account constitutes a special reason for departure from the accounting principle. Where companies prepare accounts in accordance with Schedule 4, but include unrealised exchange gains in their profit and loss account, it will be necessary for the particulars, reasons and effects of the departure to be disclosed in a note to the accounts.

10.15 Currency hedging

Where a significant amount of a broker's income is earned in foreign currency, it is appropriate for him to consider ways of protecting that income in sterling terms. Typically, the whole of a broker's expenses, including taxation and capital expenditure, is incurred in sterling and a fall in the sterling value of his income can be material. There are two main types of currency instrument used by UK brokers:

(a) a forward transaction (e.g. a sale of a certain amount of US dollars at a certain future date at a fixed exchange rate); or
(b) an option (e.g. to sell dollars at a future date at a fixed rate).

These are relatively simple transactions, usually contracted with the broker's bankers. The future exchange rate is calculated to equalise the benefits of the two currencies' interest rates and the transaction is subject to a small commission charge. On the agreed date, the set amount of foreign currency is delivered to the bank, which exchanges it for sterling at the contracted rate. Neither side has any option; they both deliver.

Where such a contract exists, brokerage to be sold should be translated for accounting purposes at the contract rate, not the average rate. If a contract straddles an accounting date, the currency assets that are covered by it should also be translated at that rate. Once a forward sale has been contracted, therefore, all currency amounts related to it are translated at the contract rate. If material, the broker's accounting policy should make this clear.

It may be, however, that a broker's currency management procedures cover more than one year and that, at the end of a year, not only will that year's brokerage have been sold forward but also a good proportion of next year's brokerage. This depends on management's view of the likely strength of sterling against the foreign currency. Providing the auditor is satisfied that the transaction is genuinely related to currency brokerage which may be expected to be earned by the time of the contracted sale, it is reasonable to accept such a contract as relating to the following year. In such a case, if it is material both in size and in effect, a note could be included in the financial statements under 'financial commitments', explaining the effect.

If, however, it appears that the broker is speculating, by selling more brokerage than he can reasonably expect to earn, then the transaction should be marked to market at the balance sheet date, any loss provided and a profit deferred.

An option is a right that one party purchases from another. In normal circumstances a broker will buy such a right from its bankers to permit the broker to require the banker to exchange currency for sterling at a fixed exchange rate, if the broker wishes. There are two types of option – European, under which the right is exercisable on a fixed future date, and American, where the option may be exercised between two stated dates. The premium payable for the grant of the option varies according to the type (American is more flexible and therefore more expensive), the volatility of the two currencies, the forward exchange rate and a number of other factors. It is in principle akin to an insurance policy where one party pays a premium to another in order that the other will protect him from certain risks.

The option rate will only be reflected in the financial statements if it provides a better return than spot. Otherwise the broker will not exercise his option, which will lapse.

The premium payable on both forward sales and options should be written off in the same period as the brokerage to be protected is taken to profit, and if necessary spread over more than one period.

Chapter 11 – Balance sheet

11.1 Introduction

The balance sheet of an insurance broker needs to comply with the same set of rules and regulations as those governing the profit and loss account. There are two formats prescribed for the balance sheet in CA 1985. Format 1 constitutes a vertical format and format 2 a horizontal format. The vertical format shows headings and subheadings in a continuous list, whereas the horizontal format displays assets separately from liabilities. Few companies have adopted format 2. Included in Appendix 4 is a pro forma format 1 balance sheet. This is not intended to be a comprehensive layout showing everything required to be disclosed, but includes items generally found in brokers' accounts. The primary accounting principles to follow when determining the value of assets and liabilities are that there should be separate determination of assets and liabilities and a minimum of offset. In this chapter some of the implications for insurance brokers of these principles are considered.

11.2 Goodwill: SSAP 22

Insurance broking is labour, not capital, intensive. In common with other service industries, the value of an insurance broking business as a whole frequently exceeds the aggregate of the fair values of the separable net tangible assets. This excess is normally referred to as goodwill. CA 1985 and SSAP 22 distinguish between two types of goodwill, that established as the result of the purchase of a company or business (purchased goodwill) and non-purchased goodwill, which is internally generated.

Non-purchased goodwill is not acceptable as an asset in the balance sheet and, accordingly, is not the subject of detailed audit tests. Total goodwill, however, must be considered when assessing the going concern of a broker. A broker relies heavily on the goodwill established by good client servicing and prompt claims settlement. If this goodwill is undermined by bad publicity, late signings, continual late settlement of claims or loss of documentation, the broker will lose business. An auditor should consider internal and external factors which may affect the goodwill of an insurance broker when assessing whether the broker is a going concern.

Purchased goodwill is that which crystallises as a result of the purchase of a broking business accounted for as an acquisition. It does not differ inherently from non-purchased goodwill but arises from an arm's-length valuation of the business. Goodwill arising on consolidation is one form of purchased goodwill. Purchased goodwill can be positive or negative although negative goodwill is often regarded as a capital reserve. A difference arising on a merger between the fair value of net assets acquired and the nominal value of shares issued by way of proceeds is not goodwill. This is explained in FRS 6 on mergers and acquisitions.

The EC's Seventh Directive requires that purchased goodwill should be amortised in the consolidated profit and loss account over a period not exceeding its useful economic life or immediately written off against reserves. SSAP 22 (as amended) adopts the same approach, although it expresses a preference for immediate write-off on acquisition against reserves and envisages that this will be the normal practice. The SSAP allows for different acquisitions to be treated differently within the same company. It is generally considered unlikely that the useful economic life of goodwill will exceed 20 years.

The auditor must ensure that the treatment of goodwill, both purchased and non-purchased, is in compliance with SSAP 22 and CA 1985. He should consider the factors which are likely to affect the useful economic life of the goodwill of a broker and determine whether the period over which any goodwill is being amortised is reasonable.

The treatment of purchased goodwill permitted in the UK, particularly the option to write it off directly to reserves, has come under criticism. The Accounting Standards Board (ASB) has therefore issued a discussion paper outlining the various options which are available with a view to revising SSAP 22. While there is no clear favourite as to which is the most appropriate treatment, what does seem certain is that a new standard will be issued which will tighten up on the treatment of purchased goodwill.

The accounting policy followed for goodwill should be disclosed in the notes to the financial statements. The amount of goodwill recognised as a result of any acquisition during the year should be shown separately for each acquisition where material. If goodwill is to be amortised the following must be considered:

(a) it should be shown as an intangible fixed asset in the balance sheet;
(b) the movement on the goodwill account should be shown, as for any other fixed asset; and
(c) the period selected for amortisation should be disclosed.

11.3 Investments

Generally, insurance brokers handle large sums of insurance monies on behalf of their clients. These monies are required to be held within specially designated IBA bank accounts but they can be invested for the benefit of the broker prior to payment to underwriters. These investments must be designated as IBA, readily realisable, free from any lien, charge or encumbrance and comply with IBRC or Lloyd's Rules (see Chapters 3 and 4). Income earned accrues to the broker and is not refunded to either the client or underwriter (see also **10.3**). The Rules applying to client monies held by PIA members are set out in Chapter 5.

Auditors should ensure that short-term IBA assets meet these requirements. IBA investments should always be shown as current assets. Where IBA assets are held by third parties, the auditor must obtain specific confirmation that the third party has designated the asset IBA. The broker should satisfy himself that the third party properly understands the significance of the IBA designation.

11.4 Insurance debtors and creditors

As the broker is the agent for the insured, he is not normally liable to pay premiums to underwriters until he has collected them. However, market practice is that the broker is usually responsible for collecting premiums and claims, and to reflect this the normal accounting practice is for premium and claim debtors and creditors to be accounted for by the broker and disclosed in the balance sheet. This reflects the commercial substance of the position, not the broker's legal position as agent. The exceptions are that the broker is legally responsible for the settlement of premiums in the following cases:

(a) direct marine business premiums under the Marine Insurance Act 1906;
(b) certain certificate type business such as motor insurance; and
(c) Lloyd's brokers who guarantee and are liable for premiums due to the Lloyd's insurance market.

If a client fails to settle premiums, the broker cannot normally bring an action against the insured to recover the monies as he is not a party to the contract. Non-payment of premiums, however, entitles the underwriter to bring an action against the insured. A similar position probably arises with claims funded by the broker (see **7.2.1**). The Institute of Chartered Accountants in England and Wales gave guidance on the treatment of debtors and creditors arising from insurance transactions

181

in Technical Release 625 following CA 85. FRS 5 *Reporting the Substance of Transactions*, published by the ASB in 1993 and applying to accounting periods ending on or after 22 September 1994, supersedes this guidance.

FRS 5 has highlighted the many anomalies in the treatment of insurance debtors and creditors in insurance brokers' accounts. Paragraph 29 of the standard requires that assets and liabilities should not be offset. Aggregation of debit and credit balances is only allowed where:

(a) the broker and another party owe each other determinable monetary amounts, denominated either in the same currency or in different but freely convertible currencies;
(b) the broker has the ability to insist on net settlement; and
(c) the broker's ability to insist on net settlement is assured beyond doubt, in particular where such settlement would survive the insolvency of the other party.

The accounting treatments set out in **11.6** show the difficulty which arises for the broker. There are a number of long-standing legal uncertainties relating to the fiduciary nature of funds flowing from insurance broking transactions, the extent of brokers' legal liabilities in certain situations and the legal effectiveness of certain rights of set-off. It is possible to argue that the broker retains no material risk or economic benefit from insurance assets or corresponding liabilities unless he has funded transactions or in the circumstances outlined earlier.

In view of these uncertainties and the fact that brokers' accounting systems may not be able to generate the gross balances required under the standard, the ASB has published an exposure draft, FRED 10, which will allow brokers more time to implement some of the requirements. It would bring application of the standard to accounting periods ending on or after 22 September 1996. It does not address the problems of comparative figures, which could effectively bring application back to September 1994 in order to comply with FRS 1 *Cash Flow Statements*. We hope the definitive statement following the exposure period will clarify this issue.

The Lloyd's Insurance Brokers Committee (LIBC) of BIIBA has recommended that, whilst brokers are deciding whether insurance debtors and creditors should appear on their balance sheets and, if so, how they should be grossed up, current reporting presentations should be retained. This will allow the development of common policy by way of a SORP (see **10.1**) which can take cognisance of the proposed IBRC accounting changes referred to in Chapter 3. However, FRED 10 requires that brokers should disclose the fact that the accounting practices set out in

FRS 5 are not applied and, where available, should quantify the effect of non-compliance.

The LIBC is considering the following possible approaches to offset:

(a) continued use of account balances to calculate creditors and debtors; however, this ignores the survival of offset on liquidation;

(b) recognition of debtors or creditors only when the related cash movement first occurs; however, this does not reflect the position where the broker is the principal;

(c) removal of all insurance debtors, creditors and funds from the balance sheet; this acknowledges the fiduciary nature of these items but does not reflect the broker as principal or comply with draft American Institute of Certified Public Accountants (AICPA) Rules;

(d) assumption of no offset at all and show aggregate of debit and credit entries; however, this would not reflect reality;

(e) retention of existing disclosure in the balance sheet with analysis in the notes to the accounts; or

(f) presentation of insurance debtors, creditors and funds in a separate section of the balance sheet under the heading 'fiduciary balances'; this could comply with IBRC and Lloyd's thinking but neither directly addresses FRS 5 issues nor complies with AICPA Rules.

Clearly there are variants on each of these possibilities. It is also probable that other ideas will be developed during the deferment period. This chapter has been written on the assumption that existing practice will continue in the short term. It is probable, however, that in the future brokers will have to disclose the extent to which their own funds are retained in the business and how much business finance is provided by funds in transit between insurer and insured. Brokers' practice regarding withdrawal of brokerage and adequate capitalisation of the business are matters the broker should consider during the deferment period on FRS 5.

11.5   Separate determination

The broker normally maintains accounts for all parties with whom or for whom he places business as if he were in a contractual relationship with each of the parties. This becomes increasingly complex where:

(a) parties are both clients and underwriters (mainly in reinsurance);

(b) the broker is only part of a chain of intermediaries; or

(c) the broker is dealing with reinsurance and bureau accounting systems such as Lloyd's and the London Processing Centre (LPC) which handles business from the London Insurance and

Reinsurance Market Association (LIRMA) or the Institute of London Underwriters (ILU), where there may be multiple underwriters.

11.6 Accounting treatment

The following accounting treatments are normally adopted by insurance brokers for insurance debtors and creditors:

(a) *Single risks (not placed through Lloyd's/ILU/LIRMA)*
The broker will treat the party from which it expects to receive a premium as the principal and record a debtor for the gross premium. In the same way, a creditor will be maintained for the net premium payable to the insurer. If at any time a claim is made against the policy and the broker is to collect it, the monies due from the insurer are shown as a debtor and those due to the insured as a creditor.

(b) *Reinsurance treaties*
Reinsurance treaties result in the insured sending the broker statements on a regular basis, detailing premiums and claims on business ceded in accordance with the terms of the treaty. These are then set up as debtors and creditors within the accounting system, with entries against the appropriate insured and insurers.

(c) *Bureau balances*
Lloyd's, ILU and LIRMA have developed centralised accounting systems whereby balances with insurers and brokers are settled periodically. Settlements are effected by calculating the net balance due on the business transacted in the particular period. For instance, the Lloyd's monthly settlement statement will show a list of all those premiums due to Lloyd's underwriters from the broker and the claims due from the underwriters to the broker, giving a net balance either due to or from Lloyd's.

The broker normally keeps one account in each main currency for each of the three bureaux, recording amounts due from and to the respective parties which need to be agreed to the settlement statements produced by Lloyd's, ILU and LIRMA.

(d) *Binding authorities*
Where the broker is the cover holder, he will accumulate premiums and claims arising under a binder and will settle on a periodic basis to the underwriter in accordance with the contract. In other circumstances the cover holder will submit the bordereau.

11.7 Funding and bad debts

Funding, the practice of paying a premium or a claim to a creditor before collecting it from a debtor, is fairly common in insurance broking, particularly when the insurance is placed with Lloyd's, ILU or LIRMA, or where the client is able to exert significant pressure on the broker to pay a claim prior to collection from the underwriters. Passive funding may occur where a net settlement account is operated and the broker 'pays' by accepting receipts net of monies payable. Under this system, controls over cheque payments alone will be insufficient and the broker may be unaware of the full extent of any funding. Passive funding may also arise where the bureau automatically debits deferred instalments.

If funding is allowed to reach significant proportions, it can have a marked effect both on the broker's cash flow and on his exposure to bad debts. Where a premium is funded the broker becomes exposed to the full amount of the premium rather than purely the brokerage element. As the brokerage is only likely to be between 2.5 per cent and 20 per cent of the total premium the increase in exposure is considerable. If a claim is funded the exposure is the total amount paid to the client. The broker should therefore ensure that the accounting system does not allow any involuntary funding. This can be achieved by posting the credits for premiums and claims to a suspense account and only releasing the amounts to client or underwriter accounts when the premium or claim has been collected.

While it is a generally accepted legal principle that balances with insurance parties should not be netted off unless there is a legal right of set off, market practice, particularly in London, is very different. Most brokers operate net accounting with parties with whom they have regular dealings, and it is often only when a party is insolvent that the legal principle is applied. The balance sheet should reflect the amount due to or from third parties with whom the broker settles in the ordinary course of business. It is therefore for consideration within the particular circumstances of each broker whether to net at all, and in particular whether to net amounts due from or to the same party:

(a) across different currencies;
(b) between client and underwriter balances;
(c) between treaty and facultative balances; and
(d) between claims and premiums.

In any case it is not currently practicable to gross up bureau balances. These reflect in each main currency all types of transaction with a number of different parties and are settled net on the basis of the regular statements on a set day, whether or not the statements are agreed or correct. The application of FRS 5 in 1996 will require these balances to be grossed up.

11.8 Disclosure

As already noted, the inclusion of insurance debtors and creditors in the financial statements may not reflect the insurance broker's legal rights and obligations but rather the commercial substance of the transactions. The inclusion of the balances is governed by the requirement for the accounts to show a true and fair view and accordingly a note should be included in the financial statements explaining the policy adopted. It might state:

> 'insurance debtors and creditors include net amounts due from or to each party with whom the company settles in the normal course of business'.

11.9 Audit of insurance debtors and creditors

The audit approach to insurance debtors and creditors is in principle similar to the approach in any other industry. There are, however, four factors perculiar to insurance brokers which may influence the auditor's approach to individual balances:

(a) whether the insurance broker is deemed at law to be acting merely as agent or intermediary;
(b) the settlement practice between client, underwriter and broker;
(c) the business nature of balances which may affect a broker's liability (e.g. Lloyd's, reinsurance, marine); and
(d) whether the broker has funded any debtor balances.

The major audit problems relating to the insurance balances flow from:

(a) the volume and types of transactions (debit notes, credit notes, cash, additional and return premiums, journal entries and exchange differences);
(b) poor cash matching with debit and credit notes, particularly where settlement is made via Lloyd's, LIRMA or ILU, or where a round sum of cash is received on account;
(c) poor reconciliation of monthly settlement statements with Lloyd's, ILU, LIRMA and reinsurance pool arrangements;
(d) direct set-off arrangements adopted by clients and underwriters in settlement of outstanding items; and

(e)   the processing, accounting and settlement delays associated with reinsurance business, especially where overseas parties are involved.

In determining the audit approach the above factors should be considered and the auditor should:

(a)   identify the precise nature and amount of individual items within balances;

(b)   consider the broker's exposure should a debt prove uncollectable, in respect of:

(i)   the brokerage element within premium debt, or

(ii)   the full premium if funded to underwriters, or

(iii) claims funded to clients; and

(c)   consider the impact of the Marine Insurance Act on premium which has not been collected.

11.10   Bureau balances

Bureau balances with Lloyd's central accounting, LIRMA and ILU must be settled on a regular, e.g. weekly, basis and are settled according to the bureau's records and not the broker's. It is therefore important for the broker to identify, reconcile and investigate differences between his account entries and those of the bureau each month. The purpose of a reconciliation is to identify and investigate the differences between what is recorded in the ledgers and what is eventually settled. Differences may arise from:

(a)   recording the settlement of convertible currency transactions in sterling at different exchange rates from the original entries;

(b)   posting several transactions together, which are then closed separately, and vice versa;

(c)   funding claims on a policy which has not been closed; or

(d)   errors in the bureau or third-party statements or the broker's accounting records.

Differences arising from convertible currency transactions should be closed to the market or written off and errors corrected as soon as they are identified.

The auditor should review the reconciling items in detail to be satisfied that transactions are accounted for completely and that balances consist of individual items that remain valid and will be settled in due course. Such reconciliations, properly monitored by management, will give the auditor considerable comfort that any unrecorded liabilities will be identified. If brokers do not produce such reconciliations, it will be necessary for the auditor to reconcile the accounts himself in order to identify unrecorded items.

It is important to obtain an aged profile of the bureau balances as the majority of the balance should arise from the last few months of the year. Any significant balances more than 12 months old indicate a problem which should be investigated. Some computerised systems provide the broker with a monthly report which gives details on an aged basis of the number and value of items brought forward, input, cleared and carried forward. Such information gives an indication of how well ledger accounts are being maintained and highlights potential problems.

There will be occasions when the auditor's opinion on bureau balances is reliant upon explanations received from management. These assurances should be included in the letter of representation. The wording of letters of representation depends on the facts of each case, but one of the following paragraphs may be appropriate:

(a) 'It is company policy in certain circumstances to settle clients' claims before payment is received from underwriters. Except as specifically provided, no losses are expected to arise from this funding.'
(b) 'All claims shown as due from reinsurers have been properly notified to them and adequate provision has been made against any such amounts which are shown to be or expected to be irrecoverable.'
(c) 'The directors recognise that reconciliation of the LCA balance is in arrears, with the result that there are a number of unmatched items and unallocated cash within the ledger balance. The directors are confident that reconciliation of these items will not result in any material amounts, including foreign exchange differences, affecting the company's profit and loss account.'

The auditor must consider whether such representations, in conjunction with other audit evidence obtained, are sufficient for him to be satisfied that proper books and records have been maintained throughout the accounting period and that the figures disclosed in the financial statements for insurance debtors and creditors, gross or net, are not materially misstated.

Unidentified or long-outstanding credits on the insurance ledger cause some difficulty. Brokers often seek to write such items back to the profit and loss account. This practice may be in conflict with IBA rules. However, exchange differences or other small amounts arising during reconciliation could be taken to profit.

11.11 Company balances

Settlement procedures to insurers vary between brokers. Monies may be settled either in accordance with the broker's records or on receipt of a statement from the insurers concerned. If settlement is on insurance companies' statements, regular reconciliation of items shown by brokers with entries on the underwriters' statements is essential. There should be some method of investigating items which are inconsistent.

Where brokers settle against their own balances, the possibility of over- or non-payment is reduced, but it is possible that legitimate liabilities arising on policy renewals are not reflected in the brokers' balances and so reconciliations with underwriters' statements are still necessary.

The insurance broker should be advised to settle balances due to insurers on the basis of the balances recorded in the broker's own accounting records and to identify the transactions recorded on the insurers' statements to ensure that bona fide liabilities are recorded in his books of account. The auditor can obtain independent confirmation of the statement direct from insurance companies and should review reconciling items between statements and ledger balances in detail.

11.12 Binders and bordereaux

The auditor's main concern is that liabilities to underwriters under binding authorities and bordereau agreements where the broker is solely responsible may not have been set up in the broker's books of account. It is not possible to obtain third-party comfort on such business. It is therefore essential to be satisfied that the broker's system of internal control will ensure the completeness and accuracy of bordereaux for all risks and claims agreed within the terms of the binder or treaty. The bordereaux should be submitted regularly to underwriters in accordance with the contract terms.

11.13 Umbrella arrangements

Where a Lloyd's broker fronts for a non-Lloyd's broker under an umbrella arrangement (see Chapter 4), the auditor should ensure that the accounting arrangements are such that the business transacted by the non-Lloyd's broker in the name of the Lloyd's broker is properly accounted for. Since the Lloyd's broker is accountable to Lloyd's for all aspects of the non-Lloyd's broker's business, including financial and accounting controls and conduct, the auditor of the Lloyd's broker will need to liaise with the non-Lloyd's broker's auditors to ensure that these are adequate. The Lloyd's broker has a contingent liability in respect of the non-Lloyd's broker's liabilities placed on the Lloyd's broker's slips. In practice, unless the non-Lloyd's broker is of doubtful solvency or his accounting records are out of control, this may not be sufficiently likely to crystallise to be worth noting, especially as the bulk of the liability will probably have been settled prior to signing the audit opinion. If the non-Lloyd's broker fails, the Lloyd's broker is responsible for running off the business written at Lloyd's.

11.14 Cash at bank and in hand

In addition to the normal audit requirements it is necessary to ensure that the regulatory rules for brokers have been complied with. IBA bank accounts must be opened with approved banks and designated so that the title of the account includes the name of the broker and 'IBA' (e.g. A Broker Ltd IBA). Written acknowledgement must be obtained by the auditor from the bank that the account is designated IBA, that it has been opened to comply with the provisions of IBRC Rules, and acknowledging that there can be no offsetting arrangements between IBA and non-IBA bank accounts, and that no lien or charge can be granted over the IBA assets.

All insurance receipts and payments must flow through the IBA account. Brokerage can only be transferred to a non-IBA account if total insurance assets are greater than insurance liabilities, and such a transfer must not result in the broker being insolvent when assessed on the same basis.

The Rules state that there can be no deposit into or withdrawal out of an IBA account unless one of the following is satisfied:

(a) the receipt is an insurance transaction;
(b) the payment is in settlement of an insurance transaction;
(c) the receipt is interest from short-term IBA assets (optional);
(d) the transfer constitutes a transfer to/from other IBA assets;
(e) the lodgement made is to maintain solvency; or
(f) the withdrawal is part of a solvency surplus.

The IBA accounts are not trust funds for the insured. In *Re Multi Guarantee Co. Ltd* (heard in the Chancery Division, July 1984) it was decided that monies derived from insurance premiums and paid into an IBA account were assets available to the company's liquidator for general purposes on winding up and were not held on trust for the benefit of insurance creditors. However, Lloyd's requires Lloyd's brokers to establish trust fund status for their IBA assets (see **11.5**).

As a result of the regulations the broker has to pay for the day-to-day running of the business out of a non-IBA bank account which is funded from:

(a) the transfer of brokerage from IBA accounts; and/or
(b) the receipt of interest from IBA or non-IBA interest-bearing assets; and/or
(c) other resources of the broker.

Cash in hand and at bank, whether an IBA asset or not, should be included in the relevant heading of assets in the balance sheet (an overdraft or loan should be included in the creditors heading, the classification depending on whether the liability will fall due within or after one year). It is not required practice to identify IBA funds separately.

The auditor should ascertain and evaluate the broker's system of recording and processing insurance and non-insurance payments and receipts, and assess its adequacy as a basis for the preparation of the financial statements. Controls should ensure compliance with IBA and solvency requirements in the following matters:

(a) any new IBAs are correctly designated;
(b) all insurance monies received are paid into an IBA;
(c) all payments made in settlement of insurance items are paid out of an IBA;
(d) withdrawals of brokerage do not result in a breach of the solvency rules; and
(e) any funding of premiums and claims is identified and recorded.

Standard bank letters should be sent to confirm the existence of the assets and to detail any other information relevant to the audit. In addition, the auditor must obtain a supplementary letter which confirms that:

(a) the bank account has been designated IBA;
(b) the terms as outlined by the broker when initially designating the account IBA have been complied with for the period being audited; and
(c) the bank has no right of set off or lien over the assets:

11.5 Trust funds

From February 1983 Lloyd's brokers dealing in US dollars were required to sign a trust deed under which all funds relating to American dollar business had to be held in trust accounts and designated IBA. The trust accounts were operated in accordance with the terms of a standard trust deed, naming the Corporation of Lloyd's as trustee. In September 1989, Lloyd's introduced a similar protection to all insurance creditors irrespective of the currency in which the debt is due.

In order for brokers to act in a continuing daily capacity, the management of the accounts is delegated by the Corporation of Lloyd's to the broker, who also enjoys any income derived. Supervision of the operation of these accounts is thus dealt with under normal IBA procedures with no direct involvement of the Corporation except in emergency.

The trust deed is in the form of a first floating charge over the insurance transaction assets of the broker. In effect, these assets are the insurance debtors, IBA bank accounts and other IBA designated assets of the broker. The US dollar deed was revoked as and when each Lloyd's broker entered into the new deed. Lloyd's has specified:

(a) the form of deed;
(b) particulars to be submitted by a company when the charge is registered with the registrar of companies;
(c) the form of board resolution authorising execution of the deed; and
(d) the form of acknowledgement by an approved bank in connection with the charged assets.

It may have been necessary for the broker to amend its memorandum and articles of association to empower it to execute charges over the property of the company for purposes other than borrowing or the giving of guarantees.

Where the Lloyd's broker is a partnership, the deed must have been executed by all partners and such execution attested by a solicitor. Lloyd's will then register the deed under the Bills of Sale Act 1878.

The presentation of the information relating to the deed is set out in the pro forma balance sheet and specimen notes to the accounts in Appendix 4.

The auditor should confirm that an account in accordance with the trust deed has been created in accordance with Lloyd's Rules and that no agreements were in existence when the trust deed was executed or thereafter which would provide a conflict of interest. He should also inspect the acknowledgement in the approved form from any banks holding insurance transaction assets for the broker that they have received a copy of the trust deed.

11.16　Directors' transactions

CA 1985 includes a general prohibition on loans and related guarantees to directors. The Act differentiates between relevant companies and others, and extends the prohibition for relevant companies to cover transactions with connected persons. There are a number of exemptions from the prohibition on loans but, whether or not they are legal, such transactions are still required to be disclosed.

There are a number of types of transactions which may arise because of the nature of insurance broking:

(a)　*Commissions*
Commissions are often paid by insurance brokers to individuals and companies introducing business. These transactions will need to be disclosed if the party receiving the commission is a director of a company controlled by or connected with a director. In the former case it should be regarded as part of his remuneration and subjected to tax and national insurance.

(b)　*Underwriting Names*
If a director or his wife is a Name at Lloyd's the broker may place business with the syndicates of which the director is a member. Such transactions are potentially disclosable subject to the exemption for transactions in the normal course of business on arm's-length terms, and the *de minimis* rules.

(c)　*Loans*
In order to underwrite at Lloyd's a Name has to lodge a deposit with the Corporation of Lloyd's. The company will have to disclose any such loans or guarantees that it has provided for its directors.

It is the duty of each director of a company to disclose his transactions with the company to his fellow directors. It is the responsibility of the auditor to:

(a)　carry out procedures which are aimed at ensuring that all transactions with directors have been brought to the auditor's attention; and
(b)　review the disclosure in the financial statements for truth and fairness and compliance with the statute.

Audit work should include reviewing the minutes of board meetings and maintaining a constant awareness of the possibility of transactions involving directors while carrying out audit work in other areas (e.g.

cheque payments, scrutinies of ledgers, cash books, commission accounts, sundry debtors and creditors).

Reference to Lloyd's 'Blue Book' will give the auditor third-party information as to whether any directors are Names at Lloyd's and therefore whether it is possible that the broker has placed business with syndicates in which the directors participate.

11.17 Going concern

One of the basic accounting concepts stated in CA 1985 and also SSAP 2 is that the company is presumed to be carrying on business as a going concern unless the accounts state to the contrary. The directors are responsible for satisfying themselves that the company is a going concern. The auditor must consider whether their assessment is reasonable and will consider whether there are any financial or other indicators that point to a possible going concern problem. In addition to the usual signs, there are certain factors which are particularly relevant to insurance brokers in the auditor's assessment of the broker's status as a going concern. These are:

(a)   dependence on a few clients and/or insurers;
(b)   goodwill;
(c)   solvency;
(d)   errors and omission insurance; and
(e)   claims servicing.

Insurance brokers trade in a competitive market, and it can be dangerous to rely on placing insurance for a limited number of clients or with a limited number of insurers. The service provided by a broker may easily be substituted in the market, and brokers must supply a good service to clients and underwriters at a competitive price. Where the client contact is not the proprietor this substitution can occur if the producer leaves one broker for employment with another.

The IBRC registers its concern in this area by requiring the following to be disclosed in the annual returns:

(a)   the number of insurers (if less than ten) with whom insurance business has been placed in the last accounting period;
(b)   the largest percentage of the brokerage in the last accounting period derived from business with a single insurer (if greater than 15 per cent); and
(c)   where the answer under (a) is four or less or the answer to (b) is 35 per cent or more, the broker has to state why it is considered that

the business is not unduly dependent on any of the insurers with whom such business is placed.

Dependence on a few clients can be even more dangerous. Another broker may attract the business away by undercutting, perhaps by effectively passing some of the brokerage back to the client.

As discussed earlier, an important asset of any insurance broker is the goodwill associated with the business. In determining the broker's ability to continue as a going concern the auditor should be aware of the existence of any factors which may undermine the goodwill of the broker. This review should include:

(a) assessment of staff continuity, especially those with major client contact;
(b) recent publicity, good or bad;
(c) consideration of the length of time taken to service claims;
(d) whether Lloyd's brokers comply with the 'terms of credit' scheme when signing policies; and
(e) profitability – classically, the existence of goodwill presupposes profits over and above a normal return on the tangible assets employed.

Insurance brokers are required to submit statements of solvency on an annual basis; Lloyd's brokers are also required to submit quarterly solvency statements. The auditor should use trends in recent solvency margins as an indication of the broker's future viability. Any change in the regulatory framework for brokers may have a significant impact in this regard. The incidence of significant bad debts or foreign currency losses can affect solvency and therefore the broker's ability to remain a going concern.

All brokers are required by the IBRC to have at least a specified level of professional indemnity errors and omissions insurance (see Chapter 3). The adequacy of the cover should be considered when the auditor completes his going concern review, as should any changes in the broker's affairs or the market that may significantly affect the availability of such cover on renewal and/or the price of such renewal. The auditor should review the broker's E & O file to identify notifications made to the insurer and consider whether provision needs to be made for the self-insured deductible. There may also be a contingent liability or requirement for further provision if the claim could exceed the limits of insurance cover provided by the E & O policy. In such extreme circumstances the broker's going concern will also be in question.

Many brokers do not make provision in their financial statements for the cost of servicing claims arising from policies already placed (see Chapters 10 and 7). In these circumstances, there may be an inherent problem relating to such costs. This may only manifest itself when the business stops growing, when a significant client or batch of clients ceases to do business with the broker, or on a change in the mix of business. At this point, the earnings from current business may be insufficient to pay both the costs of obtaining and placing such business and the servicing costs of business placed in prior periods.

11.18 Group accounts

CA85 and FRS 2 *Accounting for Subsidiary Undertakings* require a parent undertaking to prepare consolidated financial statements except where the group is small or medium sized, and not an ineligible group as defined under s248 of the Act, or where the parent undertaking is itself a wholly or majority-owned subsidiary of a parent undertaking established under the law of a member of the European Community. However, FRS 2 requires a subsidiary undertaking to be excluded from consolidation if its activities are so different from those of other under-takings in the group that its inclusion would be incompatible with the obligation to present a true and fair view. In practice, additional segmental information can usually overcome the problem of diverse activities.

The accounting problems specific to groups of insurance brokers largely relate to the reconciliation of intra-group balances. This is a particular problem where the producing broker company passes business to another placing broker company within the group. It is exacerbated where the companies are in different countries. The difficulty arises because each broker will normally account for the transaction when it first becomes aware of all the details. This may happen as follows:

(a) The producing broker, having obtained a quotation (via the placing broker) at, say, 3 per cent of market value for the fire premium for a factory in Chicago with a value of $1 to $2m, agrees with his client that the value to be insured is $1.6m. He therefore raises a debit note for $48,000, takes credit for his brokerage of $4,000 and credits his fellow group company with $44,000, being the gross premium due. The producing broker sends the credit note to the placing broker.

(b) The placing broker receives the credit note, checks it with the quotation, prepares the slip, obtains the underwriters' initials and produces his own debit note for $48,000 less $4,000 allowed to the producing broker, less $2,000 for his own brokerage and 'closes' the net $42,000 to the market.

If a year end is interposed between steps (a) and (b), which can also happen in reverse and in respect of claims as well as premiums, a reconciling entry will arise. Most brokers regard the items remaining to be put through as pipeline transactions and will adjust, on consolidation, so that intra-group balances are eliminated and the difference is reflected within debtors or creditors. In most cases the pipeline will give rise to additional income, but this will only follow additional work in placing and processing. In the example above, the imbalance of $44,000 really reflects a true external creditor of $42,000 plus brokerage not yet earned of $2,000. It is therefore usually reasonable, subject both to the quantum being relatively small and the question in each company of double or nil debiting, to treat the $44,000 as an external creditor on consolidation.

The auditor should scrutinise the reconciliation of intra-group accounts to satisfy himself that the reconciling items do represent 'true pipeline' and can therefore be fairly reflected as adjustments to external debtors and creditors. Particular care needs to be exercised in the event of a backlog of account reconciliations.

PART V

Information technology

Chapter 12 – Information technology

12.1 Introduction

The insurance industry has long been regarded as providing an appropriate environment for exploiting information technology (IT) and deriving substantial benefits from it. The sheer volume of transactions that can result from a single insurance policy has led to the development of a range of different insurance systems over the years. In many respects the insurance broker has been in the forefront, using available technology to address this problem.

In the early days of IT, only the bigger companies could afford to develop computer-based systems and purchase the necessary equipment on which to run them. These systems tended to be developed internally and run on large machines, requiring specialist programming staff and computer operators working in special air-conditioned environments. The systems themselves were often fairly inflexible and primarily used for processing large volumes of data. The cost of maintaining such facilities was high.

Over the last 20 years there have been a number of dramatic changes both in technology and in the approach adopted by the insurance broking community. The pace of change has increased in recent years. The major changes are listed below:

(a) The cost of processing power has fallen substantially. The development of personal computer (PC) technology has made computerisation a viable proposition for all sizes of broker. Larger brokers can now utilise advanced systems based on PCs linked to powerful back-room servers (client-server systems).

(b) Advances in hardware and software technology have brought graphical systems within the expectations of most users. Standardisation of 'look-and-feel' and a close integration of different systems is now commonplace.

(c) Electronic communications have become cheaper and faster. The geographical location of a broker is no longer a hindrance to the range of services that can be offered to clients. Insurance providers now market services using a range of established communication networks.

(d) There has been a migration from batch processing to the provision of full on-line systems. Computer systems are now used to support front-line broking staff in addition to the more traditional accounting and reporting systems.

(e) Software technology has advanced to the stage where the tools and methodologies used by systems developers facilitate production of flexible systems to meet user requirements.

(f) There has been a move away from costly, bespoke software to off-the-shelf packages with few modifications.

This chapter discusses the benefits of computerisation and explains the different options available to the broker considering computer systems. There is a brief summary of the issues which face different types of broker and the variety of systems available. Systems required for accounting purposes are also outlined, together with a consideration of their impact on the audit. The remainder of the chapter discusses the approach which should be adopted when choosing and implementing computer systems, and the merits of using an independent consultant for assistance.

It is beyond the scope of this book to explore the systems requirements of the insurance broker at any great length. However, there is an overview of both front-end broking and accounting requirements for the broker and the audit impact of using IT.

12.2   Benefits of computerisation

Although insurance brokers have diverse business interests, some advantages of computerisation are common to them all:

(a) a reduction in administrative costs;
(b) the ability to handle an increased volume of business;
(c) rapid access to information;
(d) availability of information for management and control purposes;
(e) availability of word processing;
(f) access to networks; and
(g) speed and quality of document production.

Brokers who have not implemented computerised systems to reap the benefits set out above will find themselves increasingly less competitive.

Although the introduction of computer systems requires an initial increase in effort for setting up, training and so on, the effective use of such systems can reduce costs substantially in the longer term by reducing the time needed for undertaking tasks and ensuring that staff are deployed effectively.

Time savings for brokers and accountants alike can be achieved by a centralised store of information which allows automatic collation and manipulation of data. This applies equally to the large number of simple tasks performed by the personal lines broker and the extremely complex information handling of the London and international broker. For example, risk information recorded once can automatically generate a number of separate documents (such as debit note, statement and renewal list) in addition to creating the underlying accounting entries.

The staffing issues which face the computerised broker are likely to be significantly different from those which face brokers using manual systems. Staff can be reallocated from the many laborious tasks now undertaken by the system. Although certain areas may require additional staff, for example quality control, the net effect will normally be that fewer staff can handle the same volume of business. Alternatively, an increased volume of business can be handled by the same number of staff with increases in profitability per staff member. This is especially true for the personal lines broker. New sources of business may be introduced by networked communication.

The insurance industry is paper intensive. The number of documents produced by even the small high street organisation has traditionally created major problems of file maintenance, poor access to information and staff availability. Proper maintenance of files is essential to avoid illegible, incomplete, improperly documented or misfiled records. Information may become out of date because of filing backlogs. File maintenance becomes less onerous and time consuming and more efficient with the use of a computer. A central information area is established and information is brought up to date, either by immediately updating files by means of an on-line process or amending files as an overnight batch process. Control can be exercised over the accuracy, completeness and authorisation of information input to a computer system.

Often paperwork storage uses expensive office space. Files and records may be defaced and physically difficult to manipulate. Archiving records will require additional storage, which may be inaccessible and costly. A computer requires less physical storage space through the use of magnetic and optical media for storing data. For example, it may be possible to put the complete records for a small company on to a PC with a single hard disk. Security and disaster recovery procedures may be easier if a computer is in place and adequate precautions taken.

A computer system improves speed of access to information. This may provide responses that are quick enough to deal with telephone enquiries and thus may improve both quality of product and service provided.

Retrieval of information, processing and reporting can all be automated, and the timeliness and diversity of reports increased. For example, computerisation of areas such as accounts and statistics has enabled companies to improve cash flow and controls over terms of credit and funding, all based on accurate, current information.

The availability and increasing sophistication of word processing software has many advantages for insurance brokers. It becomes possible to reduce the volume of typing as material can be amended, prior to printing, without destroying the rest of the document. The use of 'libraries' of standard clauses, for example, reduces the amount of time taken to produce lengthy documents such as policy wordings. Production of standard letters may assist in ensuring a uniform quality and speed of response to enquiries, and enable the use of techniques such as mailshots as a method of obtaining new business. Word processing facilities may be either an integral part of the computer system or discrete packages used independently of any existing system. The exact business requirements of an insurance broker will determine the most suitable facility.

The quality and speed of document processing has increased with new software developments and the enhancement of existing hardware peripherals, especially printers. There is an enormous variety of printers available to the market, and laser printers have facilitated quality text and graphical presentation of information. This is useful for the submission of clear statistical information, both to underwriters for placement of risks and to clients to indicate investment portfolio performances.

Examples of further improvements which brokers can expect from a computer system are listed below:

(a) control over funding, by producing reports or warnings that funding will occur as the payment details are being entered;
(b) credit control, by providing aged debtor reports faster and identifying business placed with unauthorised security;
(c) bureau accounting can be facilitated by using on-screen open item accounting;
(d) exception reporting of unauthorised or unusual transactions;
(e) greater variety, accuracy and timeliness of information supplied to both clients and underwriters;
(f) the use of document management and workflow software in

conjunction with image processing to retrieve documents on screen which look like the real document. The data can be retained in a form suitable for processing as accounting information;

(g) computerised quotations providing rapid access to a wide selection of insurers; and

(h) automated creation of policy records from accepted quotations, removing duplication of input.

12.3 Software issues

Bespoke software systems designed to meet the exact requirements of an individual broker can be an expensive and time consuming means of obtaining benefits from computer technology. Software packages, on the other hand, are off-the-shelf systems which provide adequate facilities for many brokers' needs but at a greatly reduced cost. While they can potentially overcome the disadvantages inherent in a bespoke development, problems arise where a package does not adequately fit the user's requirements. In this situation, costs and time frames can escalate rapidly. Evaluation of software is often best tackled by someone who has the necessary technical computer expertise and experience of the package, the market-place and structured evaluation techniques. Independent IT consultants may be useful in this respect and are discussed later in the chapter.

Batch-based systems require data to be input and updated periodically in batches, and are best suited to a slower-moving environment. Real-time systems involve simultaneous update of information and are particularly suitable for dynamic situations where current information is vital to the business. For this reason on-line systems are normally used by insurance brokers, although they are more costly and require more processing power to be able to operate.

12.4 Bureau services and facilities management

Many organisations, especially small businesses, lack the in-house experience to develop computer systems themselves or even to organise data so that it can be directly input to a computer system. In these circumstances, a bureau can offer a full range of services from data preparation to provision of all the necessary computer programs. These may be either pre-written software packages or programs written by bureau staff specifically to meet the user's individual requirements.

The most basic service is to process, on a regular basis, client data supplied to the bureau. The output generated is then returned within a specified time period. The cost for this service may be charged on a weekly or monthly basis, or as a fee per individual document produced.

Facilities management is the most sophisticated form of bureau service and involves the user buying both the hardware and the software and then paying the bureau a fee to operate and maintain the system. The system may be installed at either the user's or the bureau's premises.

12.5 Networks

Local area networks (LANs) provide a relatively inexpensive method of connecting computers to each other in order to exchange information and benefit from shared hardware peripherals such as printers and disk storage systems. This can be particularly useful in the departmentalised environment of an insurance broking organisation.

It is also possible to establish dial-up links between computers by using the telephone system. A special receiver, or modem, is installed at each location, and information is transferred from the computer terminal through the modem, using existing telephone cables to provide the links. Information can then be passed easily between departments that are physically separate.

Facsimile (fax) machines are now used widely by brokers to provide fast information transfer. The fax machine is essentially a photocopier which sends the copy to a remote location. As with telexes, fax messages can be sent via dedicated fax machines or via computer with a fax card. The facility is easy to use and requires no retyping before transmission across the telephone line. The quality of received fax messages can be poor in certain circumstances.

Direct communication between computers has become widespread with the formation of a number of industry networks. These include BROKERNET, LIMNET and RINET. They allow different types of computer, located either locally or internationally, to exchange information directly by electronic means. For example, a broker may transmit risk information by computer to one or many participating underwriters simultaneously. The main advantages of such networks are that they:

(a) remove the need for the transmission of paper;
(b) speed up the flow of information; and
(c) provide centrally maintained services to brokers and underwriters.

206

These networks and their applications raise various issues:

(a) standardisation of information is important in order to progress to a situation where industry-wide codes are used and translation between each computer and application is minimised, e.g. standard classes of business codes;

(b) information must be secure in transmission and brokers must secure their own computers from unauthorised access; and

(c) legal considerations and potential difficulties can occur, particularly with regard to ownership of, and responsibility for, information sent via these networks.

There are, however, significant advantages in the use of networks. These include:

(a) the faster handling of business, from risk placing to claim settlement, which can reduce costs and allow an increased volume of transacted business;

(b) minimal duplication, and thus errors, in information exchange;

(c) access to on-line services; and

(d) faster access to international markets.

The use of electronic networks in the London market has made initiatives such as Electronic Placing Support (EPS) viable and cost effective. EPS introduces potentially large cost savings into the London market, which has in the past relied on traditional (manual) methods to assist the placing process. The challenge to many brokers is to harness this technology to improve their own efficiency and to open new avenues of business, rather than viewing EPS as an additional burden.

12.6 Broking requirements: high street brokers

High street brokers are typically small businesses that have very close contact with the general public because of the nature of the personal lines and life services provided. Many of their business enquiries are *ad hoc* and will be dealt with over the telephone. A large volume of business must be handled at a low transaction cost. Speed of access to information is of great importance to provide quality of customer service in a sector of the market which is highly competitive. Provision of and access to information, in order to enable the insurance broker to give quotations over the telephone, is an important facility. This is all easily handled by computer. However, because of the initial capital expenditure outlay, which may prove unacceptable to a small business whose profit margins are not large, alternatives such as bureau services may be considered.

Where a computer is acquired, and bookkeeping and accounting procedures are computerised, the advice of both external and, where appropriate, internal auditors should be sought prior to installation of a system so that full consideration may be given to the questions of proper maintenance of books and records, and the adequacy of audit trails.

12.7 Broking requirements: London and international brokers

The requirements of London market and international brokers vary according to the variety and complexity of insurance business which is transacted. Flexibility in handling different types of business is essential. Regulation of these business functions is controlled by various accounting and administrative procedures, many of which are dictated by statute or market requirements. Computerisation has affected this area of insurance broking in many ways. There is now a considerable number of different software packages available to the market offering computerised broking, technical and accounting facilities. Some examples of the types of function which can be computerised are listed below.

(a) Broking requirements include:
- production of quotations;
- production of slips;
- production of advices, endorsements, amendments;
- production of bordereaux;
- regulation of renewals on a diary basis;
- maintenance of a quotes book;
- production of cover notes;
- production of debit/credit notes; and
- production of claims history.

(b) Technical functions include:
- production of wordings;
- maintenance of client, underwriter and third-party files;
- premium closing;
- claims processing;
- processing adjustments and amendments;
- diary for obtaining information on outstanding premiums;
- diary for maintaining information on outstanding claims;
- production of client figures and statistics; and
- production of underwriting figures and statistics.

12.8   Accounting requirements

Computerised accounting systems offer insurance brokers similar facilities to those provided by any good manual system. However, a computerised system can extend the information and controls available and reduce the amount of time needed to comply with reporting requirements. The broker's requirements must be identified in detail at the systems design stage and will include the following:

(a)   insurance ledgers;
(b)   nominal ledger;
(c)   cash requirements; and
(d)   reporting.

The computer system will need to account for clients, underwriters, third parties (e.g. producing or placing brokers), brokerage, commission and suspense accounts. The insurance ledgers should be isolated from the nominal ledger to facilitate control and statutory reporting requirements. Separate insurance and nominal ledgers can, for example, prevent the system allowing illogical journals, such as a misposting between an underwriter account and a PAYE account. Unfortunately, systems analysts and programmers may interpret a user's requirements in a manner which facilitates programming but results in control problems at a later stage. This situation often occurs when systems are being written specifically for the user, although the problem has also arisen with packaged software.

The nominal ledger should account for the insurance ledger control accounts, expenses, investments, investment income and payroll controls where the company has its own payroll system. For systems with separate insurance and nominal ledgers, there must be some means of recording insurance ledger control totals in the nominal ledger. This can be achieved by entering control totals manually or preferably by direct transfer via an interface between the two systems. A direct transfer can be at the transactional level, i.e. all individual postings within the insurance ledger are reproduced within the nominal ledger, or at grouped transaction level, e.g. a monthly total of transactions by type. Where transactions occur in different currencies, exchange rate controls are essential within a good system.

Insurance accounting systems can handle cash movements by:

(a)   allowing cash to be entered but not allocated to a specific account;
(b)   not allocating cash within accounts; or
(c)   allocating cash against specific transactions within an account.

In all cases it is necessary to be able to identify cash transactions, particularly for audit trail requirements and in those situations where cash is entered but not allocated against specific transactions within the ledger.

Computerised systems allow items to be matched with one another and a historical record of allocated items to be maintained. In smaller systems, such items are usually removed from the open ledger accounts during month-end procedures. These 'deleted' items should be retained within a history data file. At a minimum, the system should report on matched items.

Some users may require automatic cheque production, particularly where the volume of business is high. Some cheque production facilities do little more than print cheques, whereas others also raise accounting entries. Such systems will need to cater for spoilt cheques during cheque printing runs.

One of the major benefits of any computer system is that reporting on information held by the system becomes a relatively simple procedure. Depending on the type of system and the way in which the computer programs have been written, reporting can be either restricted to pre-defined formats or flexible, allowing users to request *ad hoc* reports. Reporting facilities should address:

(a) statutory requirements, including those of the IBRC;
(b) Lloyd's requirements, if applicable;
(c) audit and management control functions; and
(d) flexibility in the production of statements with the ability to suppress ledger items from inclusion within the statement, if required.

In a conventional file-based computer system the same type of data may be recorded in many different files throughout the system. This can lead to different versions of the same data being used, with consequent corruption. A database system uses one copy of each data type and has the following advantages over a conventional file-based system:

(a) As data is entered only once, duplication is avoided. Full access is provided because of the way in which the computer organises information. All the same data will therefore be updated correctly and the integrity and accuracy of the data are easy to control.
(b) Data is independent and can be used for new processes without existing processes being affected. This is particularly important when modifications are made to a system.

210

(c) There is efficient handling of *ad hoc* requests for information because it is pooled.

(d) Security of data can be improved since the database will often store items in a controlled manner. These items may have individual security access controls associated with them, which makes access more specific and effective.

However, badly-written systems will cause difficulties for the user, irrespective of the underlying systems development tools which have been employed.

A spreadsheet is a multi-purpose, off-the-shelf tool useful for decision support purposes, and particularly for the manipulation and presentation of data. It helps to establish relationships between various data items and can be either two- or three-dimensional. For example, it is possible to compare the brokerage figures of different departments by relating different geographical areas and classes of business. It provides statistical analyses and calculations, geographical presentations, and helps in solving 'what if' problems.

12.9 Audit impact

The installation of a computer does not change the objectives of an audit, but it may necessitate changes in the audit's execution. This is because computerisation may lead to:

(a) greater reliability of records;
(b) changes in information available; and
(c) different techniques for internal control.

In general, computerised records are likely to be more reliable than manual systems because many control procedures can be carried out using the computer. There are often more stringent and regular checks made on the completeness, accuracy and currency of data, with better controls over daily processing and updating of records.

Although records and, consequently, information available may be more reliable, the actual form this information may take can change. For example, the number of detailed balance lists traditionally associated with a manual system can be reduced or replaced by exception reports, and the accessibility of data is changed because the majority of information will be held on computer files and might not be in printed form.

Internal control techniques may alter and procedures which were previously sporadic or informal may be regularised. The internal controls of

211

a computer-based system can be divided into specific accounting or general controls. Specific accounting controls help check that:

(a)   there is completeness of input to the computer;
(b)   all transactions give rise to data input;
(c)   the data is correct and accurately transposed into computer media; and
(d)   proper authorisation for the validity of input material has been given.

The controls should ensure that records are updated completely and accurately with usage, that the correct files are amended, that all data is properly maintained on a master file and that it is correct and current.

Systems development controls should ensure that the system becomes operational in the manner originally specified, and that any changes or amendments made once this has occurred are properly authorised. The auditor should be satisfied that the large amount of complex documentation generated is properly prepared and kept secure. Administrative controls govern the use of the computer and storage files, maintain a division of duties within the computer department, and regulate fire precautions in order to ensure that adequate contingency arrangements have been made.

The auditor should establish whether the computerised control and processing procedures (programmed procedures) are functioning correctly. This can be achieved by testing related user controls, direct tests of significant programmed procedures or, more rarely, testing the organisational controls. In some circumstances user controls may confirm that a programmed procedure is functioning correctly. For example, checking bank statements may provide sufficient evidence that the computerised bank ledger is operating satisfactorily.

Direct testing of a programmed procedure will include the reperformance of the procedure itself. This can be done either manually or by using computer-assisted audit techniques (CAATs), such as computer audit programs or the use of test data. If the programmed procedures are functioning correctly the main audit tests can be carried out. It may be appropriate to use CAATs once again in the performance of these tests, although there are several other techniques available which can be considered.

The use of test data involves processing transactions by using the operational computer programs, thus ensuring that these are functioning as specified. The results of this process can be compared to the results obtained from manual calculations. This can be an important technique when there is a loss of audit trail.

Computer interrogation audit programs examine the data held on the computer's operational files and can be used for auditing calculation methods, creating and printing additional data for audit purposes, and producing data and reports for subsequent clerical audit. These programs may be specified by the auditor and written by the client or may be the auditor's own software package, although this latter may give rise to compatibility problems with the client's system. They remain, nevertheless, a useful technique for verifying balance sheet items.

Security of the system is an important issue where companies have become dependent on their computer systems. It is important to establish, preferably prior to installation, whether sufficient precautions have been taken against such eventualities as:

(a)   operator errors and omissions;
(b)   access of data by unauthorised personnel;
(c)   corruption or theft of data and/or software programs; or
(d)   accidental destruction of data or the system itself.

It is often the responsibility of accounting staff within the company, supplemented by the company's own auditors or experienced external consultants, to make an assessment of the suitability of such precautions or to recommend safety features which should be installed.

The principal risks associated with any computer system are accidental errors, deliberate acts of misconduct by an individual, or accidental failure of hardware or software. People are usually the weakest part of a computer system. It is very common for errors or omissions to occur at the initial stage of data preparation and input into a computer. Deliberate acts of misconduct are also relevant.

Crime may be perpetrated by individuals who have worked within a company for some time and who are familiar with the system, manipulating it to their own advantage. Industrial espionage may occur when external personnel gain access to a company's computer system or employees gain unauthorised access to files. Cases have occurred where the data storage media themselves have been stolen and used to extort money from a company. One of the easiest methods of gaining unauthorised access to information is from computer print-outs. Protection and disposal of these documents is often completely overlooked, and valuable, highly confidential information may be obtained from rubbish bins and waste-paper baskets.

213

The risk of unauthorised access to information may be reduced in a number of ways, including the use of passwords to protect entry to files. The password should be changed frequently, depending on the level of protection needed. Sometimes two passwords may be used, either in tandem or combined with other security devices such as hardware keys. Another protection is by scrambling information (data encryption) so that it cannot be read as ordinary text. This is particularly useful within database systems where there are multiple routes to unique data items. Disguising information can also be extended to cover duplicate information used for back-up purposes. Proper housekeeping routines should be adhered to, in order to prevent infection of the system by malevolent computer viruses.

The risk from deliberate acts may also be reduced by ensuring proper regulation of computer time. System usage statistics should be generated automatically, showing when the computer was used, how long it was used for, passwords required and the files accessed. In this way, persistent attempts to use incorrect passwords or access to highly confidential files may be identified. Another important consideration is the protection of the system software and application software from deliberate modification.

The risks posed by failure of hardware or software leading to the destruction of data can be reduced by making duplicate copies of all critical information. This system of 'backing up' may occur once a day, or more often if necessary, to ensure that, should the system fail, the amount of data actually lost is not large.

Since the broker's computer is of such commercial importance, there should be a systematic approach to security. It is important to make an objective assessment of all the risks affecting the system and to consider whether addition to or modification of the system would reduce the threat posed by such situations. Finally, it is prudent to ensure that those eventualities not already covered by contingent arrangements are properly insured.

It can be difficult to assess the advantages and disadvantages of insurance and maintenance to cover the computer in the event of breakdown. The maintenance policy seeks to remedy the fault while the insurance policy covers the cost of breakdowns. The latter can include either malicious or accidental damage to the system. Often both forms of cover are required to protect the company from loss. Specific aspects such as fire, flooding, theft and accidental or malicious damage should be included in the insurance policy wording. In addition, it may be appropriate to have cover for the cost of replacing the system while the cover holder's own system is replaced or repaired.

Insurance for software should cover files being accidentally erased, stolen or destroyed and the cost of reinstating the data. It may also be a requirement of the insurance policy to provide a valuation of the data stored on computer and the storage of back-up data in a separate location. It may be important to update this valuation periodically. Disaster recovery plans should be formulated and tested periodically. Service level agreements may need to be put in place with a third party, so as to allow the broker's data processing function to continue in the event of major machine problems.

12.10 Common problem areas

A number of the major problems associated with computerised systems and not already discussed are listed below.

(a) The communications requirements for multi-site operation can be complex and technical problems relating to communications can lead to severe disruption of the business.

(b) Failure to estimate future volumes of transactions may lead to problems arising some considerable time after implementation. Some practical examples of this are that the maximum number of items within one account should be specified with reference to high volume accounts (e.g. Lloyd's suspense) and the maximum monetary size should be determined with reference to currencies such as Italian lire and Japanese yen.

(c) Reference has already been made to the computer programmer's interpretation of the user's requirements. The user should try to ensure, with written specifications prepared by the software house in response to the user's requirements, that misinterpretation is avoided. Some examples of common difficulties are the use of +/− rather than DR/CR, with no standardisation applying over different screens or reports; use of standard accounting terms (e.g. nominal ledger) in a different context; lack of knowledge of statutory and other requirements; and poor controls over systems development and implementation.

12.11 Choosing a computer system

The suitability of a particular computer system for an individual organisation will be determined by its business requirements. Hardware, software and communications strategies need to be formulated. At an

215

early stage, a decision needs to be made whether to buy a packaged system or to develop it in-house, and whether a batch system is adequate or the additional cost of a real-time system is justified.

12.11.1 Statement of requirements

In any computer acquisition project it is absolutely essential to produce a detailed statement of user requirements from discussion with staff in all departments. The importance of this document cannot be over-emphasised as it forms an objective yardstick against which different systems can be compared. It will also form part of the final contract with the systems supplier.

The statement of requirements must be produced in detail. Such matters as the background of the broker, current systems and problem areas, and immediate and future requirements must be covered. Additionally, it is necessary to address volume of business transactions and hardware issues. Commercial issues relating to the supplier and system should also be addressed.

The full statement of requirements prepared as a result of these considerations will be agreed with the department concerned after drafting. At this stage it is necessary to pre-select a number of experienced and reputable suppliers and software houses whose products most closely match the needs of the prospective user. The production of the statement of requirements and submission of invitations to tender to prospective suppliers often merits the involvement of an independent consultant with a good knowledge of broking systems suppliers and experience of the selection process.

12.11.2 Evaluation of tenders

The agreed statement of requirements will be sent to a number of different suppliers and software houses as part of an invitation to tender. Meetings will be arranged with suppliers, if further clarification of the statement is required. When received, the tenders will need to be carefully compared with the original specifications. The result will be a shortlist of suitable hardware and software which can be demonstrated to the client. At this stage, there may be a negotiation phase, particularly with respect to prices quoted in the tender documents. Finally, a system will be selected from the shortlist.

12.11.3 The contract

Once the required system has been chosen, the prospective purchaser must carefully review the maintenance and purchase contracts and the

216

software licence between the broker and supplier to ensure their appropriateness.

Most computer suppliers have standard contracts establishing legally enforceable obligations and it is important that the customer, or the consultant acting on behalf of the customer, examines these in detail before committing to a particular supplier. Although the law will imply certain terms into a contract to protect the weaker party, and will both prevent the supplier from trying to escape certain obligations to the customer and refuse to enforce any oppressive provisions, it is very much in the customer's own interest to negotiate satisfactory terms with the supplier before signing any agreement rather than resorting to legal processes to resolve disputes.

There are a number of options for the customer wishing to purchase both hardware and software:

(a)   a single contract with the manufacturer to supply both hardware and software. This is usually the most advantageous option as it avoids software vendors blaming hardware vendors and vice versa;

(b)   a single contract with the manufacturer to supply both hardware and software, with the manufacturer then subcontracting to a software house for the software;

(c)   a single contract with the software house to supply the software and obtain the hardware for resale to the customer; and

(d)   two separate contracts, one with the software house for the application software and one with the manufacturer for the hardware.

The contract will determine whether the user has recourse to the supplier in order to ensure that problems are resolved and the system operates as intended. It should include, among other things:

(a)   a full definition of the hardware and software, describing user methods, procedures, system capabilities and the purposes for which the system is to be used;

(b)   warranties, both during and after installation, and whether the customer has redress should any part of the system prove to be unsuitable or defective;

(c)   details of installation specifying whether site preparation, delivery, installation and testing of the hardware and software are to be carried out by the supplier, and whether this work will incur additional costs;

(d)   a timetable for the work programme;

(e)   a trial period prior to acceptance of the system; and

(f)   maintenance agreements regulating the service and support provided by the supplier and stating the cost, together with continued support of the hardware in the event of its obsolescence.

Contractual obligations regarding the software may pose additional problems. Again, maintenance and support facilities are important. The customer's rights to use the software may be limited by the terms of the operating licence; for example, it may prohibit the customer carrying out modification or enhancements or prevent the use of the software on bureau facilities in the event of a breakdown of the customer's own hardware. Consideration needs to be given to the supplier's ability to terminate or alter the conditions of the licence. It should also establish whether any future enhancements to the software will be passed on to the customer and, if so, whether a charge is to be made.

Other aspects that should be covered in the contracts include rules governing the termination of the agreement and provisions in the event of bankruptcy of either party. Full details of all costs and whether or not VAT is included should be shown, together with information regarding risk and title to the programs and equipment.

12.12   Implementing a computer system

It is important to draw up a coherent implementation plan at an early stage to assist the efficient management of any computerisation project. This is necessary in order to monitor and control the activities required to implement the system. A senior member of staff or external consultant should be appointed to manage the project.

The implementation plan should be prepared after liaison with all interested parties and after a mutually acceptable contract has been established. In order to avoid either duplication of effort or omissions, the plan should identify who is responsible for each aspect of the project. Regular progress meetings should be organised so that the work may be reviewed and any alterations or adjustments, either to the timetable of events or to the structure of the project, can be discussed and appropriate action taken. A full systems specification should be mutually agreed and understood by all those involved, including user departments, so that there are no false expectations or misunderstandings of the system's capabilities. The company's auditors should be consulted to ensure that proper control and audit procedures exist within the proposed system.

Consideration needs to be given to the effect on staff, the availability of resources for training and the provision of adequate system tests. Once the system is in place it is useful to carry out a review of performance and at this point any operating problems should be rectified.

12.13 Delivery and installation

The final stage of implementation covers the delivery and installation of the computer system, together with advice on education and training of staff. The project manager will help ensure that computerisation proceeds as smoothly as possible and will make sure that the system is running according to the functional specification.

12.14 Staff

One important aspect of implementation is the staff's acceptance of the system. A reaction frequently encountered is fear of change or redundancy, and it is prudent to ensure that employees are aware of management's intentions to computerise well in advance. Involving staff at an early stage may alleviate many of the misconceptions that can arise and, if the question of redundancy arises, it is easier to address this before a system is chosen and implemented. The success of the computer system is largely dependent on the desire of the users to make it work.

Education and training are a major consideration in ensuring the successful implementation and ongoing benefits of a computer system. Training should relate directly to improving the individual employee's current and future performance. It must be appropriate to the individual's needs and conducted at a time when the skills acquired can be consolidated by putting them into practice as soon as possible. It is important to establish staff training requirements at an early stage of implementation planning and to ensure that sufficient funds have been allocated to this area. Unfortunately, the value of proper training is often underestimated.

Training may include the use of videos and computer-assisted techniques, and is largely dependent on the needs of the individual staff member. For example, there are a variety of courses available to acquire word processing skills, and sometimes it will be possible to arrange this type of training through the computer supplier. Other training sources include government organisations and specific training experts. There are specialist services provided by organisations catering for those individuals who need to acquire greater in-depth systems knowledge. Courses may be conducted either at the customer's own premises or at approved training centres. The ultimate object of any training scheme is to ensure that an individual is familiar with, and has confidence in, the new computer system, and to alleviate many of the misconceptions and fears that may otherwise arise.

12.15 Using an independent consultant

Increasingly, companies are turning to consultants to identify their business requirements and match these with the most suitable computer solution. The consultant will help the broker to avoid the following common problems:

(a) hardware or software houses producing information that is ill defined or may be misleading to the broker;
(b) failure by the broker to identify requirements properly;
(c) exaggerated broker expectations;
(d) failure of the computer supplier to provide technical support; and
(e) inadequate project management capability.

Computer consultants come in many guises, and not all can be considered to be independent. They may be employed by a supplier, software house, financial services adviser or specific consultancy. It is therefore important to establish the consultant's business interests before engaging his services. For example, even though not directly associated with a supplier or software house, the consultant may receive commissions on sales of the recommended system. If, however, detailed information on a specific software package and its suitability to meet precise business requirements is needed, it may be most appropriate to approach a consultant working for the software house. Often the best method of finding a good consultant is through recommendation. References should always be obtained.

A consultant will usually charge either a flat rate for the particular job undertaken or a charge per day worked on the assignment. In the latter case, it is important to ensure that time scales for the project are agreed beforehand, as daily charges can accumulate rapidly.

The consultant will usually adopt the staged approach outlined in **12.11** in order to identify the best solution to the client's needs and will seek client approval at each step. This will enable areas of uncertainty to be identified, alleviate misunderstandings or modify requirements in response to changes in user demands, and will produce a clear statement of user requirements which can then be matched against available computer options.

Using a consultant has the following benefits:

(a) in-depth and up-to-date market knowledge of computers;
(b) monitoring and adherence to specifications;
(c) controlled deadlines;

(d)   experienced review of purchase and maintenance agreements to identify where they may be prejudicial to client interests;

(e)   discounts may be obtained through personal market connections;

(f)   it may provide the least disruption to business; and

(g)   cost savings often far outweigh the fees charged by the consultant.

However, there may be disadvantages, which can include the following:

(a)   use of consultancy services is expensive if not properly controlled;

(b)   there may be a conflict of business interests for the consultant; or

(c)   the consultant may fail fully to understand customer requirements.

There are a number of circumstances in which consultants can be extremely useful to the insurance broker considering the purchase or implementation of a new computer system. A consultant may be particularly useful where senior management is unable to devote sufficient time to what must be considered a very important aspect of the infrastructure on which the business depends. Failure to implement adequate systems has resulted in many companies incurring huge costs, and even, in some cases, becoming insolvent.

PART VI

Taxation

Chapter 13 – Value added tax and insurance premium tax

13.1 Introduction

No book on accounting for insurance brokers would be complete without considering value added tax (VAT). Often the forgotten tax, VAT is complex in the way it affects the insurance industry in general and brokers in particular.

Depending on the nature and mix of supplies being made, VAT can be a significant cost to the business of a broker in terms of both the proportion of VAT paid out which cannot be recovered and the time involved in controlling VAT accounting procedures and computing VAT returns. It is therefore essential that those involved in accounting for VAT within a broking organisation should have a good understanding of the tax in order to minimise the cost of VAT to the business, while complying with the requirements of VAT legislation.

13.2 Basic principles

VAT is a tax on the value added to a supply of goods or services in the UK. A supply that is within the scope of VAT is taxable at the standard rate unless it is specifically relieved by zero rating or exemption. The practical and important difference between zero rating and exemption is that a supply which is zero rated is still a taxable supply and therefore VAT paid on goods and services involved in making the supply can be recovered. VAT paid on goods and services involved in making an exempt supply is in principle not recoverable.

VAT increasingly presents a considerable burden on the insurance industry. Although insurance transactions are free of VAT, a significant proportion of costs borne by brokers carry VAT, and this proportion is steadily increasing as the scope of VAT is extended. In recent years VAT has been added to commercial use of fuel, power and construction, and may be added by landlords to commercial rents.

An insurance broker who deals solely in UK business, which is exempt from VAT, is not eligible to register for VAT and is therefore unable to recover any VAT incurred on costs. However, an insurance broker who is involved in international business (provided to a party outside the EU) is entitled to register for VAT and obtain at least a partial recovery of VAT on his costs. He will have the additional administrative burden of complying with VAT legislation, while attempting to make best use of the legislation to reduce the cost of VAT to the business.

The effect of bringing UK legislation into line with EC Directives in respect of international services, including insurance supplies, with the advent of the single market was to a degree mitigated by consultation between Customs & Excise and representative bodies of the insurance industry. This produced a transitional period for the gradual implementation of the changes, particularly those affecting the liability of marine, aviation and transport (MAT) business, from 1 January to early July 1993. The basic changes are detailed in **13.5**.

The prime concern of brokers with regard to VAT is to obtain the best possible recovery of VAT, thus minimising the cost of VAT to the business, while keeping to a reasonable level the administrative burden of accounting for VAT.

13.3 Place of supply and the concept of belonging

Before examining the liability to VAT of supplies made by brokers, it is necessary to consider the 'place of supply' for VAT purposes. The place of supply of a service is determined by the 'belonging' of the supplier. The concept of belonging is peculiar to VAT and needs some explanation. An individual belongs where he is usually resident; a partnership or company belongs where it has its business premises. If an organisation has business premises in more than one country, it is the establishment most directly concerned with the supply in question which determines the belonging. If the company has no business premises, the registered office determines the place of belonging.

If a service is performed by someone, whether an individual or a corporate body, who belongs in the UK, the place of supply of the service is the UK, and the service comes within the scope of UK VAT.

13.4 Liability to VAT of insurance supplies

With effect from 1 January 1993, UK VAT legislation was brought into line with EC Directives as it relates to the supply of goods and services to parties outside the UK. Due to the emphasis on communicating the new rules applying to the export of goods, however, the implementation of changes to VAT on international services was delayed to enable the business community to prepare.

The insurance industry was affected more than most by the changes in how such services were treated. Not only were a number of new terms to denote VAT liability introduced – 'outside the scope with input tax recovery' and even 'exempt with credit', for example – but the way in which the liability of MAT brokerage is determined was changed to bring it much more into line with other types of brokerage.

13.5   Changes in legislation

Prior to 1 January 1993, the provision of insurance to a person belonging outside the EC was zero rated. This included direct non-MAT business and reinsurance, as well as the making of arrangements for the provision of insurance and related services such as claims handling. With regard to MAT brokerage, the liability of this was determined by the journey undertaken by the goods or passengers concerned. Where the journey was completely outside the EC, or to or from a place outside the EC, the brokerage income was zero rated. Where the journey was completely within the EC, the brokerage was exempt.

Additionally, where insurance business was placed with an overseas broker, i.e. belonging outside the UK, this brokerage too was zero rated.

Since 1 January 1993, the treatment of such transactions for VAT purposes has changed, although an extended transitional period meant that the practical implementation of the changes did not occur until early July 1993.

The liability of MAT brokerage is now determined by the place of belonging of the insured party (see **13.6**), just as with all other types of insurance business. The geography of the journey undertaken by the goods or passengers associated with the brokerage is no longer relevant.

Furthermore, the placing of risks with a broker outside the UK is also no longer relevant. The place of belonging of the insured party is now the main governing factor for almost all types of insurance business, apart from business related to the export of goods, in which case the destination of those goods will have a bearing (see **13.7**).

13.6 New terms of liability

A number of new terms of VAT liability have been introduced through statutory instrument with effect from 1 January 1993.

Insurance services fall under Schedule 5 of the VAT Act 1994 (VATA 1994) and are therefore considered supplied where received, provided the supply is made to the insured party in his *business* and not his *private* capacity. Some form of evidence of this is now required, preferably the obtaining and inclusion on documentation of the insured's VAT registration number, but alternatively some other evidence of business status, including an existing business relationship with the insured. Where the supply is made to the insured in his private capacity, it is considered supplied where the broker belongs, and for UK brokers it will therefore be exempt from VAT.

The basic rules state that where the insured is an individual, the place of belonging is where he is usually resident. Where it is a corporate body, it is where that business is established, i.e. its office premises. Where the business is established in more than one country, it is the establishment most closely connected with the supply that counts.

However, it is often more difficult to determine the location of the insured, particularly in connection with MAT brokerage, and further guidelines have been developed during consultation to assist in the practical application of the VAT legislation. These are as follows:

(a) Where the insured's address is shown on the broker's slip or equivalent document (which is normally the case), or where it can be determined by the broker or other intermediary, this address is to be taken as the place or belonging of the insured.
(b) If the insured has more than one address, the one on the slip or document should be used unless it is clear that this is simply an administrative address for payment or other purposes.
(c) Where business is written in conjunction with an overseas agent and it is not possible to identify the address of each insured dealing with the agent, the agent's address may be taken as the place or belonging of the insured parties.

The insured should still belong outside the territories of the EU to permit input tax recovery (unless the supply relates to the export of goods outside the EU, see **13.7**), but where the insured is outside the UK but within the EU, the supply is now considered outside the scope ('O/S') of VAT with no input tax recovery (as opposed to exempt where belonging within the UK and outside the scope with input tax credit where belonging outside the EU).

13.7 The export of goods

Where the supply of insurance relates to the export of goods, recovery of input tax will be determined by the destination of the goods, although the term to describe the liability of the supply will still reflect the place of belonging of the insured – that is, outside the scope of VAT where outside the UK. This leads to unusual and potentially confusing terms such as 'exempt with credit' where the insured belongs within the UK but the relevant goods are exported to a place outside the EU (see **13.8**). However, during consultations with industry representative bodies, Customs & Excise agreed that the coding of such transactions could be simplified (see **13.4**).

13.8 Summary of liability to VAT from 1 January 1993

	Underlying insurance supplied to a client belonging		
	In UK	*In EU*	*Outside EU*
Direct insurance and brokerage of all classes of insurance and reinsurance except for exported goods			
UK broker	Exempt input tax	O/S no tax credit	O/S with input tax recovery
Direct insurance and brokerage of insurance for exported goods UK broker			
(i) export to non-EU	Exempt with input tax recovery	O/S with input tax recovery	O/S with input tax recovery
(ii) export to EU	Exempt with input tax recovery	O/S no input tax recovery	O/S with input tax recovery

13.9 Partial exemption

As most brokers deal in both taxable and exempt supplies they are only entitled to recover the proportion of VAT paid on purchases and expenses which relate to the taxable supplies that they make. This is known as partial exemption and involves a restricted recovery of input tax, which is the VAT paid out on business purchases and expenses.

13.10 Direct attribution

The statutory standard method of calculating recoverable input tax is based on the direct attribution of input tax to supplies made:

(a) Input tax on supplies and imports wholly used or to be used in making taxable supplies is recoverable in full.

(b) Input tax on supplies and imports wholly used or to be used in making exempt supplies is not recoverable.

(c) Input tax on supplies and imports wholly used or to be used in connection with any other activity is not recoverable.

It is not normally possible directly to attribute or relate all input tax to various supplies in this way. Standard-rated expenditure (i.e. carrying VAT) is largely of the same character, regardless of the category of insurance supplied. Many insurance businesses do not operate cost-centre based accounting systems, nor are their staff likely to have rigidly defined rules specifying the VAT classification of the business with which they deal. For insurance brokers it is therefore likely that much of the input tax will be residual input tax.

13.11 Calculation of recoverable residual input tax

The amount of residual input tax which can be recovered depends on the extent to which it relates to the taxable supplies made. The current standard method of calculating recoverable input tax is to use the ratio that taxable supplies (i.e. any supplies which give rise to a credit for input tax) bear to total supplies made by the business. This is usually the most appropriate method, although when using this method the broker should exclude the value of any distortive supplies such as incidental land transactions and disposals of capital goods.

Brokers should generally use gross brokerage as the value for the supply when using such a method, where the commissions and discounts involved in overseas business are proportionately higher than for UK business.

230

Other methods may be devised and submitted for approval to Customs & Excise – a recovery rate based on the proportion of floor space devoted to exempt supplies, for example, or on the number of staff devoted to a particular type of business. This may be agreed to where it can be shown to produce an equitable recovery rate and where it is not too complex either to administer or for the figures to be readily verified on inspection. Any special method approved must be used for a minimum period, usually two years.

13.12   Annual adjustment

Whatever method is used, the preliminary recovery of input tax will be subject to an annual adjustment at the end of the year. This adjustment will apply the usual calculation to the figures for the whole of the partial exemption year.

13.13   De minimis

If the amount of input tax attributable to exempt supplies falls below a certain amount, the business may make full recovery of all input tax. This may be done either at the end of the accounting period or the end of the year in the annual adjustment. The current *de minimis* limit of input tax is £600 per month on average.

13.14   Coding of transactions

With the introduction of additional new terms of VAT liability effective from 1 January 1993, Customs & Excise agreed that all types of business which give rise to input tax recovery may be coded as zero rated (e.g. 'Z'), as they were before the changes, and all categories which deny input tax recovery may be coded as exempt (e.g. 'X' or 'E'). This avoids the necessity for undue reprogramming of coding systems and a further administrative burden in coping with the changes, particularly in respect of MAT business.

13.15   Accounting for output tax

It is possible that brokers may be treated as making some standard-rated supplies without being aware of it, and therefore fail to account for output tax on the value of such supplies. The most likely examples are the importation of services which fall under Sch 5 VATA 1994, which include the services of accountants, lawyers and consultants, the supply of staff or assignments of copyright or licence. Where such services are supplied to the broker from outside the UK, he must account for VAT as output tax on the value of such supplies. He may at the same time recover this VAT as input tax, to the degree that his partial exemption calculations permit him to do so. He is therefore, in effect, charging VAT to himself.

Where a broker moves into new office space and receives some consideration from the landlord to do so, the receipt may be viewed as the consideration for a supply made by the broker in agreeing to take on the lease. A capital contribution towards refurbishment costs, for example, would be liable to VAT. Where there is any doubt, brokers should stipulate when possible that amounts which may be received are exclusive of any VAT that may be chargeable.

Commissions on introductions may be liable to VAT on both insurance and investment business where the broker is not actively involved in the transaction.

13.16 Management service charges

Many brokers share accommodation, and sometimes staff, with associated companies or businesses. In these circumstances, it is common practice for one business to pay all costs and overheads and to recover a share from each of the associated companies by way of a management service charge. This creates a problem, since a management service charge is treated as a single supply taxable at the standard rate. If the business receiving the charge is partially exempt, a proportion of the VAT on the management service charge will not be recovered. One solution to this problem is group registration for VAT.

Provided certain conditions of control are met, group registration allows two or more corporate bodies to account for VAT under a single registration. One of the companies applying must be nominated as the representative member of the group and is responsible for submitting returns and tax. For the purposes of the group registration, all supplies by or to a member of the group are treated as supplies by or to the representative member. Supplies between members of the same VAT group are disregarded for VAT purposes. No tax is charged and no tax invoices must be issued. Consequently, VAT on management service charges which would otherwise be chargeable if the companies were separately registered and a proportion of which would not be recoverable if the recipient were partly exempt, would be avoided.

When group registration is either not possible or beneficial, the cost of VAT on management service charges can be reduced by breaking down the management service charge into its constituent elements as detailed below:

(a) *Accommodation*

Where a charge is made to an associated business for shared accommodation as part of a management service charge, it is taxable at the standard rate if the associated business does not occupy a separate or distinct area of the building. If, however, a licence to occupy a separate and distinct area is granted, the charge for the accommodation would then be exempt under Item 1 of Group 1 Sch 6. The same liability would apply to a sub-tenancy. If this is not practical, joint tenancy of the building may be the answer. If the associated businesses occupy the building on a joint tenancy basis and one business pays the rent and then recovers a proportion from each of the others, the recovery would be outside the scope of VAT as this business would be acting purely as a paying agent. If, however, the paying agent made a charge for his services in this respect, this would be taxable at the standard rate.

(b) *Staff*

The supply of staff is taxable at the standard rate. When employees of one company are shared with associated businesses, the recovery of a proportion of their salaries by the employer from the other companies is taxable at the standard rate, even when the recoveries are at cost. Partial exemption would restrict the recovery of VAT by the companies sharing the staff. A possible answer to this is for the staff concerned to be jointly employed by all the companies sharing their services. The company which paid the staff and then made a recovery of a proportionate share from each of the other companies would simply be acting as a paying agent and the recoveries would not attract VAT. An administration charge for acting as a paying agent would be taxable at the standard rate.

(c) *Overheads*

Recharges of expenses and overheads where associated businesses share premises are also taxable at the standard rate as part of a management service charge. If the company paying the overheads is partially exempt, it will lose a proportion of the VAT charged to it, but when it recharges the expenses it has to charge VAT in full. If the associated companies being recharged are also partially exempt they will also lose a proportion of VAT on the recharged expenses. This is the worst possible situation and would apply where the companies sharing the building did not occupy separate and distinct areas.

If, however, the company holding the head lease grants a sub-tenancy or a licence to occupy to the other companies, the position alters. As discussed above, the rent charged would be exempt, and as a result any service charges to sub-tenants or licensees to cover

233

maintenance and upkeep of common areas would also be exempt. Items of overhead expenditure directly attributable to the individual tenant's or licensee's own office would attract their usual rate of VAT. As an example, in this situation, the company holding the head lease pays for cleaning services of the building and recovers VAT on the charge subject to its partial exemption restrictions. Cleaning costs attributed to common areas would be subsumed into the service charge to the other companies and in so far as the service charge relates to the maintenance or common areas, it would be exempt. Cleaning costs which are directly attributed to individual tenant's or licensees' own offices would be standard rated.

13.17 Accounting for input tax

Input tax is not recoverable under any circumstances on certain items, such as business entertaining.

Certain assets, namely any interests in land or property of a value exceeding £250,000, and single items of computer hardware exceeding £50,000 in value, are subject to provisions known as the Capital Goods Scheme. This means that where recovery of input tax has been made, the use of that capital asset in the business has to be monitored at annual intervals for a certain period (five years for computer equipment, ten years for land and property).

13.18 Group treatment for VAT

Where insurance businesses are grouped for VAT purposes, and are therefore treated as a single entity submitting a single VAT return, a special method of calculating recoverable input tax will normally be agreed with the local VAT office. The most common methods will involve the following:

(a) Input tax must be attributed directly to taxable supplies made where possible.
(b) Input tax must be allocated to individual group members as far as possible. Where the group has an expense source company, input tax must be allocated to individual members on the basis of their use of the relevant expense.
(c) Each group member must carry out pro rata calculations for each quarter and apply the resulting recovery percentage to the input tax used by it for the quarter.
(d) A basis for calculating residual input tax will be determined for the treatment of input tax not allocated to individual group members.

(e) Input tax directly related to a dormant group member is not normally recoverable.

13.19   The meaning of a 'permitted' insurer

The exemption and outside the scope reliefs are only available where the insurance or reinsurance supplied is provided by 'persons permitted in accordance with section 2 of the Insurance Companies Act 1982 to carry on insurance business'. This section deals with restrictions on carrying on insurance business and, in conjunction with sections 3 and 4, the authorisation to carry on insurance business in the UK by the Secretary of State.

Insurance or reinsurance provided by any person who is not permitted by the Act to carry on insurance business is therefore, in principle, a supply taxable at the standard rate. A broker's services provided in respect of the supply of insurance or reinsurance by an unauthorised person would also be standard rated.

13.20   Isle of Man insurers

In practice, the position of insurers who belong in the Isle of Man for VAT purposes is somewhat peculiar. It is difficult for a Manx insurer to obtain authorisation under the Insurance Companies Act 1982, and therefore the supplied insurance would appear to be standard rated. However, Customs & Excise has confirmed that an insurance company which is permitted by the Isle of Man authorities to carry on insurance business in the island is deemed to qualify as a permitted insurer within Item 1 Group 2 of Sch 9 to the VAT Act 1994. Insurance or reinsurance provided by such an Isle of Man insurer will therefore be either exempt or zero rated depending on the belonging of the person to whom the insurance is provided. Likewise, broker's services in respect of insurance provided by such an Isle of Man insurer will be either exempt or zero rated.

13.21   Reinsurance business

All classes of reinsurance, including facultative and treaty reinsurance, are supplied to a ceding insurer. It is therefore the belonging of the ceding company which determines the VAT liability of the reinsurance and related brokerage, and not the belonging of the original insured person.

13.22   The value of a supply

For the purposes of VAT, the value of an insurance broker's services is defined as follows:

(a) for a placing broker – the gross brokerage payable by the underwriter; and

(b) for an introducing broker or co-broker when not placing the business – the gross retained brokerage, before a deduction of commissions for business introduced to them by intermediaries.

13.23 Territorial limits of the European Union

The territorial limits of the EU are of importance in establishing whether particular services supplied qualify for zero rating.

(a) For VAT purposes, the territory of the EU is as follows:
  • Belgium
  • Denmark (excluding Greenland)
  • Federal Republic of Germany (excluding the Island of Heligoland and the territory of Busingen)
  • France (excluding the overseas departments)
  • Greece
  • The Republic of Ireland
  • Italy (excluding Livigno, Campione d'Italia and the Italian waters of Lake Lugano)
  • Luxembourg
  • Netherlands
  • Portugal
  • Spain (including the Balearic Islands but excluding the Canaries, Ceuta and Melilla)
  • United Kingdom.

The full definition of the territory of the EC is given at Article 227 of the Treaty establishing the EC. (See also Article 3 of the EC Sixth VAT Directive 77/388 EEC).

(b) For VAT purposes, the following territories are not in the EU:
  • The Channel Islands
  • Andorra
  • Monaco
  • San Marino
  • Lichtenstein
  • The Vatican.

13.24 Insurance premium tax

A new tax, insurance premium tax, was introduced in 1994. The provisions of the tax were included in the Finance Bill 1994, which followed the November 1993 Budget (Part III). The tax is under the management of Customs & Excise, with an effective introductory date of 1 October 1994.

The tax is charged at the rate of 2.5 per cent on the gross receipt of a premium on certain categories of UK businesses by an insurer. In the majority of instances, therefore, it is the insurer and not the broker who is affected. However, there are some cases in which brokers might find themselves liable.

Where the insurer is liable to be registered for tax and does not have any business establishment in the United Kingdom, the broker may be considered the insurer's tax representative where:

(a) he is already acting as a representative for the insurer under the Insurance Companies Act 1982;
(b) he volunteers to be the tax representative and Customs & Excise do not object; or
(c) Customs & Excise direct that he is the tax representative.

Chapter 14 – Direct taxation

14.1 Introduction

Insurance brokers may carry on their trade as an individual, in partnership with other individuals, or through the medium of a limited company. In general, the taxation treatment of the business follows the normal rules for the particular type of concern, and it is outside the scope of this book to discuss the general taxation treatment of individuals, partnerships or companies carrying on a trade. Rather, the purpose of this chapter is to discuss some of the taxation features that are of particular relevance to insurance brokers. The relevant legislation is that extant at May 1994.

14.2 Accounting for income

There is no statutory basis for the timing of when a profit arises to a broker from introducing business to an underwriter or insurance company. One common practice is for brokerage to be brought into account in the period in which the debit note is issued. However, a variety of different bases exist, any of which may be accepted by the Revenue.

Underwriters and reinsurers will often allow or require a broker to service a contract throughout its life, and this element may be of significance in establishing goodwill or creating enforceable obligations between insurer and broker. Some brokers take the view that although the whole brokerage on an insurance contract may be received on issue of the debit note following placement, the brokerage is actually earned over the period to which the insurance relates, especially as there may be an obligation to make a partial credit of brokerage in the event of the cancellation of the insurance contract. Moreover, it is arguable that in many circumstances brokerage should be spread in a way which reflects the timing of the duties performed by the broker and therefore of the costs which he incurs.

If such a deferral is to succeed for tax purposes the broker's accounts must either defer income or provide for future expenses. However, the Revenue until recently took the view that such adjustments were not permissible for tax purposes. It considered this view to be supported by the weight of case law, notwithstanding certain other cases which support the principle that income arises for tax purposes when the obligations of the person providing the goods or services are fulfilled, rather than when the agreement to provide the goods or services is struck.

The Revenue argued that, even though the principles of commercial accountancy may support deferral to a later period, the specific principles emerging from tax case law must override this. It used the case of *James Spencer v CIR* 32 TC III to contend that income should be brought in when the right to receive that income is established. Title to income is established when all the services of introduction to the insurers have been made; title is not established over a period of time. The tax case of *CIR v Gardner Mountain and D'Ambrumenil* 29 TC 69 reinforced this view.

The Revenue may also argue that where the broker is not under a legal obligation to service a policy, but does so in the interests of convenience and furthering his own business, there can be no matching of income and subsequent costs. Here, the old case of *Zenox v Wickham [1867]* LR 2HL 296 is quoted. It established that no rule of law or usage obliged a broker who placed an insurance contract to act in collecting the payment of losses under it.

The commercial and accounting justifications for reinsurance brokers and those handling long-tail business providing for the cost of future claims servicing are discussed in Chapters 7 and 10. However, the Revenue used to seek to disallow any such provision. This could be said to have overlooked the reasoning in the case of *Owen v Southern Railway of Peru* 36 TC 602: 'what can or cannot be admitted into the annual account is not provided by any exact analysis of the legal form of the relevant obligation'. That case was decided against the company claiming deductibility for a provision for future expenditure on the basis only that the provision had not been sufficiently accurately quantified. Provided a broker's past experience enables a provision to be quantified with reasonable accuracy, it should therefore be possible to claim a deduction for such a provision where the later work can be shown to be obligatory.

The conditions to be met to satisfy the Inland Revenue are:

(a) that the broker can demonstrate an obligation to service claims;
(b) a provision for future expenses must take into account any income which may arise after the balance sheet date from that same contract; and
(c) in determining future costs a distinction should be drawn between

239

direct costs arising from 'running off' the insurance contract (such as salaries – which should be allowable) and certain fixed costs of the business which would be incurred irrespective of the existence of the obligations.

The Revenue also expects a sound statistical base to be used for projecting costs – it has been described as a 'best scientific estimate', along the lines discussed in the earlier chapters. It looks for disallowable expenses, e.g., entertaining, to be excluded.

In this developing scene, there are a number of areas still to be considered, such as discounting future costs to present value and the treatment of unearned brokerage provisions and future instalment premiums. The Revenue will also accept that a provision is deductible for brokerage which may become refundable if the policy lapses or is cancelled. Clearly, to be within the terms of the criteria laid down in *Owen v Southern Railway of Peru,* a provision needs to be calculated with substantial accuracy. It is therefore advisable for a broker considering making such a claim to keep sufficient records to enable such calculations to be made with a demonstrable degree of accuracy. The decision in *Johnston* v *Britannia Airways* [1994] STC 763 may be helpful.

14.3 Close companies

The legislation covering taxation of close investment companies in the Finance Act 1989 does not affect insurance brokers, despite their investment income often exceeding other Case I profits. This is because a normal broking company exists to trade for profit and is therefore outside the definition in s13A Income and Corporation Taxes Act 1988 of a 'close investment holding company'. It is not within the ambit of this chapter to discuss the previous apportionment legislation and its impact on close company insurance brokers.

14.4 Premiums temporarily invested

Where in an accounting period unrelieved trading losses are brought forward under ss385 (1) or 393 (I) TA 1988, relief may be available not only against current trading profits but also against income from investments under ss384 (4) or 393 (8) TA 1988.

The Revenue's view has traditionally been that interest on temporarily invested premiums is not immediately derived from the carrying on of a broker's trade. It argues that a broker does not generate interest directly from his trade and that the interest itself arises from a separate contract with the bank. However, these arguments may be disputed in appropriate circumstances because of the nature of a broker's business. If the placing on deposit of surplus monies is an integral part of his trade, the interest which accrues may often be income immediately derived from carrying on that trade, even though it may be assessed under Schedule D Case III rather than Schedule D Case I at the Revenue's option.

14.5 Anti-avoidance

There can be a charge to income tax under s776 TA 1988 on capital sums received where another person exploits the earning capacity of an individual carrying on a profession or vocation. It can apply where, for example, an individual sells shares in a company which employs him to provide the relevant professional or vocational services. This legislation is thought not to apply to insurance brokers.

14.6 Foreign currency

Premiums are often temporarily invested or retained in foreign currency investments. If making those investments forms part of the trading operations of the broker, the profits or losses are taken into account in computing the trading income. However, if (unusually) the temporary investment of surplus funds is outside the ambit of the trading operations, the profits or losses fall to be dealt with as capital gains or losses. This is unlikely to be advantageous unless the company has substantial capital losses available for relief. There is a risk that losses will accrue which are not capable of being used, which may significantly increase the effective rate of tax.

Until the Finance Act 1993 fundamentally alters the taxation treatment of exchange differences on year end balances, it may be necessary to determine which of such differences in a broker's accounts arise on trading balances.

For balance sheets on or after a date yet to be decided, differences on monetary balances, as defined in s153 Finance Act 1993, will form part of a broker's Case I profits or losses.

14.7 Old balances

The Inland Revenue take the view that old balances may belong to brokers and become taxable when they are statute-barred.

Appendix 1 – Lloyd's brokers: solvency

This appendix gives examples of the calculation of solvency margins for two Lloyd's brokers, Broker A and Broker B.

Broker A

		Profit and loss account (12 months) £'000
Net retained brokerage		36,772
Other fees and income		–
	A	36,772
Interest and investment income		7,365
		44,137
Expenses		
Commissions payable and other normal expenses		28,478
	B	28,478
Exceptional expenses		–
Total expenses		28,478

Solvency margins

IBA (based on percentage of A)		£'000	£'000
5% on first	£ 1m	1,000	50
4% on next	£ 2m	2,000	80
3% on next	£ 2m	2,000	60
2% on next	£ 5m	5,000	100
1% on next	£21m	21,000	210
	£31m		500 (Minimum £25,000)

		£'000	£'000	
NCA (based on percentage of B)				
10% on first	£ 1m	1,000	100	
7.5% on next	£ 2m	2,000	150	
5% on next	£15m	15,000	750	
	£18m		1,000	(Minimum £50,000)
Add IBA margin			500	
			1,500	(Minimum £75,000)
NTA (based on the higher of A and B)				
30% on first	£ 1m	1,000	300	
15% on next	£ 2m	2,000	300	
5% on next	£28m	28,000	1,400	
	£31m		2,000	(Minimum £250,000)

	Balance sheet £'000	Lloyd's tests		
		IBA £'000	NCA £'000	NTA £'000
FIXED ASSETS				
Tangible	3,097			3,097
Intangible	79			
	3,176			
CURRENT ASSETS				
Debtors:				
Less than 12 months				
Insurance	81,530	81,530	81,530	81,530
Other	25,067		25,067	25,067
	106,597			
Over 12 months	–			
	106,597			
Cash				
IBA	50,000	50,000	50,000	50,000
Other	523		523	523
Investments				
IBA	4,296	4,296	4,296	4,296
Other	4,000		4,000	4,000
	165,416			
TOTAL ASSETS	168,592	135,826	165,416	168,513

	Balance sheet £'000	IBA £'000	Lloyd's tests NCA £'000	NTA £'000
CURRENT LIABILITIES				
Creditors:				
Less than 36 months				
Insurance	133,420	133,420	133,420	133,420
Other including taxation	25,094		25,094	25,094
Contingent liabilities				200
	158,514			
Bank loans and overdrafts:				
IBA	–			
Other <36 months	4,343		4,343	4,343
Over 36 months	–			
Deferred liabilities (under 36 months)	–			
TOTAL LIABILITIES	162,857	133,420	162,857	163,057
NET ASSETS	5,735	2,406	2,559	5,456
Margin required		500	1,500	2,000
Surplus (deficiency)		1,906	1,059	3,456

Broker B

		Profit and loss account (12 months) £'000
Net retained brokerage		460*
Other fees and income		–
	A	460
Interest and investment income		26
		486
Expenses		
Commissions payable and other normal expenses		498
	B	498
Exceptional expenses		(11)
Total expenses		487

* *Includes brokerage retained by umbrella and related companies from business broked on Lloyd's broker B's slips.*

Solvency margins

IBA (based on percentage of A)   £'000   £'000

5% on first	£ 1m	460	23
4% on next	£ 2m		
3% on next	£ 2m		
2% on next	£ 5m		
1% on next	£21m		
	£31m		25 (Minimum £25,000)

NCA (based on percentage of B)

10% on first	£ 1m	498	50
7.5% on next	£ 2m		
5% on next	£15m		
	£18m		50 (Minimum £50,000)
Add IBA margin			25
			75 (Minimum £75,000)

NTA (based on the higher of A and B)

30% on first	£ 1m	498	150
15% on next	£ 2m		
5% on next	£28m		
	£31m		250 (Minimum £250,000)

	Balance sheet £'000	IBA £'000	Lloyd's tests NCA £'000	NTA £'000
FIXED ASSETS				
Tangible	75			75
Intangible	9			
	84			
CURRENT ASSETS				
Debtors:				
Less than 12 months				
Insurance	906	906	906	906
Other	50		50	50
	956			
Over 12 months	27			27
	983			
Cash				
IBA	300	300	300	300
Other	44		44	44
Investments				
IBA	–			
Other	–			
	1,327			
TOTAL ASSETS	1,411	1,206	1,300	1,402
CURRENT LIABILITIES				
Creditors:				
Less than 36 months				
Insurance	1,074	1,074	1,074	1,074
Other including taxation	100		100	100
Contingent liabilities				15
	1,174			
Bank loans and overdrafts				
IBA	–			
Other <36 months	105		105	105
Over 36 months	–			
Deferred liabilities – not lease or HP instalments (under 36 months)	52		52	52
TOTAL LIABILITIES	1,331	1,074	1,331	1,346
NET ASSETS	80	132	(31)	56
Margin required		25	75	250
Surplus (deficiency)		107	(106)	(194)

Appendix 2 – Lloyd's brokers: application for registration checklist

Set out below are suggested matters to be considered by the auditor before signing his opinion on a Lloyd's broker's application for registration.

1 Systems and controls

Schedule reference

(a) Records

    (i) Do the records maintained by the broker of each contract of insurance contain the information specified by paragraph 47 of Byelaw No. 5 of 1988, in particular:

- the details to be recorded on and the copies to be retained of documents relating to an insurance contract;
- the procedures to be followed where the broker assists in arranging or processing details of a contract of insurance arranged by another person, other than by way of an umbrella arrangement;
- the records to be made where a broker assists in notifying, processing or resolving a claim made by an assured or reassured;
- the records to be made where a broker operates a binding authority as cover holder or arranges a binding authority; and
- the period for and manner in which the records must be kept?

    (ii) Does the broker have adequate arrangements for retaining records for the required periods of time?

(b) IBA accounts

    (i) Are there controls to ensure that all insurance monies are paid into and out of IBA bank accounts?

    (ii) Is the withdrawal of brokerage from IBA accounts monitored against the broker's accounting policy?

    (iii)   What controls are there to ensure that IBA accounts are opened in accordance with Lloyd's requirements?

    (iv)   Are IBA investments properly controlled in accordance with Lloyd's requirements?

(c) Solvency margins

    (i)   Is the broker able to meet Lloyd's margins at the time of registration, in all currencies?

    (ii)   What procedures are there to ensure that the year end margins are maintained throughout the year or that breaches are reported to Lloyd's?

    (iii)   Will the broker need to request Lloyd's to apply lower margins?

(d) Funding

Are there adequate controls over funding of premiums and claims?

(e) Currency exposure

Does the broker monitor the potential risk of adverse exchange rate movements?

(f) Insurance ledgers

    (i)   Are the ledgers regularly reconciled?

    (ii)   Are there controls to monitor and identify potential bad debts?

(g) Motor direct dealing agreements

Are there adequate controls and monitoring procedures over direct dealing agreements?

2 Umbrella arrangements

(a) Are the terms of the arrangement set out in writing?

(b) Does the broker exercise proper control and supervision over the non-Lloyd's broker's activities?

(c) Does the non-Lloyd's broker have the necessary level of E & O cover?

(d) Are there any other potential problems likely to affect the registration of the umbrella arrangement?

(e) How does the broker monitor the proportion of brokerage earned through umbrella arrangements?

3 Insurance connections

How does the broker monitor the need to disclose any insurance connections to the potential insured?

Other matters*

4 IBRC

(a) Is the broker registered with the IBRC?

(b) Are there any matters in dispute with the IBRC?

5 E & O insurance

Does the broker's E & O cover meet Lloyd's requirements?

6 Compliance officer

(a) Is the proposed compliance officer a director or partner of the broker?

(b) Does the proposed compliance officer have sufficient authority or status to carry out his duties?

7 Code of Practice

(a) Are all executives and staff of the broker familiar with the Code of Practice?

(b) Is compliance with the Code of Practice effectively monitored throughout the broker's activities?

* Although the auditor has no reporting responsibilities in connection with points 4 to 7, any problems should be discussed with the broker.

Appendix 3 – Extract from Insurance Brokers Registration Council (Accounts and Business Requirements) Rules Approval Order 1979 (SI 1979 No. 489)

NOTES
   Made: 19 April 1979
   Authority: Insurance Brokers (Registration) Act 1977, ss 27(1), 28(1)

1. This Order may be cited as the Insurance Brokers Registration Council (Accounts and Business Requirements) Rules Approval Order 1979 and shall come into operation on 1st July 1979.   **[752]**

NOTES
Commencement: 1 July 1979.

---

2. The Insurance Brokers Registration Council (Accounts and Business Requirements) Rules 1979 made by the Insurance Brokers Registration Council in exercise of their powers under section 11(1), (2), (3) and (7) of the Insurance Brokers (Registration) Act 1977 are hereby approved as set out in the Schedule to this Order.   **[753]**

NOTES
Commencement: 1 July 1979.

SCHEDULE
THE INSURANCE BROKERS REGISTRATION COUNCIL (ACCOUNTS AND BUSINESS
REQUIREMENTS) RULES 1979

The Insurance Brokers Registration Council, in exercise of their powers under section 11(1), (2), (3) and (7) of the Insurance Brokers (Registration) Act 1977, hereby make the following Rules:

PART I—PRELIMINARY

1. These Rules may be cited as the Insurance Brokers Registration Council (Accounts and Business Requirements) Rules 1979.

2.—(1) In these Rules, unless the context otherwise requires:
'the Act' means the Insurance Brokers (Registration) Act 1977;
'brokerage' means any remuneration originating from insurance broking business;
'business' means an insurance broking business or any business which includes an insurance broking business.

(2) For the purposes of these Rules, unless the context otherwise requires, every business carried on by a partnership shall be deemed to be carried on jointly and severally by all the partners thereof.

PART II

REQUIREMENTS AS TO WORKING CAPITAL, ASSETS AND INDEPENDENCE
(PURSUANT TO SECTION 11(1) OF THE ACT)

3.—(1) Practising insurance brokers and enrolled bodies corporate shall ensure that at all times they have working capital of not less than £1,000 in each of their businesses.

(2) For the purposes of this rule:

    (i) practising insurance brokers and enrolled bodies corporate carrying on a business in partnership shall ensure that at all times there is working capital of not less than £1,000 in such business but so that the liability of each such partner to ensure compliance with this rule shall be a joint and several obligation on each of the partners; and

    (ii) 'working capital' shall mean the aggregate of the current assets of the business, being the figure to be shown in Total K in paragraph 2 of Part I of the Statement of Particulars set out in the Appendix to these Rules calculated in accordance with the provisions of such Appendix, less the aggregate of the current liabilities of the business, being the figure to be shown in Total X in paragraph 2 of Part I of the said Statement of Particulars calculated in accordance with the provisions of such Appendix.

4.—(1) Practising insurance brokers and enrolled bodies corporate shall ensure that at all times the value of the assets of each of their businesses exceeds the amount of the liabilities of that business by not less than £1,000.

(2) For the purposes of this rule:

    (i) practising insurance brokers and enrolled bodies corporate carrying on a business in partnership shall ensure that at all times the value of the assets of such business exceeds the amount of the liabilities of that business by not less than £1,000 but so that the liability of each such partner to ensure compliance with this rule shall be a joint and several obligation on each of the partners;

(ii) 'the value of the assets' shall mean the aggregate of the value of the assets of the business being the figure to be shown in Total M in paragraph 2 of Part I of the Statement of Particulars set out in the Appendix to these Rules calculated in accordance with the provisions of such Appendix; and

(iii) 'the amount of the liabilities' shall mean the aggregate amount of the liabilities of the business being the figure to be shown in Total Z in paragraph 2 of Part I of the Statement of Particulars set out in the Appendix to these Rules calculated in accordance with the provisions of such Appendix.

5.—(1) Practising insurance brokers and enrolled bodies corporate shall ensure that the number of insurance companies with which each of their business place insurance business, and the amount of insurance business which each of their businesses place with each insurance company, is such as to prevent each such business from becoming unduly dependent on any particular insurance company.

(2) For the purposes of demonstrating to the satisfaction of the Council that the provisions of paragraph (1) of this rule are being complied with practising insurance brokers and enrolled bodies corporate shall at the same time as they submit any accounts or statement to the Council in respect of a business in accordance with the provisions of rule 8 of these Rules complete and submit the Questionnaire in Part II of the Statement of Particulars set out in Appendix to these Rules in respect of such business.

PART III

REQUIREMENTS AS TO ACCOUNTS AND ACCOUNTING RECORDS (PURSUANT TO SECTION 11(2) OF THE ACT)

6.—(1) For the purposes set out in this rule one or more separate bank accounts shall be maintained with approved banks by each practising insurance broker and enrolled body corporate for each separate insurance broking business which they carry on. Each such account shall contain in its title the name of the practising insurance broker or enrolled body corporate or the names of the partners or the name of the partnership if the practising insurance broker or enrolled body corporate carries on the business in partnership. Each such account shall be designated and is hereinafter called an 'Insurance Broking Account', and money standing to the credit of such an Insurance Broking Account shall be used solely for the purposes set out in this rule.

(2) A practising insurance broker or enrolled body corporate opening an Insurance Broking Account with an approved bank shall inform such bank in writing and forthwith obtain a written acknowledgement therefrom:

> (i) that the account shall be designated 'Insurance Broking Account' and that the title of the account shall contain the name of the practising insurance broker or enrolled body corporate or the names of the partners or the name of the partnership if the practising insurance broker or enrolled body corporate carries on the business in partnership;
>
> (ii) that the Insurance Broking Account is being opened to comply with the provisions of these Rules; and
>
> (iii) that the bank is not to be entitled to any charge, encumbrance, lien, right of set-off, compensation or retention against money standing to the credit of the Insurance Broking Account or any approved short term assets held for the Insurance Broking Account of the practising insurance broker, enrolled body corporate or partnership except in the circumstances set out in paragraph (7) of this rule.

(3) Practising insurance brokers and enrolled bodies corporate shall without delay pay or cause to be paid into the Insurance Broking Account and into no other account all moneys paid to or received by them from all sources and which relate to insurance transactions of any kind in connection with their insurance broking business, including brokerage.

(4) Practising insurance brokers and enrolled bodies corporate shall use the Insurance Broking Account and no other account for payment to an insured or an insurance company of all moneys due under insurance transactions of any kind in connection with their insurance broking business.

(5) In addition to the purposes set out in paragraphs (3) and (4) of this rule and always subject to there being no breach of paragraph (8) of this rule at the time the Insurance Broking Account is used, the Insurance Broking Account shall be used for the following purposes and for none other:

> (i) for all transactions relating to approved short term assets as provided for in paragraph (6) of this rule;
>
> (ii) for the withdrawal of brokerage;
>
> (iii) for the withdrawal of any money paid into the Insurance Brokering Account in error;

(iv) for the receipt of funds necessary for the operation of the account;

(v) for the withdrawal of any surpluses arising on the Insurance Broking Account.

(6) (i) [Subject to the provisions of sub-paragraph (v) of this paragraph] practising insurance brokers and enrolled bodies corporate are permitted to hold moneys standing to the credit of the Insurance Broking Account in, or to purchase out of such moneys, any approved short term assets. Such approved short term assets shall be:

EITHER

(a) registered in their name or the partnership name if appropriate and designated 'Insurance Broking Account';

(b) so far as the approved short term assets defined in paragraph (9)(ii), (vii) or (viii) of this rule are concerned, held for the Insurance Broking Account of the practising insurance broker, enrolled body corporate or partnership if appropriate at the approved bank at which such Insurance Broking Account is held.

(ii) Approved short term assets must be readily realisable, that is to say, within a period of not more than one month, they can be readily and easily converted into or sold or realised for cash which can be immediately credited to or is immediately eligible for credit to an Insurance Broking Account.

(iii) Moneys, other than interest, arising from approved short term assets or their realisation, sale or disposal shall be paid into an Insurance Broking Account and no other account.

(iv) For the purpose of this rule, unless the context otherwise requires, the expression 'Insurance Broking Account' shall include all approved short term assets so designated or held for such Insurance Broking Account in accordance with the provisions of this paragraph (6).

[(v) No money standing to the credit of the Insurance Broking Account shall be held in any approved short term assets defined in paragraph (9)(i) of this rule until the practising insurance broker or enrolled body corporate shall have informed in writing the approved bank or licensed institution with whom the deposit account is to be opened or from whom the deposit receipt is to be obtained and forthwith obtained a written acknowledgement therefrom:

(a) that the deposit account and deposit shall be designated 'Insurance Broking Account' and that the title of the

255

account shall contain the name of the practising insurance broker or enrolled body corporate or the names of the partners or the name of the partnership if the practising insurance broker or enrolled body corporate carries on the business in partnership; and

(b) that the approved bank or licensed institution is not to be entitled to any charge, encumbrance, lien, right of set-off, compensation or retention against money standing to the credit of the deposit account or represented by the deposit receipt except in the circumstances set out in paragraph (7) of this rule.]

(7)　(i)　(a) No advance, whether by way of loan, overdraft or otherwise, may be obtained by a practising insurance broker or an enrolled body corporate for any purpose relating to the Insurance Broking Account except on a bank account with an approved bank in circumstances which do not give rise to a breach of the requirements of paragraph (8) of this rule.

(b) Any advance obtained shall be of a temporary nature and repaid as soon as reasonably practicable and the bank account itself shall be designated 'Insurance Broking Account' and be used only for the purposes set out in paragraph (4) of this rule and the withdrawal of brokerage but not for the withdrawal of any surpluses on the Insurance Brokering Account.

(c) Subject to the provisions of paragraph (7)(ii) of this rule approved short term assets may only be charged to or deposited with an approved bank to secure an advance by way of loan, overdraft or otherwise on a bank account obtained in accordance with the provisions of this rule but not otherwise.

(d) An approved bank making an advance by way of loan, overdraft or otherwise on an Insurance Broking Account in accordance with the provisions of these Rules shall be entitled to any lien, right of set-off, compensation or retention in respect of such advance to which that bank is otherwise entitled at law over or against moneys standing to the credit of another Insurance Broking Account of the same business held with that bank.

(ii) Approved short term assets may be charged to or deposited with an approved bank to secure the issue of a letter of credit by an approved bank PROVIDED THAT such letter of credit shall only be obtained in circumstances which do not give rise to a breach of the requirements of paragraph (8) of this rule and shall be used only for the purposes set out in paragraph (4) of this rule but not for the withdrawal of brokerage or surpluses on the Insurance Broking Account.

(iii) Nothing in these Rules shall be construed as requiring an approved bank making an advance or issuing a letter of credit in accordance with the provisions of this rule to make any enquiry or satisfy itself that the provisions of these Rules are or will be complied with by the practising insurance broker or enrolled body corporate to whom or to whose partnership such an advance is to be made or for whom or for whose partnership such letter of credit is being issued.

(8) (i) Practising insurance brokers and enrolled bodies corporate shall ensure that at all times the value of the insurance transactions assets of each of their businesses is not less than the amount of the insurance transactions liabilities of that business.

(ii) For the purposes of paragraph (8)(i) of this rule:

'insurance transactions assets' shall mean the aggregate of balances on banking accounts designated 'Insurance Broking Account', approved short term assets designated 'Insurance Broking Account' or held for the Insurance Broking Account of the practising insurance broker, enrolled body corporate or partnership at an approved bank at which such Insurance Broking Account is held and debtors in respect of insurance transactions being the figure to be shown in Total H in paragraph 2 of Part I of the Statement of Particulars set out in the Appendix to these Rules and calculated in accordance with the provisions of such Appendix; and

'insurance transactions liabilities' shall mean the aggregate of creditors in respect of insurance transactions and bank advances designated 'Insurance Broking Account' being the figure to be shown in Total V in paragraph 2 of Part I of the Statement of Particulars set out in the Appendix to these Rules and calculated in accordance with the provisions of such Appendix.

(9) For the purposes of this rule 'approved short term assets' shall be those assets purchased with or provided from moneys drawn from an Insurance Broking Account and which fall into one of the following categories:

(i) [deposit accounts and deposit receipts with approved banks and licensed institutions;]

(ii) [certificates of deposit of approved banks and licensed institutions];

(iii) deposits with a building society which has been designated for the purpose of section 1 of the House Purchase and Housing Act 1959;

(iv) loans to and deposits with any local authority in the United Kingdom;

(v) fixed or floating rate interest marketable securities which will mature for repayment within five years from the date of purchase and (a) are issued or guaranteed by Her Majesty's Government in the United Kingdom; or (b) are issued in the United Kingdom by any local authority or public authority or nationalised undertaking in the United Kingdom; or (c) are issued by any water authority or statutory water company in the United Kingdom; or (d) are issued by the International Bank for Reconstruction and Development being securities registered in the United Kingdom;

(vi) British Savings Bonds:

(vii) British Treasury Bills and Northern Ireland Treasury Bills;

(viii) Bills accepted by any public or local authority or nationalised undertaking in the United Kingdom or bank acceptances eligible for rediscount at the Bank of England.

(10) Except as provided by these Rules, practising insurance brokers or enrolled bodies corporate shall not by their own act or omission create, nor so far as they are legally able shall they permit to arise, any charge or encumbrance upon any Insurance Broking Account, or upon any approved short term assets, or upon debtors in respect of insurance transactions, nor shall they create or permit to arise by their own act or omission, nor so far as they are able shall they by their own act or omission permit to arise as a matter of law, any lien, right of set-off, compensation or retention in favour of any other person over or against money standing to the credit of an Insurance Broking Account, or any approved short term assets, or upon debtors in respect of insurance transactions.

(11) For the purposes of this rule:

(i) 'approved bank' means:

[(a) a recognised bank within the meaning of the Banking Act 1979; and]

(b) a trustee savings bank as defined by section 3 of the Trustees Savings Bank Act 1969; and

(c) the National Girobank being the name under which the Post Office provides its banking services;

(ii) 'insurance' includes assurance, reinsurance or reassurance and 'insured' shall be construed accordingly;

(iii) 'insured' and 'insurance company' include agents of an insured or insurance company, and any other person to whom payments are due under, or in connection with, a contract of insurance;

(iv) 'moneys which relate to insurance transactions' and 'moneys due under insurance transactions' include the following individual items or balances representing the same:

(a) premiums, additional premiums and return premiums of all kinds,

(b) claims and other moneys due under contracts of insurance;

(c) refunds and salvages;

(d) fees, charges, taxes and similar fiscal levies relating to contracts of insurance;

(e) all forms of reserves under contracts of insurance and any adjustment of them;

(e) all forms of reserves under contracts of insurance and any adjustment of them;

(f) discounts and brokerage.

[(v) 'licensed institution' means a licensed institution within the meaning of the Banking Act 1979.]

7. Practising insurance brokers and enrolled bodies corporate shall ensure that accounting records are kept in respect of each of their businesses in accordance with the following requirements:

(i) the accounting records shall be sufficient to show and explain the transactions of the business;

(ii) the accounting records shall be such as to:

(a) disclose with reasonable accuracy, at any time, the financial position of the business at that time; and

(b) ensure that any balance sheet, profit and loss account or other statement of the financial position of the business prepared is capable of giving a true and fair view of the state of affairs of the business as at the date to which the balance sheet is drawn up and of the profit or loss for the accounting period then ended;

(iii) the accounting records shall in particular contain:

(a) entries from day to day of all sums of money received and expended in the course of the business and the matters in respect of which the receipt and expenditure takes place; and

(b) a record of the assets and liabilities of the business;

(iv) the accounting records shall be such as to enable compliance with the relevant provisions of these Rules to be demonstrated at any time.

(v) the accounting records shall be preserved for at least three years from the date of the last entry made therein.

NOTES

Rule 6: amended by SI 1981 No 1630, art 2, Schedule.

Appendix 4 – Statutory accounts

FINANCIAL STATEMENTS FOR THE YEAR ENDED
31 DECEMBER 19X2

A BROKER LIMITED

DIRECTORS:

SECRETARY:

AUDITORS:

CONTENTS

Page

(Note that the company's registered number should appear on the front
cover of the financial statements.)

DIRECTORS' REPORT

The directors present their report and the financial statements for the year ended 31 December 19X2.

Statement of directors' responsibilities

Company law requires the directors to prepare financial statements for each financial year which give a true and fair view of the state of affairs of the company and of the profit or loss of the company for that period. In preparing those financial statements, the directors are required to:

- select suitable accounting policies and then apply them consistently;
- make judgements and estimates that are reasonable and prudent;
- state whether applicable accounting standards have been followed, subject to any material departures disclosed and explained in the financial statements; and
- prepare the financial statements on the going concern basis unless it is inappropriate to presume that the company will continue in business.

The directors are responsible for keeping proper accounting records which disclose with reasonable accuracy at any time the financial position of the company and to enable them to ensure that the financial statements comply with the Companies Act 1985. They are also responsible for safeguarding the assets of the company and hence for taking reasonable steps for the prevention and detection of fraud and other irregularities.

Review of the business

The principal activity of the company continued to be that of insurance broking.

(A fair review of the development of the business of the company (and its subsidiary undertakings) during the financial year ended 31 December 19X2 and of the position at 31 December 19X2. Include, for example, particulars of acquisitions and disposals of subsidiary and associated undertakings.)

For example:
Both the level of business and the year end financial position were satisfactory, and the directors expect that the present level of activity will be sustained for the foreseeable future.

Future developments

(An indication of the likely future developments in the company's business.)

For example:
The directors consider that 19X3 will be another year of difficult trading conditions. Their aim is to continue to implement the management policies which have been introduced in recent years and which have assisted in successfully overcoming the difficulties and uncertainties in the market place in 19X2.

Post balance sheet event(s)

(Particulars of any important events which have occurred since the end of the financial year.)

Results and dividends

The profit (loss) for the year after taxation (and extraordinary items) was £ .....

Alternative wording:
The results of the company for the year ended 31 December 19X2 are set out in the financial statements on pages ..... to .....

After payment of the preference dividend of £....., the profit attributable to ordinary shareholders was £.....

An interim dividend of ..p per share on the issued ordinary share capital amounting to £ ..... was paid during the year. The directors propose a final dividend of ..p per share amounting to £ ..... making a total dividend for the year of ..p per share (19X1 ..p) amounting to £ ..... (The directors do not recommend the payment of any dividend.)

Retained profits of £ ..... have been transferred to reserves. (The loss for the year has been charged to reserves.) (The loss for the year has been added to the accumulated losses on the profit and loss account at the beginning of the year.)

Fixed assets

(Particulars of significant changes in fixed assets.)

For example:
During the year the company sold its motor vehicle fleet and entered into arrangements with a finance company under which its fleet is now leased. Details are set out in notes ..... and ..... to the financial statements.

Alternatively if there are no significant changes, the following statement may be included:
Details of changes in fixed assets are given in note ..... to the financial statements.

Where market value is substantially different from book value:
The directors estimate that the open market value (*or give details of independent professional valuation*) of the freehold (and leasehold) properties stated at a book value of £ ..... in the balance sheet at 31 December 19X2 amounted to £ ..... If these properties were disposed of at this valuation, there would be a liability to corporation tax on chargeable gains amounting to approximately £ ..... (*The last sentence may be unnecessary where roll-over relief is available or there are losses brought forward.*)

Share capital (and debentures)

(Give particulars of the acquisition by the company or its nominee, or an individual/ entity receiving financial assistance from the company, of its own shares.)

Directors
The directors set out in the table below have held office during the whole of the period from 1 January 19X2 to the date of this report unless otherwise stated.

(The following is optional here, as detail may be given in notice of Annual General Meeting.)
Mr ..... and Mr ....., having been appointed directors since the last annual general meeting, retire in accordance with the articles of association and, being eligible, offer themselves for re-election. In accordance with the articles of association, Mr ..... retires by rotation and, being eligible, offers himself for re-election. (*Listed companies only*: None of the directors offering themselves for re-election have service contracts of more than one year's duration.)

Mr ..... retired as a director on 31 January 19X2.

Mr ..... was appointed as a director on ..... (*post balance sheet date but prior to date of directors' report*).

The interests of the directors holding office on 31 December 19X2 in the shares of the company (group companies), according to the register of directors' interests, were as shown below:

					Ordinary (Preference) shares (stock) of ..... each		
					1 January 19X2		
	Date of				or date of		
	appointment		31 December 19X2		appointment if later		
Director's	(if after	Beneficial	Other	Under	Beneficial	Other	Under
name	1 January 19X2)	interests	interests	option	interests	interests	option

(For listed companies give details of any changes in directors' interests in shares or options between the end of the financial year and a date not more than one month prior to the date of the notice of the AGM. A nil statement is required if there has been no change.)

(*Listed companies only*: None of the directors had an interest in any contract of significance with the company during the year.)

(*Note: Details of directors' interests in shares and options may be disclosed instead in the notes to the financial statements.*)

Indemnity insurance

The company purchased insurance for ..... (*officers or directors*) during the year to indemnify them against liabilities arising as a result of (*negligence, etc.*) of which they may be guilty in relation to the company.

Substantial shareholdings *(other than those of directors – for listed and USM companies only)*

The directors have been advised of the following shareholdings at ..... 19X2 (*not more than one month before the notice of the annual general meeting*) of 3 per cent or more in the company's issued share capital:

Shareholder   %

or:

The directors are not aware of any person (other than a director) who is interested in 3 per cent or more of the issued share capital of the company.

Disabled persons

(*Statement as to the policy applied in respect of disabled persons.*)

For example:
The company's policy is to give full and fair consideration to applications for employment made by disabled persons, having regard to their particular aptitudes and abilities.

Disabled employees receive appropriate training to promote their career development within the company. Employees who become disabled are retained in their existing posts where possible or retrained for suitable alternative posts.

Employee involvement

(*Statement as to the policy on employee involvement if average UK weekly workforce exceeds 250.*)

For example:
Quarterly meetings are held between senior management and employee representatives to discuss matters of concern. Employees are kept well

informed about the progress and position of the company by means of regular departmental meetings, newsletters and journals.

An employee share scheme is operated which is open to all full-time employees.

Donations

During the year the company made the following payments:

(a) Political purposes (*specify recipient and amount for individual amounts over £200*) £

(b) Charitable purposes £

Auditors

A N Auditor & Co. have signified their willingness to continue in office and a resolution to re-appoint them as auditors will be proposed at the forthcoming annual general meeting.

Approved by the board on 19X3
and signed on its behalf by

....
(*Name*), Secretary/Director

A BROKER LIMITED

PROFIT AND LOSS ACCOUNT FOR THE YEAR ENDED
31 DECEMBER 19X2
EXAMPLE 1

	Note	*19X2*	*19X2*	*19X1 as restated*
		£	*£*	*£*
TURNOVER	2			
Continuing operations				
Acquisitions				
Discontinued operations				
Other operating income	3/5			
Trading expenses	3/4			
Less: 19X1 provisions			( )	( )
OPERATING PROFIT (LOSS)				
Continuing operations				
Acquisitions				
Discontinued operations				
Less: 19X1 provision		( )		
Profit (loss) on sale of fixed assets	6			
Provision for loss on operations to be discontinued				
Profit (loss) on disposal of discontinued operations	6			
Less: 19X1 provision		( )		
Other interest receivable and similar income				
Amounts written off investments			( )	( )
Interest payable and similar charges	7		( )	( )
PROFIT (LOSS) ON ORDINARY ACTIVITIES BEFORE TAXATION	4			
Taxation on profit (loss) on ordinary activities	10			
PROFIT (LOSS) ON ORDINARY ACTIVITIES AFTER TAXATION				
[Extraordinary items]*	11			

	Note	19X2	19X2	19X1 as restated
		£	£	£
PROFIT (LOSS) FOR THE FINANCIAL YEAR	27			
Dividends paid and proposed	12			
RETAINED PROFIT (LOSS) FOR THE YEAR	26			

* Included to show the statutory position of such an item. It is most improbable that this caption will ever be used.

Where all activities are from continuing operations and there have been no acquisitions, omit the continuing operations/acquisitions/discontinued operations analysis and add the following statement:

'The company's turnover and expenses all relate to continuing operations'.

(NB: The only significant difference between the above format (format 2) and format 1 is that the 'other operating income' line is dropped below the 'trading expenses' to highlight a 'gross' or 'trading profit'. Clients may choose whichever treatment they wish.)

A BROKER LIMITED

PROFIT AND LOSS ACCOUNT FOR THE YEAR ENDED 31 DECEMBER 19X2
EXAMPLE 2

	Notes	Continuing operations 19X2 £	Acquisitions 19X2 £	Discontinued operations 19X2 £	Total 19X2 £	19X1 as restated £
TURNOVER	2					
Other operating income	3/5					
Trading expenses	3/4					
Less: 19X1 provision	3			( )	( )	( )
OPERATING PROFIT (LOSS)						
Profit (loss) on sale of fixed assets	6					
Provision for loss on operations to be discontinued						
Loss on disposal of discontinued operations	6					
Less: 19X1 provisions					( )	
Other interest receivable and similar income						
Amounts written off investments					( )	( )
PROFIT (LOSS) ON ORDINARY ACTIVITIES BEFORE INTEREST						
Interest payable and similar charges	7					
PROFIT (LOSS) ON ORDINARY ACTIVITIES BEFORE TAXATION	4					
Tax on profit (loss) on ordinary activities	10					

	Notes	Continuing operations 19X2	Acquisitions 19X2	Discontinued operations 19X2	Total 19X2	19X1 as restated
		£	£	£	£	£
PROFIT (LOSS) ON ORDINARY ACTIVITIES AFTER TAXATION						
[Extraordinary items]*	11					
PROFIT (LOSS) FOR THE FINANCIAL YEAR	27					
Dividends paid and proposed	12					
RETAINED PROFIT (LOSS) FOR THE YEAR	26					

* Included to show the statutory position of such an item. It is most improbable that this caption will ever be used.

(Where all activities are from continuing operations and there have been no acquisitions omit the continuing operations/acquisitions/discontinued operations analysis and add the following statement:)

'The company's turnover and expenses all relate to continuing operations.'

(NB: The only significant difference between the above format (format 2) and format 1 is that the 'other operating income' line is dropped below the 'trading expenses' to highlight a 'gross' or 'trading profit'. Clients may choose whichever treatment they wish.)

A BROKER LIMITED

STATEMENT OF TOTAL RECOGNISED GAINS AND LOSSES
FOR THE YEAR ENDED 31 DECEMBER 19X2

	Note	*19X2*	*19X1 as restated*
		£	£
Profit (loss) for the financial year			
Unrealised surplus (deficit) on revaluation of properties*			
Unrealised (loss)/gain on trade investment*		——	——
Currency translation differences on foreign currency net investments*		——	——
TOTAL RECOGNISED GAINS AND LOSSES RELATING TO THE YEAR			
Prior year adjustment*	26	——	——
TOTAL GAINS AND LOSSES RECOGNISED SINCE THE LAST ANNUAL REPORT		══	══

NOTE OF HISTORICAL COST PROFITS AND LOSSES FOR
THE YEAR ENDED 31 DECEMBER 19X2

	19X2	*19X1 as restated*
	£	£
Reported profit (loss) on ordinary activities before taxation*		
Realisation of property revaluation gains of previous years*		
Difference between the historical cost depreciation charge and the actual depreciation charge for the year calculated on the revalued amount*	——	——
HISTORICAL COST PROFIT (LOSS) ON ORDINARY ACTIVITIES BEFORE TAXATION	══	══

	19X2	*19X1*
		as restated
	£	£

HISTORICAL COST PROFIT (LOSS) FOR THE YEAR RETAINED AFTER [TAXATION, EXTRAORDINARY ITEMS AND DIVIDENDS*]

Where there are no gains or losses other than those shown in the profit and loss account and/or the profits/losses are recorded at historical cost then the above tables may not be necessary. Instead either or both the following statements should be inserted at the end of the profit and loss account:

'The company has no recognised gains or losses other than the profit (loss) for the year. The profit for the year has been calculated on the historical cost basis.'

Or:

'There is no material difference between the profit (loss) on ordinary activities before taxation and the retained profit (loss) reported in the profit and loss account and the equivalent figures calculated on the historical cost basis.'

* These captions are for illustrative purposes only, and are not meant to be an exhaustive list of items to be included within these statements. The write off to reserves of purchased goodwill is not a recognised loss and would not therefore be included within the statement of total recognised gains and losses.

A BROKER LIMITED

BALANCE SHEET AT 31 DECEMBER 19X2

	Notes	19X2 £	19X1 £
FIXED ASSETS			
Intangible assets	13		
Tangible assets	14		
Investments	15	____	____
		____	____
CURRENT ASSETS	16		
Debtors	17		
Investments	18		
Cash at bank and in hand	19	____	____
		____	____
CREDITORS: AMOUNTS FALLING DUE WITHIN ONE YEAR	20	( )	( )
NET CURRENT ASSETS (LIABILITIES)		____	____
TOTAL ASSETS LESS CURRENT LIABILITIES			
CREDITORS: AMOUNTS FALLING DUE AFTER MORE THAN ONE YEAR	21	( )	( )
PROVISIONS FOR LIABILITIES AND CHARGES	22	( )	( )
ACCRUALS AND DEFERRED INCOME	24	( )	( )
		════	════
CAPITAL AND RESERVES			
Called-up share capital	25		
Share premium account	26		
Revaluation reserve	26		
Other reserves	26		
Profit and loss account	26		
SHAREHOLDERS' FUNDS	27	════	════

Approved by the board on 19X3
and signed on its behalf by

....
(*Name*), Director

A BROKER LIMITED

CASH FLOW STATEMENT FOR THE YEAR ENDED 31 DECEMBER 19X2

	Notes	19X2		19X1	
		£	£	£	£
NET CASH INFLOW (OUTFLOW) FROM OPERATING ACTIVITIES	28a				
RETURNS ON INVESTMENTS AND SERVICING OF FINANCE					
Interest received					
Interest paid					
Interest element of finance lease rentals					
Dividends received from associated undertakings					
Dividends paid		—		—	
NET CASH INFLOW (OUTFLOW) FROM RETURNS ON INVESTMENTS AND SERVICING OF FINANCE					
TAXATION					
UK Corporation tax paid (including advance corporation tax)					
Overseas tax paid		—		—	
TAX PAID					
INVESTING ACTIVITIES					
Purchase of intangible fixed assets					
Sale of tangible fixed assets					
Sale of trade investments		—		—	
NET CASH INFLOW (OUTFLOW) FROM INVESTING ACTIVITIES		—		—	
NET CASH INFLOW (OUTFLOW) BEFORE FINANCING					
FINANCING					
Issue of ordinary share capital					
Repurchase of debenture loan					
New secured loan repayable in 19XX					
New unsecured loan repayable in 19XY					
New short-term loans					
Repayment of amounts borrowed					
Capital element of finance lease rental payments					
Expenses paid in connection with share issues		—		—	
NET CASH INFLOW (OUTFLOW) FROM FINANCING		—		—	
INCREASE (DECREASE) IN CASH AND CASH EQUIVALENTS	28b				
		=		=	

A BROKER LIMITED

NOTES TO THE FINANCIAL STATEMENTS FOR THE YEAR
ENDED 31 DECEMBER 19X2

1. Accounting policies

The financial statements have been prepared in accordance with applicable accounting standards (except as indicated in note 35).

(a) *Accounting convention*

The financial statements are prepared under the historical cost
convention (modified to include the revaluation of land and
buildings).

(b) *Revenue and expense recognition*

It is impracticable to devise accounting policies which consistently
match revenue from brokerage with the related expenses. Accordingly the following bases are adopted:

(i) *Turnover*

Turnover represents brokerage and fees which are (mainly)
taken to credit when debit or fee notes are issued irrespective
of the inception date or period of insurance, with the following
principal exception(s):

1. Life and pensions brokerage and other commissions which
are credited when received

2. Treaty business
(per quarterly advice on statements)

3. Direct motor agency business
(as 1 above)

4. Deferred premium business
(per policy wording)

Alterations in brokerage arising from return and additional
premiums and adjustments are taken into account as and
when these occur.

*(Reference to any of items 1 to 4 above should only be made where they
constitute a material part of turnover and consideration may need to be
given to the inclusion/exclusion of the word 'mainly', bracketed above,
depending upon the outcome. Items 2 to 4 will need appropriate wording.)*

(ii) *Expenses*

Costs are written off as incurred, except for costs of servicing
claims on long-term business where provision is made for
future expenses when brokerage is brought to account.

(c) *Depreciation*

Depreciation is calculated to write off the cost or revalued amount
less estimated residual value of fixed assets on a straight-line basis

275

over their estimated useful lives. No depreciation is charged on freehold and long leasehold land.

(Where zero depreciation of freehold buildings is appropriate)
Freehold buildings are depreciated to write down the cost less estimated residual value over the remaining useful life by equal annual instalments. Where buildings are maintained to such a standard that their estimated residual value is not less than their cost or valuation, no depreciation is charged as it is not material.

(d) *Deferred taxation*
Deferred tax is provided in respect of the tax effect of all timing differences, to the extent that it is probable that a liability or asset will crystallise in the foreseeable future, at the rates of tax expected to apply when the timing differences reverse.

Deferred tax is provided in respect of pensions and other post-retirement benefits on the full provision (*or* partial provision) basis.

(e) *Goodwill*
Goodwill represents the excess of cost of acquisition over the fair value of the separable net assets acquired. Goodwill is:

either:

written off to reserves immediately upon acquisition.

or:

amortised through the profit and loss account in equal instalments over its estimated useful life.

(f) *Insurance debtors and creditors*
In the normal course of business, settlement is required to be made with certain markets, market settlement bureaux or insurance intermediaries on the basis of the net settlement due to or from the market, bureau or intermediary in question, rather than the amounts due to or from the individual parties which it represents. Insurance debtors and creditors reflect this basis of settlement.

FRS 5 *Reporting the Substance of Transactions* precludes assets and liabilities being offset, unless net settlement is legally enforceable. The application of this requirement to insurance brokers in connection with the offset of balances between insurers and insureds has been deferred until accounting periods ending on or after 22 September 19X6. It is not practical to quantify the gross value of assets and liabilities if this requirement were to be strictly applied.

(g) *Investments*
Investments held as fixed assets are stated at cost less provision for any permanent diminution in value. Investments held as current assets are stated at the lower of cost and net realisable value.

(h) *Foreign currencies*

Assets, liabilities, revenues and costs expressed in foreign currencies are translated into sterling at rates of exchange ruling on the date on which transactions occur, except for:

(i) monetary assets and liabilities which are translated at the rate ruling at the balance sheet date (other than those in (ii) below); and

(ii) transactions to be settled at a contracted rate and trading transactions covered by a related or matching forward contract which are translated at those contracted rates.

Differences arising on the translation of such items are dealt with in the profit and loss account.

(i) *Leases*

Accounting by lessees

Finance leases

Assets held under finance leases and the related lease obligations are included at the fair value of the leased assets at the inception of the lease. Depreciation on leased assets is calculated to write off this amount on a straight-line basis over the shorter of the lease term and the useful life of the asset.

Rentals payable are apportioned between the finance charge and a reduction of the outstanding obligation for future amounts payable so that the charge for each accounting period is a constant percentage of the remaining balance of the capital sum outstanding.

Operating leases

Rentals payable under operating leases are charged on a straight-line basis over the term of the lease.

Accounting by lessors

Operating leases

Assets held for use in operating leases are included as a separate category in fixed assets at cost and depreciated over their useful life.

Rental income from operating leases is recognised on a straight-line basis over the term of the lease.

Finance leases

Amounts due under finance leases are included as a debtor at the amount of the net investment in the lease.

Lease payments receivable are apportioned between repayments of capital and interest so as to give a constant periodic rate of return on the net cash investment in the lease.

277

(j) *Repurchase of own debt*
The gain or loss arising on the repurchase of fixed rate debt is recognised in the profit and loss account in the period to which it relates. Where fixed rate debt is replaced by other fixed rate debt, the gain or loss arising is deferred and amortised through the profit and loss account in equal instalments over the period of the original debt.

(k) *Pension costs and other post-retirement benefits*

(Where the company operates a defined benefit scheme)
Contributions payable to the company's pension scheme are charged to the profit and loss account in the period to which they relate.

Payments in respect of other post-retirement benefits are charged to the profit and loss account so as to spread the cost of pensions over the service lives of employees in the scheme. The pension charge is calculated on the basis of actuarial advice.

or:

Contributions payable to the company's pension scheme are charged to the profit and loss account in the period to which they relate.

Payments in respect of other post-retirement benefits are charged to the profit and loss account so as to spread the cost over the service lives of employees to which the benefits relate.

or:

Payments in respect of other post-retirement benefits are charged to the profit and loss account in the period to which they relate.

(l) *Cash equivalents*
Cash equivalents include readily convertible short-term highly liquid investments less advances from banks repayable within three months from the date of the advance.

2. Segmental information

Classes of business	Class A		Class B		Other		Company	
	19X2	*19X1*	*19X2*	*19X1*	*19X2*	*19X1*	*19X2*	*19X1*
	£	£	£	£	£	£	£	£
TURNOVER								
Total brokerage (and fees)								
Inter-segment brokerage	( )	( )	( )	( )	( )	( )	( )	( )
Brokerage derived from third parties	══	══	══	══	══	══	══	══
PROFIT BEFORE TAXATION								
Segment profit	══	══	══	══	══	══	══	══
Common costs							( )	( )
Operating profit								
Net interest							( )	( )
Profit before taxation							══	══
NET ASSETS								
Segment net assets	══	══	══	══	══	══		
Unallocated assets							──	──
Total net assets							══	══

Geographical segments	UK		North America		Europe		Other		Company	
	19X2	*19X1*	*19X2*	*19X1*	*19X2*	*19X1*	*19X2*	*19X1*	*19X2*	*19X1*
	£	£	£	£	£	£	£	£	£	£
TURNOVER										
Turnover by destination:										
Brokerage derived from third parties	=	=	=	=	=	=	=	=	=	=
Turnover by origin:										
Total brokerage										
Inter-segment brokerage	( )	( )	( )	( )	( )	( )	( )	( )	( )	( )
Brokerage derived from third parties	=	=	=	=	=	=	=	=	=	=
PROFIT BEFORE TAXATION										
Segment profit	=	=	=	=	=	=	=	=		
Common costs									( )	( )
Operating profit										
Net interest									( )	( )
Profit before taxation	=	=	=	=	=	=	=	=		
NET ASSETS										
Segment net assets	=	=	=	=	=	=	=	=		
Unallocated assets									—	—
Total net assets									=	=

Where there is only one class of business and one geographical segment:
The turnover, profit before taxation and net assets are attributable to the principal activity of ..... The company operates in the UK and the whole of its turnover is to the UK market.

3. Analysis of operations

Profit and loss account: Example 1

	19X2			19X1 (as restated)		
	Continuing	Discontinued	Total	Continuing	Discontinued	Total
	£	£	£	£	£	£
Other operating income	( )	( )	( )	( )	( )	( )
Trading expenses	—	—	—	—	—	—
Less: 19X1 provision	( )	( )	( )			
	=	=	=	=	=	=

The total figures for continuing operations in 19X2 include the following amounts relating to acquisitions: other operating income £ ..... and trading expenses £ .....

Where there have been NO discontinued operations, only use the 'continuing' columns above, and below the table include the following:

There were no discontinued operations, so the turnover, cost of sales and net operating expenses are all in respect of continuing operations.

Profit and loss account: Example 2

		19X1 (as restated)	
	Continuing	Discontinued	Total
	£	£	£
Turnover			
	=	=	=
Other operating income	( )	( )	( )
Trading expenses	—	—	—
	=	=	=

4.   Format 2 – Trading expenses

Format 2 – Included in trading expenses are:

	19X2 £	19X1 £

Staff costs (note 9)
Exchange losses
Depreciation of owned tangible fixed assets
Depreciation of assets held under finance leases
    and hire purchase contracts
Loss on sale of tangible/intangible fixed assets
    (unless disclosed on the face of the profit and loss account)
Amortisation of goodwill
Hire of plant and machinery – operating leases
Hire of other assets – operating leases
Amount set aside to provisions *(specify)*
Amounts written off fixed asset investments
Amounts written off current asset investments
Other exceptional charges *(give details)*
Auditors' remuneration:
    Audit fee
    Fee(s) for non-audit services

'Included in the audit fee is the estimated money value of the following benefits in Kind: .....

5.   Other operating income

	19X2 £	19X1 £

Income from fixed asset investments
Income from other (i.e. current asset) investments
Other interest receivable (and similar income)
Exchange gains
Rents receivable
Amount released from provisions *(specify)*
Exceptional income *(give details)*
Profit on sale of tangible/intangible fixed assets
    *(unless disclosed on the face of the profit
    and loss account)*

6. Profit (loss) on disposal of fixed assets/operations

	19X2 £	19X1 £
Profit (loss) on sale of tangible fixed assets (analysed by category)		
Profit (loss) on sale of intangible fixed assets (analysed by category)		
Profit (loss) on disposal of discontinued operations	—	—

7. Interest payable and similar charges

	19X2 £	19X1 £
Bank loans and overdrafts, and other loans wholly repayable within 5 years		
Other loans		
Finance charges – finance leases and hire purchase contracts		
Gain (loss) on repurchase of own debt	—	—

8. Staff costs

	19X2 £	19X1 £
Wages and salaries		
Social security costs		
Other pension costs	—	—

	19X2 Number	19X1 Number
The average number of persons, including executive directors, employed by the company during the year was:		
Management		
Administration		
Broking and technical	—	—

Transactions of officers
(Disclosure required of loans and credit transactions involving the company and its officers, e.g. company secretary and employees overseeing the affairs of the company as

a whole, other than directors, where these exceed £2,500 per officer at the end of the financial year.)

For example:
The company has guaranteed an undertaking totalling £15,000 given by a bank in relation to the Lloyd's underwriting membership of Mr C. O. Seck.

9. Directors

	19X2 £	19X1 £
Emoluments:		
Management services		
Fees	—	—
Total emoluments	═══	═══
Pensions to present and past directors:		
For services as a director		
For other services	—	—
Compensation to directors or past directors for loss of office:		
For services as a director		
For other services	—	—
	═══	═══

The emoluments of directors disclosed above
  (excluding pensions and pension contributions)
  include amounts paid to:

	£	£
The chairman	═══	═══
The highest paid director	═══	═══

The number of other directors who received emoluments
  (excluding pensions and pension contributions)
  in the following ranges were:

	Number	*Number*
Up to £5,000		
£5,001 to £10,000		
£10,001 to £15,000		
£15,001 to £20,000		
etc.		

284

(Number) (*19X1 (Number)*) directors have waived their entitlement to directors' emoluments amounting to £ ..... (*19X1 £* .....).

Note that there are additional disclosures for clients following the Cadbury Code.

Transactions

For example:
(i)   Prior to his appointment as a director in June 19X2, Mr A. N. Other was granted a house purchase loan from the company. The loan amounted to £..... at the date of his appointment as a director and this was the maximum amount outstanding at any time during the period. The balance at 31 December 19X2 was £...... .

In addition Mr D. E. Minimis had a £..... fixed house purchase loan throughout the year. The maximum amount outstanding during the year was £...... . The balance at 31 December 19X2 was £..... (31 December 19X1: £.....).

(ii)   During the year the company disposed of its leasehold interest in premises at Artillery Lane, London E1, to Mr A. N. Other for the sum of £....., the company having first obtained professional valuers' advice that the consideration received fairly represented the property's open market value.

(iii) The company places risks with syndicates at Lloyd's on which Mr I. M. Deguvna, Mr D. E. Minimis and Mr A. N. Other are members, on the same basis as the company deals with other Lloyd's syndicates.

10. Taxation

	19X2 £	19X1 £
Based on the profit (loss) for the year:		
Corporation tax at ..% (19X1 ..%)		
Less: Relief for overseas taxation	⎯	⎯
Tax attributable to franked investment income		
Deferred taxation		
Overseas taxation		
Advance corporation tax written off		
Under (over) provision in respect of prior years	⎯	⎯
	══	══

The tax charge for the year has been reduced by £..... as a result of .....

11. Extraordinary items

	19X2	19X1
	£	£
Extraordinary income (*analyse*)		
Extraordinary charges (*analyse*)	——	——
Extraordinary profit (loss) before taxation		
Taxation on extraordinary profit (loss)	——	——
	══	══

12. Dividends

	19X2	19X1
	£	£
Preference dividend paid		
Ordinary dividends:		
Interim dividend paid of ..p (*19X1 ..p*) per share		
Proposed final dividend of ..p (*19X1 ..p*) per share	——	——
	══	══

13. Intangible fixed assets

Goodwill

	£
COST	
At 1 January 19X2	
Additions	
Disposals	( )
	——
AMORTISATION	
At 1 January 19X2	
Charge for the year	
Eliminated on disposals	( )
At 31 December 19X2	——
NET BOOK VALUE	
At 31 December 19X2	══
At 31 December 19X1	══

Goodwill arose on the purchase of an unincorporated business in 19XX and is being amortised over ..... years. In the opinion of the directors, this represents a prudent estimate of the period over which the company will derive direct economic benefit from the products acquired as part of that business.

14. Tangible fixed assets

	Land and buildings*	Plant and machinery leases held for use in operating leases	Others	Fixtures, fittings and equipment	Total
	£	£	£	£	£
COST OR VALUATION					
At 1 January 19X2					
Surplus on revaluation					
Additions					
Disposals	( )	( )	( )	( )	( )
At 31 December 19X2	═	═	═	═	═
Comprising:					
Cost					
Valuation 19XX					
19XX	─	─	─	─	─
	═	═	═	═	═
ACCUMULATED DEPRECIATION					
At 1 January 19X2					
Eliminated on revaluation	( )	( )	( )	( )	( )
Charge for the year					
Eliminated on disposals	( )	( )	( )	( )	( )
At 31 December 19X2	═	═	═	═	═
NET BOOK VALUE					
At 31 December 19X2	═	═	═	═	═
At 31 December 19X1	═	═	═	═	═
Depreciation rates**:	..% on freehold/ leasehold buildings over the unexpired term of the lease	..% - ..%	..% - ..%	..% - ..%	

Where details of finance leases and hire purchase contracts are not analysed above a note such as the following should be included:

The net book value of plant and machinery of £ ..... (19X1 £ .....) includes an amount of £ ..... (19X1 £ .....) in respect of assets held under finance leases and hire purchase contracts.

*Where space permits the analysis given on the following tables could be incorporated within the main table.
**Alternatively, this information could be given within the accounting policies.

	Freehold properties £	Land and buildings* Leasehold properties Long-term £	Short-term £	Total £
COST OR VALUATION				
At 1 January 19X2				
Surplus on revaluation				
Additions				
Disposals	( )	( )	( )	( )
At 31 December 19X2	===	===	===	===
Comprising:				
Cost				
Valuation 19XX				
19XX				
	—	—	—	—
	===	===	===	===
ACCUMULATED DEPRECIATION				
At 1 January 19X2				
Eliminated on revaluation	( )	( )	( )	( )
Charge for the year				
Eliminated on disposals	( )	( )	( )	( )
At 31 December 19X2	—	—	—	—
	===	===	===	===
NET BOOK VALUE				
At 31 December 19X2	===	===	===	===
At 31 December 19X1	—	—	—	—
Depreciation rates:	..% on freehold buildings	..% on leasehold buildings	over the unexpired term of the lease	

The comparable amounts of land and buildings included above at valuation determined according to the historical cost accounting rules are as follows:

	Freehold properties £	Land and buildings* Leasehold properties Long-term £	Short-term £
COST			
Accumulated depreciation	—	—	—
NET BOOK VALUE			
At 31 December 19X2	===	===	===
At 31 December 19X1	===	===	===

Freehold and leasehold properties were revalued during the year by Messrs ....., Chartered Surveyors, on the basis of the open market value for existing use.

No provision has been made for additional United Kingdom taxation of £..... which would arise if the land and buildings were disposed of at their revalued amount.

*Alternatively, where space permits (e.g. where there is only one class of land and buildings) this could be incorporated within the main fixed asset analysis illustrated on the previous page.

15. Fixed asset investments

Other investments other than loans:

	Listed £	Unlisted £	Total £
COST			
At 1 January 19X2			
Additions			
Disposals	( )	( )	( )
At 31 December 19X2			
PROVISIONS FOR DIMINUTION IN VALUE			
At 1 January 19X2			
Charge for the year			
Amount written back	( )	( )	( )
At 31 December 19X2			
NET BOOK VALUE			
At 31 December 19X2			
At 31 December 19X1			

At 31 December 19X2 the aggregate market value of listed investments (all of which are listed on a recognised investment exchange in Great Britain) was £ ..... (*19X1* £ .....).

No provision has been made for the liability to corporation tax on chargeable gains that would arise if the above investments were disposed of at market value. A tax liability of £ ..... would arise if the investments were disposed of at the above valuation.

Included in the listed investments above is a ..... (*not less than 10*) per cent (*19X1* ..... *per cent*) interest in the issued ordinary share capital of ..... Plc, a company registered in England and Wales.

The unlisted investments above include a ..... per cent interest in the issued ordinary share capital of ..... Limited, a company registered in England and Wales. The cost of the investment is £..... (*19X1* £ .....) and it is valued by the directors at £ ..... (*19X1* £.....). This amount represents ..... (*not less than 10*) per cent (*19X1* ..... *per cent*) of the total assets of A B Company Limited.

Included in unlisted investments is a ..... per cent interest in the ordinary shares of ..... Limited (a subsidiary undertaking) held by the company. Group accounts have not been prepared as the group qualifies as a small/medium-sized group.

Or:

the company is a subsidiary of ..... BV, a company incorporated in the Netherlands.

Or:

all of its subsidiary undertakings are permitted/required to be excluded from consolidation because (*reason*).

The value of this/(these) subsidiary(ies) calculated on an equity basis is £.....

The accounts of the subsidiary were qualified because ..... (*give reasons for qualification*). The aggregate capital and reserves are £..... and its profit for the year £.....

During the course of the year the accounting reference date of ..... Limited was changed to be coterminous with that of the company. Consequently its accounting period to 31 December 19X2 was for a period of ..... months.

16. Current assets

As required by Lloyd's Brokers Byelaw (No. 5 of 1988) the company has entered into a trust deed under which all insurance broking account assets are subject to a floating charge held on trust by the Society of Lloyd's for the benefit of the insurance creditors, which at 31 December 19X2 amounted to £..... (*19X1* £.....). The charge only becomes enforceable under certain circumstances as set out in the deed. The assets subject to this charge were:

	19X2	19X1
	£	£
Cash at bank		
Insurance debtors		
Other assets		

17. Debtors

	19X2 £	19X1 £
DUE WITHIN ONE YEAR		
Insurance debtors		
Other debtors		
Prepayments and accrued income		
Advance corporation tax/taxation receivable	——	——
	——	——
DUE AFTER ONE YEAR		
Insurance debtors		
Other debtors		
Prepayments and accrued income		
Advance corporation tax/taxation receivable	——	——
	——	——
TOTAL DEBTORS	══	══

18. Current asset investments

	19X2 £	19X1 £
Listed		
Unlisted	——	——
	══	══

At 31 December 19X2 the market value of listed investments (all of which are listed on a recognised investment exchange in Great Britain) was £ ..... (*19X1 £ .....*).

No provision has been made for the liability to corporation tax on chargeable gains that would arise if the above investments were disposed of at the valuations given in the previous paragraph. A tax liability of £ ..... would arise if the investments were disposed of at the above valuation.

Included in the listed investments above, is a ..... (*not less than 10*) per cent (*19X1 ..... per cent*) interest in the issued ordinary share capital of ..... Plc, a company registered in England and Wales.

Included in the unlisted investments above, with directors' valuation of

291

£..... (*19X1* £ .....), is a ..... per cent interest in the issued ordinary share capital of ..... Limited, a company registered in England and Wales, amounting to £ ..... (*19X1* £ .....). This amount represents ..... (*not less than 10*) per cent (*19X1 ..... per cent*) of the total assets of A B Company Limited.

19. Cash

	19X2 £	19X1 £
Call and short-term deposits		
Cash at bank and in hand		

20. Creditors: amounts falling due within one year

	19X2 £	19X1 £
Debenture loans		
Bank loans and overdrafts		
Obligations under finance leases and hire purchase contracts		
Insurance creditors		
Bills of exchange payable		
Corporation tax		
Other taxation		
Social security costs		
Other creditors		
Directors' loan accounts		
Accruals and deferred income*		
Proposed dividend		

Include appropriate proportion of any deferred premiums accounted for, together with brokerage not yet brought into account (if material).

The bank loan/overdraft is secured by a fixed (and floating) charge on .....

21. Creditors: amounts falling due after more than one year

	19X2 £	19X1 £
Debenture loans		
Bank loans		
Payments received on account		
Obligations under finance leases and hire purchase contracts		
Insurance creditors		
Bills of exchange payable		
Social security costs		
Other creditors		
Directors' loan accounts		
Accruals and deferred income	——	——
	══	══

Included above are the following:

(Separate disclosure is required for **each** *item in this classification unless this would be excessively lengthy)*

	19X2	19X1
Amounts repayable otherwise than by instalments in more than five years	══	══
Amounts repayable by instalments:		
Not wholly repayable within five years:		
Repayable within five years		
Repayable after five years	——	——
Wholly repayable within five years	——	——
	══	══

The bank loan bears interest at a rate which fluctuates in line with the inter-bank rate. At the year end the rate was ..... per cent.

The bank loan is secured by a fixed (and floating) charge on .....

The debenture stock is secured by a fixed charge on .....

The claims servicing costs total £..... and represent the anticipated cost of servicing claims on long tail business. The proportion of such costs falling due within 12 months amounts to £..... and is included in creditors under note 20.

	19X2	19X1
	£	£

Obligations under finance leases
  and hire purchase contracts
Amounts payable:
Within two to five years
After five years

22. Provisions for liabilities and charges

	Pensions and similar obligations	Deferred taxation (see also note 23)	Other provisions	Total
	£	£	£	£
At 1 January 19X2				
Charge for the year				
Utilised during the year	( )	( )	( )	( )
Other movements (*describe*)				
At 31 December 19X2				

The provision for pensions at 31 December 19X2 includes £ ..... (*19X1 £ .....*) in respect of pensions payable to past directors.

(Any provision for future service costs (if not included in creditors) or amount set aside for brokerage on any long-term contracts (say three years) should be included here and appropriate details given by way of a note.)

23. Deferred taxation

	19X2		19X1	
	Asset recognised/ amount provided	*Amount unprovided*	*Asset recognised/ amount provided*	*Amount unprovided*
	£	£	£	£
Excess of capital allowances over depreciation				
Property revaluations				
Investment valuations				
Interest and other timing differences (*specify if individually material*)				
Losses carried forward	( )	( )	( )	( )
Advance corporation tax recoverable	( )	( )	( )	( )

(An asset has been recognised for those timing differences which are expected to crystallise in the foreseeable future. No reversal of capital allowances is expected.)

Deferred taxation movements

	£
Balance at 1 January 19X2	
Transfer to/from profit and loss account	
Other movements (*identify the nature*)	――
Balance at 31 December 19X2	

24. Accruals and deferred income

	Deferred income (specify) £
At 1 January 19X2	
Received during the year	
Released to profit for the year	――
At 31 December 19X2	

25. Share capital

	Authorised		Allotted, issued and fully paid	
	19X2	*19X1*	*19X2*	*19X1*
	£	£	£	£
.. per cent cumulative preference shares of £ ..... each				
Ordinary shares (stock) of £ ..... each	____	____	____	____
	════	════	════	════

No dividend has been paid on the cumulative preference shares since 19..; the arrears amount to £ .....

The cumulative preference shares are redeemable at par at the option of the company on or after 1 January 19XX.

On (*date*) (*number*) ordinary shares (stock) of £ ..... each were (was) issued for cash at £ ..... each (per £ ..... of stock) to provide additional working capital.

The company has a share option scheme under which options for ..... ordinary shares have been granted as follows:

Number of shares	*Option price per share*	*Option period ending*
════	════	════

26. Reserves

	Share premium account	Revaluation reserve	Other reserves	Profit and loss account	Total
	£	£	£	£	£
At 1 January 19X2:					
– as previously reported					
– prior year adjustment (see below)					
As restated:					
Premium arising on the issue of ..... ordinary shares of £ ..... each less expenses					
Retained profit for the year (loss for the year)					
Net surplus arising on revaluation of tangible fixed assets					
Transfer of amount equivalent to additional depreciation on revalued assets		( )			
Goodwill written off					
Other movements (*describe*)					
At 31 December 19X2					

Of the total reserves, £ ..... is not available for distribution.

(*Give details of the nature of the prior year adjustment and the effect on reported profits.*)

27. RECONCILIATION OF MOVEMENTS IN SHAREHOLDERS' FUNDS

	19X2	*19X1 as restated*
	£	*£*
Profit (loss) for the financial year		
Dividends paid and proposed	( )	( )
Other recognised gains and losses (net)		
New share capital subscribed		
Goodwill written off	( )	( )
Net addition to shareholders' funds		
Opening shareholders' funds		
Closing shareholders' funds		

WHERE THE ONLY reserve is the profit and loss account, and there have been no movements in shareholders' funds other than profit for the year, REPLACE notes 26 and 27 above with the following:

26. RECONCILIATION OF MOVEMENTS IN SHAREHOLDERS' FUNDS

	Share capital	*Profit and loss account*	*Total shareholders' funds*
	£	*£*	*£*
Balance at 1 January 19X1			
Profit/(loss) for the year			
Dividends paid			
New share capital subscribed			
Balance at 31 December 19X1			
Profit for the year			
Dividends paid and proposed			
New share capital subscribed			
Balance at 31 December 19X2			

Notes 28 and following and cross-references to them will require amendment if this option is taken.

28. CASH FLOW STATEMENT

(a) Reconciliation of operating profit
to net cash inflow/(outflow) from
operating activities

	19X2 £	19X1 £
Operating profit		
Depreciation charges		
Loss on sale of tangible fixed assets		
(Increase) in insurance debtors		
(Increase) in other debtors		
Increase in insurance creditors		
Increase in other creditors		
Net cash inflow/(outflow) from operating activities		

(b) Analysis of movements in cash and
cash equivalents during the year

	£	£
Balance at 1 January 19X2		
Net cash inflow/(outflow) before adjustments for the effect of foreign exchange rate changes		
Effect of foreign exchange rate changes		
Balance at 31 December 19X2		

(c) Analysis of the balances of cash and cash equivalents
as shown in the balance sheet

	19X2 £	19X1 £	19X2 Change in year £	19X1 Change in year £
Cash at bank and in hand				
Bank accounts and short-term investments designated IBA				
Short-term investments				
Bank overdrafts				

(d) Analysis of changes in financing during the year

	Share capital	Finance leases	Debenture loan
	£	£	£
Balance at 1 January 19X1			
Cash inflow/(outflow) from financing			
Inception of finance lease contacts			
Shares issued for non-cash consideration			
Profit on repurchase of debenture loan for less than its book value			
Balance at 31 December 19X1			
Cash inflow/(outflow) from (*specify*)			
Balance at 31 December 19X2			

(e) Major non-cash transactions

During the year the group entered into finance lease arrangements in respect of assets with a total capital value at the inception of the leases of £ .....

29. Pension commitments and other post-retirement benefits

(These disclosures are based on examples given in the Appendix to SSAP 24.)

Defined contribution scheme
The company operates a defined contribution pension scheme. The assets of the scheme are held separately from those of the company in an independently administered fund. The pension cost charge represents contributions payable by the company to the fund and amounted to £..... (*19X1* £ .....). At 31 December 19X2 contributions amounting to £..... (*19X1* £ .....) were payable to the fund and are included in creditors.

Defined benefit scheme
The company operates a pension scheme providing benefits based on final pensionable pay. The assets of the scheme are held separately from those of the company, being invested with insurance companies. Contributions to the scheme are charged to the profit and loss account so as to spread the cost of pensions over employees' working lives with the

company. The contributions are determined by a qualified actuary on the basis of triennial valuations using the projected unit method. The most recent valuation was at 31 December 19X1.

The pension charge for the period was £ ..... (*19X1 £* .....). (*Give a brief description of the main actuarial assumptions.*) This included £ ..... (*19X1 £*.....) in respect of the amortisation (allocation) of experience surpluses (deficits) which are being recognised over ..... years, the average remaining service lives of employees in the scheme.

The most recent actuarial valuation showed that the market value of the scheme's assets was £ ..... and that the actuarial value of those assets represented ..... per cent of the benefits that had accrued to members, after allowing for expected future increases in earnings. The contributions of the company and employees will remain at ..... per cent and ..... per cent of earnings respectively.

A provision of £ ..... (*19X1 £* .....) is included in creditors, representing the excess of the accumulated pension cost over the amount funded.

Other post-retirement benefits
The company provides post-retirement benefits, other than pensions for its employees, which include:

Description of benefit	*Approximate number of employees*

During the period, the amount payable by the company in respect of these post-retirement benefits amounted to £ ..... (*19X1 £* .....). At 31 December 19X2 costs in respect of post-retirement benefits amounting to £ ..... (*19X1 £* .....) were payable by the company and are included in creditors. The company expects the costs of meeting the liability to attract taxation relief of approximately £ ...... (*Or:* The company does not expect the costs of meeting the liability to attract taxation relief.)

30. Capital commitments

	19X2 £	19X1 £
Capital expenditure contracted for but not provided for in the financial statements		
Capital expenditure authorised by the directors but not yet contracted for		

31. Other financial commitments

(Particulars must be disclosed of any other financial commitments which have not been provided for and are relevant to assessing the company's state of affairs, e.g. commitments to purchase goods extending more than one year from the balance sheet date, leasing commitments, commitments to acquire companies or to form a joint venture or to purchase own shares.)

For example:
At 31 December 19X2 the company was committed to making the following payments under non-cancellable operating leases in the year to 31 December 19X3:

	Land and buildings		Other	
	19X2	*19X1*	*19X2*	*19X1*
	£	£	£	£
Operating leases which expire:				
Within one year				
Within two to five years				
After five years				

32. Contingent liabilities

At 31 December 19X2 there were contingent liabilities in respect of bills receivable discounted and performance bonds which amounted to £ ..... (*19X1 £ .....*).

Bank and other guarantees given by the company amounted to £ ..... (*19X1 £ .....*).

33. Post balance sheet event(s)

(Give details of all material adjusting (except where referred to elsewhere) and non-adjusting events and 'window-dressing' transactions.)

34. Parent undertakings

The ultimate parent company is X Limited, a company registered in England and Wales.

The immediate parent company is Y BV, a company incorporated in the Netherlands.

35. Departure from Accounting Standard/Companies Act requirements true and fair override

(Particulars of and reasons for departure from accounting standard or Companies Act requirements along with the effect on profit and/or balance sheet).

Appendix 5 – Glossary

The following glossary of insurance broking terms is not comprehensive but is intended to provide broad definitions of some of those terms referred to in the guide and some of those that the reader may come across in practice.

Absolute net claims
Claims paid less returns less reinsurance recoveries.

Absolute net premiums
Premiums plus additional premiums less return premiums less re-insurances, brokerage and commission.

Acceptance
Notification by a party to a proposed contract that he accepts the offer of the other party of the terms proposed, as where an underwriter initials a slip or where the proposer of a life assurance, on receiving an offer of cover from assurers, signifies his acceptance by paying the premium.

Accident year
The calendar year in which the accident or loss occurred.

Accommodation business
Business accepted by an insurer not because he thinks it desirable in itself but to oblige an agent or policyholder whose other business he values.

Accountants' clause
A clause in a business interruption policy entitling the insured to employ his own accountants to prepare a claim.

Accountants' (accountancy) fees
Within Lloyd's, the amount included in Names' personal expenses, usually in respect of accountancy fees of the Name's personal accountant.

Accumulation
Concentration of risk, as where an insurer finds that he has many policies on properties in adjacent locations that could result in losses arising from one event, e.g. fire.

Acquisition costs
The insurer's expenses incurred in acquiring business, including commission to agents and brokers.

Act of God
An accident or event which happens independently of human intervention and is due to natural causes, such as a storm or earthquake. It will relieve from liability if it amounts to circumstances which no human foresight can provide against, and of which human prudence is not bound to recognise the possibility.

Active underwriter
In relation to a Lloyd's syndicate, the person at, or deemed by the Committee to be at, the underwriting box with the principal authority to accept risks on behalf of the members of the syndicate.

Actual total loss
An actual total loss occurs when:

(a) the subject matter of insurance is completely destroyed;
(b) it ceases to be a thing of the kind insured;
(c) the insured is irretrievably deprived of it; or
(d) a ship is posted 'missing', in which case both the ship and its cargo are deemed to be an actual total loss.

Actuarial valuation
A valuation by an actuary of the present value of future liabilities, made by using probability tables and other statistical techniques to evaluate long-term business liabilities.

Actuary
A specialist who applies the mathematical theory of probability to the statistics on which the premium rates for life assurance, annuity and analogous undertakings are based.

Additional premium
Extra premium due from the insured either because the insurance is more hazardous than normal or arising from an endorsement because additional benefits are added to the policy.

Adjustable premium
1 A premium that varies according to the extent of the subject matter of insurance – for example, according to variations in the number of persons insured or the value of goods covered.
2 Premiums under an LPSO scheme, the 'Adjustable Scheme',

305

whereby a premium not having been agreed but a risk having incepted, the underwriter accepts an estimated premium to allow the risk to proceed.

Admitted assets
The assets of an insurance company that are recognised by a supervisory authority for the purpose of determining the company's financial condition (USA).

Admitted insurer
An insurer authorised to do business in a state (USA).

Advance entry
Entries set up by Lloyd's syndicates, usually in respect of reinsurance transactions, where the reinsurance premium on a claim recovery has not been received through the central accounting system but the syndicate wishes to take the items into account. When the closing from the broker or the computer notification is received, the advance entry should be reversed before the entry is finalised.

Advance premium
US description of **deposit premium**.

Agency agreement (*or* **Names agreement**)
See **underwriting agency agreement**

Agency system
System of producing business through a network of agents. Such agents have a contract to represent the underwriter and are of three classes: part-time, brokers and general. Brokers (but not part-time and general agents) are also agents for the client and therefore may encounter problems of conflict of interest. Agents are compensated at differing rates of commission, and general agents have much greater responsibilities and duties than part-time agents and brokers. In the UK, general agents are usually confined to marine and home foreign business.

Agent
An insurance intermediary.

Agent, co-ordinating
An underwriting member of Lloyd's who writes business under more than one underwriting agent is required to nominate an agent to co-ordinate the allocation of his **premium income limit**.

Agent, Lloyd's underwriting
A company, firm or person approved by Lloyd's and authorised to manage the affairs of syndicates or Names at Lloyd's.

Agent, Managing
The agent who manages a syndicate, appointing the underwriter and other staff, investing syndicate funds and preparing accounts. A Managing Agent may also act as a Members' Agent.

Agent, Members'
The agent who looks after the interests of the Name to ensure he derives maximum benefit from his participation in syndicates.

Agent's account
A statement of the period's business showing each premium transaction, the policy number, the insured's name, the premium or return premium and claims in the appropriate column, together with commission, postage and other charges and the balance due either to the company or to the agent, in accordance with the contract between the agent and the underwriter.

Agents' balances
Net balances, i.e. premiums less commissions and claims, due from agents and brokers.

Agent's salary
Within Lloyd's, the amounts charged to a Name by the Members' and Managing Agents for dealing with his affairs as a member of a syndicate.

Aggregate Excess of Loss reinsurance
A form of reinsurance, providing excess of loss cover for losses arising from any one event (or vessel) in excess of the reinsured's retention up to an agreed limit, but only when the aggregate of claims otherwise recoverable under the excess of loss treaty exceeds a stated amount.

Aggregate Stop Loss reinsurance
This is a wider application of the ordinary stop loss treaty in that it applies to the entire portfolio of one branch of the reinsured's activities (*see* **Stop Loss reinsurance**).

Aggregation
The process of accumulating claims as specified by an excess of loss reinsurance agreement for the purpose of establishing the amount recoverable.

All risks insurance
Insurance of property against loss or damage however caused, subject only to stated exceptions.

Annual report, Lloyd's
A document prepared by the managing agent of a syndicate for the underwriting members participating therein. The annual report comprises:

(a)   the underwriting accounts;
(b)   a balance sheet;
(c)   a seven-year summary;
(d)   a disclosure of interests statement; and
(e)   such other information as is necessary for a proper understanding of the annual report (e.g. a statement of accounting policies), as defined in the syndicate accounting rules.

Annual subscription
A subscription paid by a Name each year to Lloyd's (to cover expenses incurred by Lloyd's). It is geared to the Name's premium income limit and is normally paid by the syndicate on behalf of each Name.

Annuity
1   A contract of insurance to provide an income to the annuitant for a set period (commonly for life or for joint lives). The contract will provide for periodic payments, e.g. monthly or quarterly.
2   The annual sum paid under (1).

Annuity consideration
The premium(s) an annuitant pays to purchase an annuity.

Antedating
Where a policy is expressed as operating from a date before final agreement was reached on its terms, it is said to be antedated.

Any one bottom (*or* any one policy)
A term applied by a reinsurer to a limit in a marine reinsurance treaty to avoid a potential accumulation of liability (bottom = hull).

Arbitration clause
A clause in a policy providing that certain differences which may arise between the parties shall be determined by arbitrators chosen in some specified way.

Arranged total loss (compromised total loss)
A compromise settlement where a total loss has not in fact occurred, but is deemed to have done.

As original
'Terms as original' is used in reinsurance to denote the fact that the reinsurance is on the same conditions as the original insurance.

Assurance
A term interchangeable with insurance but generally used in connection with life business, because assurance implies the certainty of an event and insurance the probability.

Assured
Same as **insured**.

Attachment
1   The coming into force of an insurance.
2   The seizure of property.

Attachment date
The date on which insurance cover comes into force.

Attachment of risk
Same as **attachment**.

Attachment slip
A supplementary slip, attached to the original slip, used when it is necessary to obtain an insurer's agreement, by signature, to an amendment or addition.

Audit categories
The headings under which different types of risk are grouped for analysis.

Audit codes
Each audit category of risk is given a one-letter audit code, the purpose of which is to ensure that there are clearly defined categories for audit, accounting and reporting purposes.

Audit reserves
Reserves created according to rules laid down by Lloyd's and approved by the DTI. They are made on open years of account to ensure that Names have sufficient funds to wind up their accounts after 36 months have elapsed. This solvency must be on an individual Name basis (i.e.

aggregating the Name's participation in all relevant syndicates) and any deficiency must be covered by the lodgement of additional assets.

Automatic reinsurance treaty
See **obligatory treaty**.

Average
1 In marine insurance a partial loss.

   (a) *General average* is a loss which arises in consequence of an extraordinary sacrifice made, or expenses incurred, for the preservation of the ship and cargo. All underwriters involved in the ship and cargo will participate to indemnify the insured against the actual loss incurred.

   (b) *Particular average* is partial loss of the subject matter insured, caused by a peril insured against, and which is not a general average loss.

2 A clause in non-marine insurance policies (mostly for fire business) whereby, in the event of under-insurance, the claim paid out by the insurer is restricted to the same proportion of the loss as the sum insured under the policy bears to the total value of the insured item.

Average adjuster
One who assesses and apportions losses in marine insurance, notably general average losses.

Aviation hull insurance
In aviation insurance, hull insurance (i.e. of the aircraft's structure) is distinguished from cargo, passenger and liability insurance.

Avoidance
The right of the underwriter to treat an insurance contract as though he had never accepted the risk. This can occur in cases where there is a breach of good faith, a significant change in the actual risk involved or a delay in the commencement of a voyage.

Back-to-back
A term used to describe complementary transactions in the nature of hedging, as where a life policy and an annuity are effected simultaneously on the life of one person.

Balanced portfolio
The total business of an insurer that has been so arranged by selection and reinsurance as to safeguard the financial equilibrium of the underwriter.

Bank guarantee
An undertaking by a bank that liability under a document will be honoured or a contractual obligation met.

Base premium
A ceding company's premiums to which the rate of premium for reinsurance is applied.

Beneficiary
The person named on a life policy to receive the proceeds (benefit) at maturity.

Binder
1   American expression for an agreement to insure. It contains the details of the insurance and is used in the same way as the 'slip' in the London market between the time of acceptance by the insurer and the closing of the policy.
2   Same as **binding authority**.

Binding agreement
The agreement by which a **binding authority** is operated.

Binding authority (binding cover)
An authority given by an underwriter to an agent (known as the cover holder) to grant cover on the underwriter's behalf within agreed limits. Such authorities are used more in the non-marine and aviation markets than in the marine market.

Binding clause
1   A clause in a reinsurance treaty setting out the parties and the extent of each underwriter's liability.
2   A clause in the SG (ship & goods) form of marine policy in which it is agreed that the policy shall have as much force and effect as a policy made in London.

Binding cover
See **binding authority**.

Blanket policy
A policy in which a single sum insured covers a number of separate items, such as buildings in a fire policy or employees in a fidelity guarantee policy, without being divided up among them.

311

Block policy
1   A policy used primarily for inland transit risks on cargo issued for a fixed premium without the need for sendings to be declared.
2   An 'all risks' policy issued to certain trades, e.g. jewellers (USA).

Block reserves (*also* **block holding**)
Forms of personal investment holding. In the case of syndicates, however, Names contribute to a 'pool' which the Agent then invests.

Bordereau(x)
Detailed listings of premiums and/or loss transactions usually prepared monthly or quarterly and rendered to interested parties. Frequently rendered by ceding companies to reinsurers and by general agents and cover holders.

Bottomry bond
A shipping term. If the captain of a ship finds it necessary to incur expenditure, such as for the repair of his ship, he may give a bond mortgaging his ship as security for a loan obtained to cover this expenditure. Loss of the ship would extinguish the mortgage.

Bouquet (of treaties)
Reinsurances of different classes of insurance transacted by an insurer offered as a package deal to a reinsurer.

Box, the
The area used in Lloyd's by the active underwriter and his assistants. The box has evolved from the booths in Edward Lloyd's coffee-house. Here underwriters sign business and accept notification of claims.

Branch
1   A class of insurance, e.g. life, marine.
2   A local office of an insurance company.

British Insurance and Investment Brokers' Association (BIIBA)
A professional organisation formed by an amalgamation of four earlier trade associations to represent the interests of insurance brokers.

Broker
See **insurance broker**.

Brokerage
The remuneration payable to a broker. This is normally agreed by the insurer and paid as a deduction from the premium.

Burning cost

A method of calculating the premium for reinsurance whereby within certain limits the reinsurance premium paid by a cedant is related to the claims made under the policy. The adjustment factor works to the advantage of the reinsurer until the maximum level of reinsurance premium is reached. There are minimum and maximum levels of premium payable, usually expressed as a percentage of the cedant's underlying premiums. Within these limits, if the cedant makes a claim the reinsurer will collect an additional premium calculated in accordance with a formula contained in the policy. When the maximum premium has been paid the reinsurer has full liability for further claims with no recourse.

Burning ratio

The ratio arrived at by comparing losses with the amount insured, a term generally found in treaty reinsurance.

'C' Account

A Lloyd's broker's US$ account with Citibank N.A. in London, designated 'Lloyd's American Trust Fund'.

Call

1   The sum payable by a member of a Protection and Indemnity Club (*see* **protection and indemnity risks**) for his right to indemnity by the club. A call payable at the outset of each period is termed an advance call. Additional payments (supplementary calls) in respect of a period may be made subsequently if required to meet claims arising.
2   A request/demand by a Lloyd's syndicate to participating Names for funds to enable it to pay claims and expenses.

Cancellation

1   A termination of an existing policy by notice prior to expiry. In most cases this will result in a return premium being paid by the insurer to the insured.
2   If the risk does not attach and the subject matter is not imperilled the insurance is cancelled. Once the subject matter has been imperilled cancellation can only be effected by agreement between both parties, except where one of the parties is at fault in circumstances where the aggrieved party is entitled to avoid the policy (*see* **cancellation clause**).

Cancellation clause

The purpose of this clause is to protect the interests of either party to the contract in the event that one of them might be unreasonably prejudiced by the continuation of the contract.

Capacity
The maximum amount of insurance that an insurer of the insurance market will be prepared or is permitted to accept.

Capital appreciation
1   'Gross': the increase in value at the year end over the value at the previous 1 January or subsequent cost of syndicate investments, including realised gains (less losses).
2   'Net': gross capital appreciation less provision for capital gains tax.

Captive insurance company
An insurance company formed by a trading company, a trade association or the like, primarily for the insurance of the founder's own risks.

Cargo
This can be underwritten by marine, non-marine or aviation syndicates. Cargoes can be covered against loss, theft or destruction, including special cover for carriers entering war zones.

Cash-in value
Same as **surrender value**.

Cash loss
An arrangement whereby if a large claim arises it is settled immediately without waiting for a periodic adjustment of accounts.

Cash loss reserve
See **loss reserve**.

Casualty
A loss; notably a marine sinking.

Casualty insurance
US term for non-life insurance other than fire, marine or surety business.

CA tabulation sheet
Central Accounting document issued by Lloyd's as a summary of underwriting transactions for one or more days. Tab sheets are for advice only, actual cash movement being given by settlement sheets every week.

Catastrophe
Conflagration, earthquake, windstorm, explosion and other sudden and severe disasters resulting in substantial losses. Catastrophic losses (the whole loss of an insurance company arising out of a single catastrophic event) are usually protected by excess of loss reinsurance treaties in order

to limit an underwriter's exposure to any one such event to a specific amount.

Cedant
An insurer who lays off risks by means of reinsurance.

Ceding company
An insurance company that lays off risks by means of reinsurance.

Cede
To buy reinsurance. The proportion of the original premium which the underwriter pays over (cedes) to his reinsurer under the terms of a reinsurance contract is known as the 'ceded line'. The proportion kept by the insurer is the 'retained line'. A ceded line is called a 'cession' or a 'declaration'.

Central Accounting system
The department at Lloyd's responsible for the accounting of all the underwriting business of its syndicates. Underwriters receive all their tabulation sheets and settlement sheets from this department. Lloyd's brokers also receive daily statements and weekly settlement sheets. Both underwriters and brokers settle the net balance on the settlement date.

Central solvency
The method used by Lloyd's of expediting and simplifying the earmarking process for Names by means of a central computerised facility.

Cession
See **cede**.

Charge note
Same as **debit note**.

Citibank schedules
These schedules give all the details of the purchases and sales of LATF investments and the investment income arising therefrom.

Claims
Death, injury, destruction or damage covered by insurance gives rise to a claim, i.e. the mandatory indemnity payable to the insured under the terms of the policy.

Claims bureau
1 Lloyd's Claims Office, used by underwriters at Lloyd's to handle claims, including reinsurance matters.
2 Any other office set up by insurers to handle claims.

315

Claims co-operation clause
Where the reassured agrees to consult and co-operate with reinsurers on claims handling and settlement.

Claims expenses
The expenses incurred in the investigation, adjustment and settlement of claims. There are two types of claims expenses: allocated and unallocated.

Allocated claims expenses are generally considered to cover expenses incurred in settling claims that can be attributed to specific cases, including such items as actual court costs, lawyers' fees, medical examinations and independent adjusters' fees.

Unallocated claims expenses are generally considered to cover expenses incurred in settling claims that cannot be attributed to specific cases, including salaries of claims department employees and other direct and overhead expenses of the claims department as a whole.

Claims file
Data relating to a claim is placed together in a folder or stapled together, for example, and is referred to as the claims file.

Claims notified/reported
Claims resulting from accidents or events which have taken place and on which the insurer has received notices or reports of claim.

Claims outstanding
Claims not yet settled.

Claims ratios
Expression in terms of ratio of the relationship of claims to premiums. Two ratios in common usage are:

1 Paid claims ratio – paid claims divided by written or earned premiums.
2 Incurred claims ratio – incurred claims divided by earned premiums.

These can be expressed as either gross (i.e. before insurance premium and recoveries), or net.

Claims reserve
1 The provisions made by an insurer for outstanding claims and losses that have been incurred but not reported (IBNR).
2 Under a reinsurance contract the amount retained by the reassured

against payment of claims which will be recoverable under the contract in due course. (*See also* **outstanding claims advance**, **outstanding claims reserve** and **premium reserve**).

Claims year
The underwriting year of account to which a claim is allocated. This is not necessarily the year of occurrence, as claims are allocated to the year the premium is credited.

Class
A category of insurance business defined by the nature of the cover provided or by the nature of the object at risk.

Closed line
A broker is said to close a line when he attributes the cover to underwriters who have written lines. The total lines written may have exceeded 100 per cent of the insurance required, or the value provisionally stated may have proved to be an overestimate (*see* **signing down**).

Closed year (of a Lloyd's syndicate)
An underwriting year of account all of whose outstanding benefits and liabilities have been transferred to a succeeding year or another Lloyd's syndicate by means of a reinsurance to close. This is normally after 36 months (occasionally 48 months with special permission from Lloyd's). The ascertained profits or losses of a closed year are available for distribution to or are collected from the Names.

Closing
When an insurance has been placed the broker 'closes' the insurance to the insurer by presenting a premium advice note, together with the slip, to the insurer for signing. In the case of Lloyd's underwriters the closing is made to the LPSO. In the case of companies the closing is made either to the ILU (Policy Department), if the company is a member, or direct to the company. In closing the risk to a non-Institute company the broker prepares a closing slip for submission to the company, retaining his placing (or signing) slip. The policy may be submitted for signing at the same time that the risk is closed, or it may be signed later.

Closing instructions *or* Closing advice
An advice sent by a broker to an insurer who has taken a line on a slip, specifying the actual proportion of a risk that has been allocated and the actual premium receivable. If the slip was over-subscribed by underwriters a pro rata scaling-down will have taken place in the broker's office.

Closing reinsurance
Reinsurance of an entire portfolio of outstanding liabilities and outstanding claims to close a syndicate's underwriting account by transfer of the outstanding liability to the next open underwriting account, normally by the end of year 3.

Closing slip
A form of advice to an insurer from a broker detailing an insurance so that a policy can be prepared. Its use dropped off considerably when the Institute of London Underwriters formed a policy signing department to sign combined company policies but it is still used for non-Institute signings.

CMR form
Lloyd's goods in transit (CMR) policy. This form is designed to cover the insured's legal liability as a carrier under the provisions of the CMR. Marine insurers are interested in this only in so far as they are prepared to cover liabilities of road carriers, such as container operators, in connection with a sea voyage.

Co-insurance
1 Where a number of insurers each cover part of a risk, or where a policy requires the insured to bear a part of each loss, there is said to be co-insurance except in certain circumstances. A co-insurer is not obliged to follow the decision of another co-insurer. Each co-insurance is a separate contract with the insured.
2 In the USA, the term is used to describe the application of an average condition (*see* **average**) whereby if a sum insured is inadequate the insured has to bear a proportionate part of a claim.
3 Reinsurance on the same terms as the original insurance (USA).

Collective policy
A form of policy for several co-insurers sharing the same risk. The policy is issued by the leading insurer in the joint names of all co-insurers. On renewal a collective renewal receipt is issued for all co-insurers.

Commission
1 Remuneration to an agent for services such as arranging an insurance.
2 Remuneration on the same terms as the original insurance (USA).

Committee of Lloyd's
The governing and supervisory body which controlled the activities of Lloyd's and its Names up to 31 December 1982. On 1 January 1983 a separate committee, consisting of the 16 working members of the Council of Lloyd's and having substantial delegated powers, was formed

under the Lloyd's Act 1982 to take over this role (*see also* **Council of Lloyd's**).

Common account
When an original insurer who already has reinsurance effects further reinsurance with another reinsurer it may be either wholly for his own protection or also for the protection of the first reinsurer. In the latter case it is said to be reinsurance for the common account.

Commutation
The finalisation of an outstanding loss by payment of an agreed figure in settlement.

Comprehensive cover
Cover that is not, in fact, 'comprehensive', but covers a wide range of specified risks.

Consequential loss
A loss following and consequent on a loss caused by a peril insured against. The insurer is not always liable for consequential loss. Neither is consequential loss allowed in general average except where it is directly consequential on the general average act. Loss of profits as a consequence of the destruction of a factory by fire is an example of consequential loss.

Constitution of Lloyd's syndicates
See **stamp**.

Constructive total loss
In marine insurance a constructive total loss occurs where the subject matter insured is reasonably abandoned because its actual total loss appears unavoidable or because it could not be preserved from actual total loss without an expenditure which would exceed its total value after the expenditure had been incurred. In non-marine insurance the insurer has no right of abandonment, but the term is used when repair of the subject matter would be uneconomic.

Contingency insurance
Insurance of loss due to a contingency, e.g. non-performance, cancellation of event.

Contingent commission
Profit commission or share of profits on a reinsurance.

Contract signing scheme
A scheme in operation at LPSO whereby underwriters can receive bulk entries of items for which they do not require individual advices (e.g. where there is a large volume of similar risks).

Contractors' all risks
Insurance in respect of contract works covering damage to property on the site however caused (though with exceptions) and third party liability.

Contributing business
Where reinsurers' liability for claims is proportional to premium ceded.

Convertible currency
Within Lloyd's, any currency other than sterling and US and Canadian dollars.

Co-reinsurance
Retention by a reassured in his own reinsurance.

Cost, insurance and freight (CIF)
A quotation of a price for goods covering the price ex-warehouse, and including delivery to the docks, dock dues, carriage and insurance as far as the port to which the goods are to be consigned, but excluding delivery from the docks to the purchaser's premises (*see* **free on board**).

Council of Lloyd's
The ruling body of Lloyd's formed under the Lloyd's Act 1982 and consisting at that time of 16 elected working Names, eight elected external Names, and three nominated members not being Names, annual subscribers or associate members of Lloyd's. With effect from 1 January 1994, following Council and Committee (Amendment No. 2) Byelaw (No. 27 of 1993), the composition of the Council became six elected working Names, five elected external Names and seven nominated members. Of the nominated members, one shall be the Chief Executive Officer at Lloyd's and one the Director of Regulatory Services. The Council has powers to delegate, to make additional byelaws, and to carry out disciplinary measures over members, Lloyd's brokers, underwriting agents and employees thereof.

Since 1 January 1993 the Council has devolved the majority of its functions to the Market Board (whose primary purpose is to advance the interests of Lloyd's members) and the Regulatory Board (whose primary purpose is to regulate the Lloyd's market), although it has retained exclusive power to make Byelaws and to make decisions on certain specific matters. It may revoke or vary the devolution of power to the two Boards.

Cover (when used in relation to Names at Lloyd's)
1 To cover. To guarantee indemnity as an insurer in the event of a loss.
2 If the Open Year's solvency calculations show an audit deficiency for individual Names this deficiency must be funded, i.e. covered by assets. Such funding is termed 'cover', and may be obtained from the following:

   (a) surpluses on other syndicates;
   (b) the Lloyd's Deposit;
   (c) Special Reserve Fund investments;
   (d) Personal Reserve investments; and
   (e) direct funding (the transfer of cash or investments, or by letter of credit).

3 Same as binding authority.

Cover holder
The agent under a binding authority.

Cover note
An interim document evidencing the grant of insurance cover.

Custom of Lloyd's
Practice peculiar to the Lloyd's market which binds those taking part, but not if it is unreasonable (unless they have assented to be bound) or unlawful.

Cut-off
1 The date after which a reinsurer is not liable under a reinsurance contract.
2 Separation between buildings so that each is assumed to be a separate fire risk.

Cut-through clause
A clause in a reinsurance contract providing that in the event of the ceding insurer's insolvency the reinsurer will be liable for his share of the loss to the insured and not to the ceding insurer's liquidator.

Debited income
The premium income debited by an insurer during any period.

Debit note
An advice that an account is to be debited with a sum of money.

Deceased Name
A Name who has, before an audit is completed, died. Reference should be made to the Agency Agreement for the method of calculating the Name's share in the syndicate for that year of account.

Declaration
1   A statement by the insured giving details of the risks required to be covered. This may be incorporated in the proposal form or made later. If made later, the policy will be issued subject to declaration and will be endorsed with the details of the declaration.
2   *See* **cede**.

Deductible
On direct insurance the first part of an insurance loss paid by the assured and thus not insured (*see also* **excess**).

Deferred account
An account where premiums are paid in instalments. It is part of the Central Accounting system.

Deferred annuity
An annuity which will become payable on a future date either at the expiration of a fixed number of years after its purchase or at the attainment of a stated age.

Deferred premium
Premium paid by an insured or reinsured by instalments.

Deficit clause
1   A clause in a reinsurance contract under which profit commission is payable, whereby if the reinsurer makes a loss in any year, his deficit is carried forward for the purpose of calculating the profit commission in a subsequent year or years.
2   A clause in an **underwriting agency agreement** whereby a Name's syndicate results are aggregated, either over a number of years ('vertical' deficit clause) or in a single year across some or all of his syndicates ('horizontal' deficit clause), before the amount of profit commission payable by the Name to his agent is determined.

Deposit premium
A payment in advance as a deposit pending determination of the actual premium.

Development statistics
A statement by an original insurer showing details of claims falling within a proposed reinsurance with figures for the amounts paid and

outstanding at the end of each period from the date of occurrence until final settlement.

Direct business
1 Insurance placed with an insurer by the insured directly and not through an intermediary.
2 Insurance, as opposed to reinsurance.

Direct dealing
An arrangement for motor syndicates whereby a non-Lloyd's broker is permitted to arrange insurance for the public to be placed at Lloyd's directly and not via a Lloyd's broker. Such activities must be guaranteed by a Lloyd's broker.

Direct insurance
Insurance, as opposed to reinsurance.

Direct liability clause
(*See* **cut-through clause**.) Clause making a reinsurer directly liable to an original insured, bypassing the cedant.

Disability
Incapacity because of accident or sickness.

Discovery period
The period within which a loss covered by a policy has to be discovered and notified to the insurers. The period may be longer or shorter than the term of the policy.

Domestic company
An insurance company established in the country where it is doing business. In the USA, the term is used in each state to describe a company established in that state, a company established elsewhere in the USA being described as a foreign company, while a company established outside the USA is an alien company.

Early signing/early signing account
Where a broker has difficulty in getting money from a particular country, the underwriter may agree to the signing of a policy before the actual premium can be noted.

Earmarking of Lloyd's funds
Method of funding (obtaining cover for) deficiencies on open years of account or losses on a closed year. Lloyd's funds consist of surpluses on

other syndicates in which a Name participates, the Special Reserve Fund, Personal Reserves and the Name's Deposit.

Earned-incurred basis
A basis for calculating an insurer's loss ratio by comparing the premiums earned in a period with the estimated cost of claims arising during the period.

Earned premium
Premium in respect of that part of the insurance where the adventure has attached and terminated and during which the insurer was on risk. Where time is of the essence, the premium is 'earned' pro rata to the time on risk. If the policy pays a total loss the whole premium is deemed earned.

Eighths basis
A basis used for the calculation of unearned premiums involving the assumption that the average date of issue of all policies written during a quarter is the middle of that quarter. So at the end of the year premium arising in the first quarter is $\frac{1}{8}$ unearned, $\frac{3}{8}$ for the second quarter, and so on.

Endorsement
Documentary evidence of a change in an existing policy. This may give rise to a premium adjustment.

Endowment policy
A life assurance policy under which the sum insured is payable on a date specified in the policy or on death should that occur sooner.

Enrolled body corporate
A firm or company registered under the IBRA. Only such firms may use the description 'insurance brokers'.

Entrance fees
See **Lloyd's entrance fees**.

Equity linked policy
A life assurance policy, the benefits of which are calculated according to the value from time to time of certain specified equity investments.

Estimated future liabilities (EFL)
This is the total of each of the open year's audit reserves calculated in conducting the Lloyd's Solvency Audit.

Excess
The first part of the cost of a claim which is not covered by a policy. It may be borne by the insured or by another party.

Excess of loss insurance
An insurance where the insurer's liability only attaches when a loss exceeds a certain figure and then only for liability in excess of that figure.

Excess of loss reinsurance
A type of reinsurance whereby an insurer limits his loss for a specific risk (facultative) or class of risk (treaty), beyond and up to specific limits. The lower limit is called his retention. The premium payable is usually a percentage of the underlying premiums accepted by the insurer for the risk or class covered, but it may be a moving percentage (*see* **burning cost**). This form of reinsurance may be placed to cover any one loss or each and every loss, in which case claims are made on the reinsurer for the aggregate of the amounts by which individual losses paid out exceed the retention. Because of the wider range of cover required, excess of loss reinsurance is usually arranged in layers.

Exclusion
A clause in a policy excluding certain losses, e.g. war perils, frustration, nuclear weapons, dangerous drugs and earthquakes.

***Ex gratia* payments**
A payment made by an insurer to a policyholder where there is no legal liability or proof of legal liability so to pay.

Expenses
1 Name's expenses – expenses incurred by a Lloyd's syndicate or agency on behalf of a specific Name and therefore, charged to that Name in his Personal Account for a Closed Year.
2 Syndicate expenses – expenses incurred by a syndicate in the normal course of running its affairs and therefore apportioned to Names in accordance with their share of the stamp.

Expense ratio
The proportion that the expenses, other than claims and reinsurance premiums, of the insurer bear to his income from premiums.

Experience
The comparison of claims, or claims and premiums, over a period, in respect of a particular insured or a group of insurances.

Extra-contractual obligations (ECO)

An ECO (inclusion or exclusion) clause in a reinsurance contract normally covers the eventuality of damages arising out of delay in payment of claims, and other ECO liabilities mentioned in the wording of the clause.

Facultative

Single named risks (e.g. single voyages) are effected on a facultative basis whereby the underwriter assesses the risk. Most hull insurance is effected facultatively but the majority of cargo insurance is effected on an 'open cover' basis, whereby the underwriter agrees in advance to accept all shipments coming within the period and scope of the cover (*see* **open cover**). The acceptance by the underwriter of declarations under an open cover is obligatory rather than facultative.

Facultative obligatory treaty

A reinsurance treaty under which an insurer may elect to offer a risk of a specified type for reinsurance, the reinsurer being obliged to accept it if offered.

Facultative reinsurance

1 The reinsurance of risks that the original insurer may elect whether or not to offer for reinsurance, the reinsurer being free to accept or reject the offer.
2 Reinsurance of a single risk negotiated and placed individually.

Facultative treaty

A contract setting out how facultative reinsurance shall be handled by an insurer and a reinsurer.

Failsafe

See **Lloyd's deposit**.

Fidelity guarantee

Cover provided to an employer against loss arising from dishonesty of employees.

Fire insurance

Term used to cover not only insurance against fire, but also the insurance of additional perils such as explosion and weather.

First line reinsurance

Same as **flat line reinsurance**.

First reserve

See **Lloyd's deposit**.

First surplus reinsurance/first surplus treaty
The name given to an ordinary surplus treaty; the surplus must be allotted to that treaty first and in priority to any other reinsurers. Sometimes treaties are arranged as second surplus treaties, and these would receive a share of the surplus only after the first surplus treaty had received the full amount to which it is entitled.

Flat line reinsurance
Reinsurance of a fixed amount, whether the whole or part of the insurer's line.

Flat rate
Where a contract is rated at a fixed rate rather than a rate adjustable according to premiums or tonnage, for example.

Fleet
Originally a group of ships, but applied now to groups of other vehicles, and in the USA to a group of insurance companies in one ownership.

Follow the lead
The custom in an insurance market, e.g. Lloyd's, whereby once a **leading underwriter** who is sufficiently well known as being versed in the type of risk involved has accepted part of an insurance, other underwriters will tend to follow him, and accept part of the insurance.

For declaration only
The issue of a policy with no premium charge being made or specific insurance stated. Subsequent declarations are then made and premiums assessed within the general framework of the policy.

Foreign insurance legislation
A series of codes appearing on advice cards primarily used to distinguish between taxable and non-taxable US business for American tax purposes.

Forty per cent basis
A basis used for the calculation of unearned premiums, being 40 per cent of written premiums. It is used for treaty business when there is not enough information about inception dates to use a more accurate method.

Franchise
Where an insurance or reinsurance covers only losses exceeding a certain agreed size.

327

Free on board
Prices quoted on these terms include carriage only from the suppliers' premises as far as the port from which the goods are to be despatched, the remainder of the cost of carriage having to be borne by the purchaser of the goods (*see* **cost, insurance and freight**).

From the ground up (FGU)
A statement of an original insurer's experience of a class of business offered for reinsurance is said to be from the ground up when it shows the number and distribution by amount of all claims, however small, even though reinsurance is large claims only.

Fronting agreement
The system whereby a non-Lloyd's broker is permitted to place business with Lloyd's syndicates by agreement with, and guarantee of, a Lloyd's broker. The Lloyd's broker 'fronts' for the non-Lloyd's broker.

Fronting insurer/company
An insurer who accepts direct insurance in its own name and reinsures all or most of it with a reinsurer.

Full signed line
When an insurer accepts a line on a slip this is called his written line. It frequently occurs that the broker over-places the insurance, i.e. the total of the lines he receives exceeds the amount of insurance required. This is accepted market practice, but it means that when the insurance is finally closed (or signed) each insurer's written line must be reduced in proportion so that the total of the lines agrees exactly with the amount of insurance required. The line so arrived at is called the full signed line. An insurer may use the expression 'full signed line' in a reinsurance order in place of the term 'full written line'. When used in this manner both terms mean the same because ultimately the full written line will be reduced to the full signed line when the reinsurance is closed. In cargo insurance, a further reason for reducing the written line to a lower amount when signing occurs is when the value which is subsequently shipped is less than the value contemplated by the insurance.

Full written line
The amount which an insurer writes on a slip when he accepts an insurance. The term is often to be seen in a facultative reinsurance order where the insurer wishes to reinsure the whole of the line he has written. The broker, when closing the reinsurance, must take care to ensure that, in the event of a short closing on the original, the reinsured line is reduced in the same proportion as the reinsured's line on the original insurance (*see* **full signed line**).

328

Fund
A provision or reserve.

Funding
In a broker, the practice of paying a premium or a claim to a creditor before collecting it from the debtor.

Funds held by company under reinsurance treaties
The deposit or retention by a company out of funds due to a reinsurer as a guarantee that a reinsurer will meet its loss and other obligations.

Funds held by or deposited with ceding reinsurers (treaty reserves)
An asset account used in connection with reinsurance agreements. The reinsurer uses this account to record deposits made with ceding companies or withholdings by ceding companies of a portion of premiums due as a guarantee that the reinsurer will meet its loss and other obligations. Such accounts are also used when pools and associations withhold funds from reinsurers for the same purposes mentioned above. The member companies use the asset account and the liability account (funds held by company under reinsurance treaties) to record this information on their books.

General average
See **average**.

General business
The classes termed general business are defined in Part I of Schedule 2 to the Insurance Companies Act 1982.

Global excess
An excess of loss contract covering a reassured's whole operation, or embracing a number of different departments and classes.

Global return
The statement of business required by the Department of Trade and Industry covering the activities of all Lloyd's syndicates. The managing agent of each syndicate is responsible for submitting a return, audited by the syndicate auditor, to Lloyd's. These returns are consolidated by Lloyd's and give rise to the published Lloyd's market underwriting results.

Goods in transit
See **CMR form**.

Green card
A document evidencing the existence of third party motor insurance, issued to a motorist for use internationally.

Gross earned premium
Premiums received by or due to an insurer, without deduction of the cost of any reinsurance, but adjusted to take account of the differences between the unexpired risk reserves at the beginning and end respectively of the period concerned.

Gross line
The share of an insurance accepted by an underwriter before a deduction is made for any reinsurance by him.

Gross net premium
The gross premium for a marine insurance, before deduction of brokerage and discounts, but less gross returns of premiums.

Gross premium
The total premium before deduction of brokerage or discounts.

Gross premium underwriting limit
The volume of insurance business which may be underwritten on behalf of a Lloyd's Name for any one year of account. It is dependent on the amount of wealth (net eligible means) confirmed by the Name on entry into Lloyd's and at three-yearly intervals thereafter.

Gross written premiums
Premiums received by or due to an insurer without deduction of the cost of any reinsurance or any adjustment for the fact that some of the income has to be reserved for the unexpired element of the policy.

Guarantee (salvage)
See **salvage guarantee**.

Hold-harmless agreement
An agreement by one party to indemnify another against claims of a defined nature.

Honeycomb slip
At Lloyd's, a slip with a honeycomb of boxes in which the syndicate numbers of insurers on the risk are inserted in the same order as they appear on the original slip to ensure that none of the original underwriters has been omitted.

Hull
A classification of risks referring to a hull of a ship or boat, or the fabric of a hovercraft or aircraft, including its machinery and equipment. Marine hull insurance commonly includes indemnity for $\frac{3}{4}$ of collision liability.

Illinois reserve/deposit
Where business is accepted through the State of Illinois, the syndicate is required to place a dollar deposit into a trust fund to cover any liabilities arising. Such deposit is based on the Premium Income arising from Illinois business in the previous year.

ILU closing date
The date on which a particular risk is closed by the ILU and the policy is issued.

Immediate annuity
An annuity beginning from the date of completion of the contract.

Inception date
The date when a risk commences.

Incidental non-marine
Non-marine insurance written by a marine underwriter as an adjunct to his marine insurance account.

Incurred but not reported (IBNR)
At the end of a period of account a reserve is necessary in respect of losses that have occurred but have not yet been reported to the insurer.

Incurred claims (losses)
Losses arising during a period whether settled or not.

Incurred claims (loss) ratio
Percentage of incurred losses to earned premium.

Indemnity
1 A principle whereby the insurer seeks to place the insured in the same position after a loss as he occupied immediately before the loss (as far as possible). The principle does not apply to life assurance.
2 The cover given by an insurance policy or amount of claim paid to indemnify an insured.

Indirect business
1 Business accepted by way of reinsurance.
2 Insurance received by an insurer through a broker or agent entitled to commission.

Industrial business
Insurance written in relatively small amounts covering life, total and permanent disability, and accidental death benefits, the premiums on which are usually collected on a weekly or monthly basis by an agent of the insurance company.

Instalment premium
A premium that is expressed as annual but is met by a series of payments at more frequent intervals (*see also* **deferred premium**).

Institute clauses
Standard clauses used in the insurance of all main forms of marine hull and cargo and air cargo insurance written in London, and adopted by many underwriters outside the United Kingdom.

Institute of London Underwriters (ILU)
A bureau of insurers transacting marine, aviation and transport insurance in London.

Instructions for the annual solvency test of underwriting members of Lloyd's
A document issued annually by the Council of Lloyd's with the approval of the Department of Trade and Industry in respect of general business reserves. It gives instructions and guidance concerning the Lloyd's solvency test and is accompanied by a covering letter which amplifies and explains the instructions.

Insurable interest
For a contract of insurance to be valid the (potential) policyholder must have an interest in the insured item to the extent that its loss, death, damage or destruction would cause him loss. This is called insurable interest and must exist as follows:

Marine insurance	At the time of the loss
Life assurance	At the time the policy is taken out
Other insurances	At the time the policy is taken out and also at the time of the loss

Insurable value
The value of the insurable interest which the insured has in the insured occurrence or event. It is the amount to be paid out by the insurer (assuming full insurance) in the event of total loss or destruction of the item insured.

Insurance agent
A representative of an insurer, whether an employee or an independent contractor, who negotiates, effects and sometimes services contracts of insurance.

Insurance broker
One who advises persons on their insurance needs and negotiates insurances on their behalf with insurers, exercising professional care and skill in so doing (*see* **Lloyd's broker** and **Insurance Brokers (Registration) Act 1977**). A registered broker sometimes acts as an insurance agent.

Insurance Brokers (Registration) Act 1977
The Act provides for the setting up of an Insurance Brokers Registration Council to register individuals ('registered persons'), firms ('practising insurance brokers') and companies ('enrolled bodies corporate') who use the description 'insurance broker' or 'reinsurance broker', and to set professional standards for them.

Insurance broking account (IBA)
1   A bank account maintained with an approved bank by a practising insurance broker or an enrolled body corporate for the receipt and payment of insurance transactions monies. Each such account must be designated an 'insurance broking account'. The use of the insurance broking account is restricted by Rule 6 of the Insurance Brokers Registration Council (Accounts and Business Requirements) Rules 1979 and by the Lloyd's Brokers Byelaw.
2   *See* **solvency margin (2).**

Insurance certificate
A document evidencing the fact of insurance where it is convenient to have such evidence separate from the policy, for example:

(a)   for issue to a person covered under a group policy;
(b)   for shipments under a cargo open cover;
(c)   for users of motor vehicles to produce to show that they have the third party cover required by the Road Traffic Acts.

Insurance contract
A contract whereby one party, the insurer, in return for a consideration, the premium, undertakes to indemnify the other party, the insured, against loss upon the happening of a specified event that is contrary to the interest of the insured.

Insured
The person whose life or property is insured or in whose favour the policy is issued.

Insurer
An insurance company or Lloyd's underwriter who, in return for a consideration (a premium), agrees to make good in a manner laid down in the policy any loss or damage suffered by the person paying the premium as a result of some accident or occurrence.

Intermediary
An agent or broker through whom a transaction is arranged between parties.

Investment appreciation
See **capital appreciation**

Investment depreciation
See **capital appreciation**. A fall in value rather than an increase.

Investment income
Interest and dividends arising from the investing of premium monies pending claims being made.

Inwards reinsurance
Reinsurance business written, as opposed to ceded.

Jeweller's block policy
A policy covering a jeweller's stock and goods entrusted to him against all risks, with certain exceptions.

Judgement rating
Rating an insurance on a discretionary basis without dependence on a tariff or schedule of rates.

Keyman insurance
Insurance of a business against financial loss caused by the death or disablement of a person whose work has a material effect on the profitability of the concern.

Kidnap and ransom insurance
Insurance to provide reimbursement of ransom for a kidnapped person. A fundamental condition of the policy is that the existence of the policy must not be disclosed to any third party.

Knock-for-knock agreement
An agreement between motor insurers that in the event of an accident involving their respective policyholders neither party shall seek to recover the insured cost of repairing the damage caused to the vehicle it insured from the other insurer, whoever is to blame for the accident.

Known outstanding losses
Where claim notifications have been received for potential loss.

Lapse
The termination of a policy either:

(a) by failure to pay a premium due (if the policy has no cash value, cover is terminated; if the policy has a cash value, the protection may be continued in a modified form); or
(b) because the insurer does not invite renewal.

Lapse ratio
The proportion of policies lapsed or surrendered during the year to those in force at the beginning of the year.

Layer
Term used to denote a stratum of cover, e.g. for claims between £50,000 and £250,000.

Lead
See **leading underwriter.**

Leading underwriter (leader)
The underwriter who first accepts a share or line of an insurance. He will be involved in more detailed discussions with the brokers than the other underwriters.

Leading underwriters' agreement
An agreement whereby, when there are alterations to a risk that do not materially affect it, they may be accepted by leading underwriters only, whose acceptance will bind the others.

Letter of credit
A document authorising payment of an agreed sum to a named person at the risk of the issuer (normally a bank). If expressed as irrevocable, the authority cannot be withdrawn.

Liability insurance
Insurance in respect of liability to third parties, most commonly for accidents resulting in bodily injury and damage to property.

Life assurance policy
A contract between an assurer and a policyholder whereby the assurer, in return for an agreed premium, which may be a single payment or a series of regular payments, undertakes to pay a sum of money on the death, or in the case of endowment assurance, on the survival to a date specified in the contract, of the person assured who may, but need not, be the policyholder.

Life expectancy
The average number of years of life remaining for persons of a particular age, according to a particular mortality table.

Life fund
A pool of assets owned by a life company, out of which it meets claims under life assurance policies as and when they arise.

Limitation of liability
A statutory limitation to the amount of the liability of the owner or operator of a vehicle for claims against him, e.g. under the Carriage of Goods by Sea Act 1971.

Line
A share of an insurance or of reinsurance business. The proportion of an insurance accepted is termed a line. In reinsurance the original insurer's retention is termed a line. Thus a ten-line reinsurance treaty is one under which the insurer retains one line and can place ten lines with the various reinsurers.

Line slip
An arrangement entered into between underwriters and brokers whereby, for a given type of risk, the broker needs to approach only the leading and second underwriter, who will accept or reject each risk on behalf of all the underwriters concerned in their agreed proportions. This is an administrative convenience where a broker is placing a large number of similar risks with the same group of underwriters.

Line stamp
A stamp impressed by a Lloyd's underwriter on a slip and bearing his syndicate pseudonym and number.

LIRMA
A bureau providing policy signing and central accounting services for its members (insurance and reinsurance companies) in respect of non-marine business.

Lloyd's, Corporation of (Lloyd's of London)
A society incorporated under the Lloyd's Act 1871 which provides services and premises for the transaction of insurance business. It does not carry on insurance business and is not itself liable for insurance business transacted within its premises.

Lloyd's, Council of
See **Council of Lloyd's**.

Lloyd's Acts
Acts of 1871, 1911, 1925, 1951 and 1982 which regulate the constitution of Lloyd's.

Lloyd's agency system
An international network of persons appointed by Lloyd's to provide intelligence (mainly in relation to shipping) and to perform certain services for underwriters when so instructed by them.

Lloyd's agent
A person appointed by Lloyd's to provide intelligence, e.g. as to shipping movements, and, when so instructed by underwriters, to carry out surveys and adjust claims.

Lloyd's American Trust Fund
The fund in which the US dollars forming part of a Name's Premium Trust Fund are required to be held under the Lloyd's regulations. Funds are transferred to/from Lloyd's Central Accounting by direct debit on the settlement date.

Lloyd's associates (*or* associate members of Lloyd's)
Individuals, not being insurers, who are admitted to the Lloyd's Underwriting Room for business purposes, e.g. as accountants or solicitors.

Lloyd's audit
Not an audit in the true sense, but a solvency test of Lloyd's syndicates conducted by auditors approved by Lloyd's who report to the Council of Lloyd's on the solvency of each and every Name on the basis laid down in the instructions for the Annual Solvency Test of Underwriting Members of Lloyds. ('Solvent' Names are said to have passed the Lloyd's audit.)

Lloyd's broker
A firm or individual who is authorised to place insurance at Lloyd's and who in doing so represents the insured. Lloyd's brokers must be formally registered with Lloyd's, pass solvency tests and comply with Lloyd's

regulations. With limited exceptions, all business in and out of Lloyd's must pass through Lloyd's brokers.

Lloyd's Brokers Security and Trust Deed
IBA funds, including designated cash and investments and insurance debtors, of Lloyd's brokers are required to be kept under a separate trust deed for the benefit of insurance creditors.

Lloyd's Canadian Trust Fund
The fund in which the Canadian dollars forming part of a Name's Premium Trust Fund are required to be held under the Lloyd's regulations. Funds are transferred to/from Lloyd's Central Accounting by direct debit on the settlement date (*see also* **Lloyd's American Trust Fund**).

Lloyd's central accounting
A central accounting facility provided by the Corporation of Lloyd's enabling syndicates and brokers to receive or pay money centrally each week. Effectively this provides Lloyd's syndicates with a broker's ledger accounting service since all business signed each day is processed for the account of each syndicate and each broker.

Lloyd's central fund
A fund set up to meet any underwriting deficit of a Lloyd's member whose Lloyd's deposit, premium trust fund balance, reserves and personal assets prove inadequate to meet his liability to policyholders. All Lloyd's underwriters make annual contributions to this fund.

Lloyd's certificates
Insurance certificates issued by Lloyd's. They facilitate the payment of claims abroad.

Lloyd's claims office (LCO)
LCO provides to underwriters a quick and efficient service of advice of claims and agreement to settle. Where several syndicates are involved, the broker, instead of agreeing a claim with each of them, will show the claim to the leading underwriter and then present it to LCO, which will act on behalf of the remaining underwriters, keeping them informed of their individual liabilities.

Lloyd's deposit
A deposit of cash, approved securities, bank or insurance company guarantees or letters of credit made by an underwriter before he can become a member of Lloyd's. It is held in trust for policyholders by the Corporation of Lloyd's under a deposit trust deed which entitles the member, as beneficial owner, to receive the dividends or interest. The

amount of the deposit determines the level of premium income a member may write. Overseas members are required to deposit more than UK residents.

Lloyd's entrance fees
The sum payable on becoming a member of Lloyd's (not allowable as a deduction for UK income tax). See Lloyd's Manual for Members, Section A Appendix B.

Lloyd's minimum percentages
See **minimum percentage ratios**.

Lloyd's policy signing office
A central service provided by the Corporation of Lloyd's. Its main functions are to:

(a) validate and number transactions;
(b) sign policies on behalf of underwriters;
(c) take down entries and process syndicate reinsurances;
(d) produce daily tabulations of transactions;
(e) produce periodic settlement statements;
(f) provide special schemes (as required);
(g) provide statistics, manuals, circulars and advices; and
(h) operate LCA.

Lloyd's syndicate
A group of underwriting members of Lloyd's who are bound by the signature of an active underwriter on their behalf. When an insurance is accepted on behalf of the syndicate each member is liable for his stated fraction only of the insurance, not for the fractions of other members. His personal liability is unlimited, unless he is a corporate vehicle with limited liability.

Lloyd's Underwriters' Association (LUA)
LUA was formed in 1909 and officially acts for marine underwriters at Lloyd's in all technical matters relating to their business. It neither effects nor underwrites marine insurances. All Lloyd's marine underwriters are members.

Lloyd's US Dollar Trust Fund
US IBA funds of Lloyd's brokers required to be kept under a separate trust deed for the benefit of US dollar trade creditors. This has now been revoked and replaced by the **Lloyd's Brokers Security and Trust Deed**.

Load (*or* loading)
1 Charging a higher rate of premium than normal because of some adverse feature of an insurance.
2 The addition to known outstanding claims of Lloyd's and other long-tail business to allow for IBNR.
3 An addition to pure premium (the amount to pay losses without taking expenses into account) to allow for expenses, contingencies or profit desired.

London market excess
Excess loss reinsurance on business written entirely in the London market.

Long-tail claims
Claims notified or settled normally a long time after the expiry of a period of insurance.

Long-term business
Business in which the period covered by the policy is capable of exceeding the short term, e.g. life assurance or, in fire insurance, a contract that is expressed at the outset as being for a term of two or more years.

Loss
1 An event giving rise to a claim under an insurance.
2 A claim.
3 The disappearance of the subject matter of insurance through theft or some other cause, as opposed to its survival in a damaged state.

See also **actual total loss, constructive total loss, general average loss, particular average loss**.

Loss adjuster
An independent and highly trained claims expert who acts as a consultant to insurers in assessing the true extent and value of any loss which has resulted in a claim being made against them. Although paid a fee by the insurer, a member of the Chartered Institute of Loss Adjusters is required to act with the claimant's legitimate interests in mind.

Loss occurrence
1 An occurrence of a single loss.
2 An occurrence of several losses in the same incident, catastrophe or disaster.

Loss ratio
The proportion of claims paid or payable to premiums earned.

Loss reserve

1   Where it is agreed that the reassured shall retain a proportion of the net premiums for a given period to provide a fund to settle gross claims without recourse to the reinsurer. Sometimes called cash flow reserve.

2   A fund set aside to pay claims outstanding at the end of a period of account.

Losses occurring basis

A provision in a reinsurance treaty whereby the reinsurance applies to all losses occurring during the treaty period even if the risk attached before that period. The reinsurance does not apply to claims occurring after the reinsurance period even though the underlying insurance began to run during that period. Professional indemnity insurance is usually under-written on this basis, although 'claims occurring' are usually advised and accepted on a potential claim basis.

Managing agent

See **agent, Lloyd's underwriting**.

Margin of solvency

See **solvency margin**.

Marine insurance

The insurance of ships (including oil-rigs at sea) and their cargoes.

Marine Insurance Act 1906

An Act that codified the law relating to marine insurance.

Market agreement

An agreement subscribed to by all underwriters in a given section of the Lloyd's market.

Market association

An association of those engaged in some particular trading activity at Lloyd's, e.g. marine underwriters or underwriting agents.

Market capacity

The amount of insurance that can be absorbed by all the insurers in the relevant market.

Master policy

A single policy in respect of a number of persons or insurances. In some circumstances certificates of insurance or even separate policies may be issued to persons concerned with a portion of the cover.

Material fact
A fact that would influence the mind of a prudent insurer in deciding whether to accept a proposed insurance and, if so, on what terms.

Maturity
The time when payment of the sum assured under a life assurance policy becomes due. A life insurance policy matures on the death of the assured. An endowment policy matures upon the death of the assured or at the end of a specified period of time, if earlier.

Maximum possible loss
The largest loss thought possible under a given insurance.

Means test
An evaluation of the assets and/or income of a person for the purpose of determining his eligibility for underwriting membership of Lloyd's and the volume of premium income which he can write.

Member of Lloyd's
An individual elected to membership of the Corporation of Lloyd's either as an underwriting member (a 'Name') or, very rarely, as a non-underwriting member.

Members' agent
See **agent, Lloyd's underwriting.**

Members' solvency
The requirement for a Name to show that he can meet the financial requirements of Lloyd's based on a summary of his open and closed year results (*see also* **syndicate solvency).**

Member's syndicate premium limit
1   The limit prescribed by or on behalf of a member of a syndicate on the amount of insurance business allocatable to a year of account which is to be underwritten on his behalf through that syndicate (such limit being expressed as the maximum permissible amount of his member's syndicate premium income allocatable to that year of account); or
2   Where a limit lower than that referred to in (1) above is prescribed by or under the authority of the Council or the Committee, that lower limit.

Minimum and deposit premium
See **minimum premium.**

Minimum percentage ratios
The quantum of the reserve for the Lloyd's solvency test, based upon the application of percentages set out in the Instructions for the Annual Solvency Test of Underwriting Members of Lloyd's to a syndicate's net premium income for each year of account.

Minimum premium
Usually specified in conjunction with a deposit premium. The agreed minimum is customarily paid as a deposit in advance.

Minimum reserve
A nominal provision made where a claim has been notified to an insurer but insufficient details have been supplied to enable him to make a reasonable assessment of his liability thereon.

Mode
The frequency of premium payment (e.g. monthly, quarterly, half-yearly, annual).

Morbidity
The state of being mentally or physically impaired.

Morbidity table
A statistical table showing the incidence, by age, of a given sickness or accident in the population or in a selected group, based on the assumed morbidity which is being defined by the table. It is an instrument for measuring the probabilities associated with the given event and is one factor in computing premiums and reserves for policies providing cover for such events.

Mortality table
A statistical table showing the proportion of persons expected to die at each age, based on the assumed mortality which is being defined by the table, usually stated as so many deaths per thousand, as well as other mortality functions such as the rate of mortality and the expectation of life. It is the instrument for measuring probabilities of life and death. It is used as one factor in determining the amount of premium required at each age at issue of a policy.

Multiple line insurer
An insurer who writes a number of classes of insurance (USA).

Mutual insurance
Insurance undertaken by a group of persons for their own benefit, without risk capital being provided by outside sources.

Mutual insurance company

A company conducting mutual insurance. In non-life insurance, business may be confined to insuring the risks of persons in the group who formed it (e.g. a trade association), who may have subscribed capital. In life assurance the policyholders (especially holders of with-profits policies) commonly become members of the company on effecting a policy. A mutual life assurance company has no risk capital.

Names (members of Lloyd's)

The persons of proven means carrying ultimate financial responsibility for the underwriting operations of Lloyd's. Names join together in syndicates, on whose behalf underwriters, through underwriting agencies, write business. A Name is responsible only for his share of liabilities.

Neill Report

The report of the Committee of Inquiry, chaired by Sir Patrick Neill, into the regulatory arrangements at Lloyd's. The report, published in January 1987, made 70 recommendations as to how the regulatory arrangements at Lloyd's should provide protection for Names comparable to that proposed for investors under the Financial Services Act 1986.

Net absolute(ly)

1 Term used in marine insurance to emphasise that all discounts, without exception, have been taken off (the word 'absolutely' is added to the word 'net' when referring to premiums net of discounts). The expression is frequently used in connection with premium returned to the assured, where it is understood that the broker shall retain his brokerage when making the return of premium.
2 Term used in facultative aviation reinsurance when no reinsurance commission is allowable.

Net earned premiums

The premiums received or due to an insurer less the cost of reinsurance and after adjustment to allow for the cost of any unexpired risk.

Net eligible means

See **means test**.

Net line

The amount of liability under a line of insurance that is retained by an insurer after cession by way of reinsurance.

Net loss

A loss after deduction of recoveries, salvage and reinsurance.

Net premium
1 In marine insurance, the premium after all discounts have been taken off; alternatively, the premium following the deduction of a return of premium. The latter, if before deduction of discounts, may be called the 'gross net premium' (*see also* **net absolutely**).
2 In life assurance valuation, a hypothetical premium calculated as sufficient to secure the guaranteed benefits on the valuation bases of mortality and interest, but without allowance for commission, expenses or bonus.
3 In Lloyd's syndicate accounting, premiums net of brokerage, agents' costs or ceding commission, return premiums and reinsurances.
4 In brokers, the amount due to underwriters after declaration of brokerage.

Net retained line
The amount an insurer retains for his own account after having arranged all reinsurances.

Net written premiums
The premiums received or due to an insurer less the cost of reinsurance but without allowance being made for the cost of any unexpired risk.

No claims bonus
The reduction allowed in a renewal premium in recognition of no claims having been paid by the insurer during the recent past period of insurance.

Non-admitted company
An insurance company not admitted to do business in a state (USA).

Non-marine
General business other than marine, aviation and transport business. (Motor business is also usually considered as falling outside the non-marine class.)

Non-proportional reinsurance
Reinsurance such as excess of loss reinsurance where the reinsurer's liability is not calculated as a proportion of the insurer's.

Noting limits
1 The amounts above which it is agreed that an estimated claim will be notified to and/or recorded by the underwriter by brokers or by agencies such as ILU and LCO.
2 The amount, to be determined by the underwriter, above which each transaction shall be separately identified in a syndicate's accounting

records in the manner prescribed by Lloyd's Byelaw No. 11 of 1987.

Obligatory treaty

A treaty where a reassured is obliged to cede and a reinsurer is obliged to accept.

Off risk

An insurer is said to be off risk when an insurance has been terminated.

Open cover

1 Reinsurance where the reinsurer agrees to accept obligatorily a share of any business of a specified kind that is offered.
2 A contract for cargo insurance to cover all shipments from time to time as declared, a policy being issued in respect of each. The arrangement is subject to cancellation on notice by either party.

Open market

Used to refer to a risk that is individually placed in the market, as opposed to one that is covered under a binding authority, line slip or treaty.

Open policy

A marine insurance policy which covers such risks as may be declared during the currency of the policy with no aggregate limit of cover.

Open slip

A form of slip used to cover a merchant contractor with a large contract to fulfil by several shipments, the total value of which is known in advance. Each shipment is declared and policies issued until the insured value is exhausted.

Open year

A year of account or insurance in respect of which the financial outcome remains to be determined. Particularly at Lloyd's, any year which has not been closed by **reinsurance to close**.

Original gross premium

The premium charged by the reassured to the original assured before any discounts have been taken into account. The reinsurer usually requires to know the original gross premium to ensure that he is not backing the liability of a reassured who is retaining high commissions and thus encouraging bad underwriting.

Original gross premium income
Referred to in long-term reinsurance contracts such as treaties. When the contract is being placed, the reinsurer will wish to know the gross and net premium income over the preceding years in order that he may compare the claims ratio and assess the desirability of the reinsurance. The original gross premium income is the total premium charged to the original assured by the reassured, excluding all discounts over a period of time.

Original gross rate
In reinsurance, the original rate of premium (as a percentage) charged to the assured by the reassured before any deductions or discounts.

Original net premium income
A reinsurance treaty term indicating the net premium income over a period of time to the reassured.

Original net rate
In reinsurance, the original gross rate charged to the original assured by the reassured less the original deductions, that is, the net rate of premium received by the reassured.

Outstanding claims/losses
The total of losses or claims which have been advised but which at a given time are still outstanding and, as such, are only estimated amounts.

Outstanding claims advance
A payment made by underwriters under a reinsurance contract or treaty whereby an advance payment is made in respect of outstanding claims that will come into account in a subsequent periodic settlement when the actual claim amount has been determined.

Outstanding claims portfolio
An amount payable by a cedant to a reinsurer in consideration of the reinsurer accepting liability arising under a contract of reinsurance in respect of reinsurance claims incurred and arising prior to a fixed date.

Outstanding claims reserve
A reserve held by an insurer to meet claims notified but not yet paid (*see also* **outstanding claims advance**).

Outwards reinsurance
Business ceded by an insurer by way of reinsurance to other insurers or reinsurers.

Overrider
Same as **overriding commission**.

Overriding commission
A discount allowed to an agent or ceding insurer in addition to normal commission. In reinsurance it is commonly by way of contribution to the direct insurer's overheads. In direct insurance it may be payable to an employee or agent in respect of insurances written within his territory, even without his mediation.

Overseas deposits
Deposits required under local legislation to be made by insurers in overseas countries for the security of policyholders in those countries.

Paid losses or claims
The total of claims or losses which have been settled during a given period.

Participating assurance policy
An assurance policy where the policyholder is entitled to share in the insurer's earnings by dividends or bonus, which reflect the difference between the premium charged and the actual experience.

Peril
Classification of possible causes of loss insured against, such as fire, windstorm, collision, hail, bodily injury, property damage and loss of profits.

Period of risk
The period during which the insurer can incur liability under the terms of the policy.

Personal accounts
A statement prepared for each underwriting member participating in a Lloyd's syndicate, showing *inter alia* how that member's net result was determined.

Personal Reserve
A reserve of cash or investments held on behalf of a Name by his Lloyd's underwriting agent to provide funds to meet future losses. Normally this reserve is built up by the agent, in accordance with the underwriting agency agreement, setting aside a proportion of a Name's past profits, but a Name may put up funds direct from other sources. A Personal Reserve is in addition to amounts set aside in any Special Reserve Fund which the Name may have.

Placing
1 Effecting an insurance.
2 An insurance which has been effected.

Policy
A document detailing the terms and conditions applicable to an insurance contract and constituting evidence of that contract. It is issued by an underwriter for the first period of risk. On renewal, a new policy may not be issued, but the same conditions would apply and the current wording would be evidenced by the renewal receipt. A change of conditions is evidenced by an endorsement.

Policy loan
A loan made by a life assurance company to a policyholder on the security of the cash surrender of his policy.

Policy proof of interest
A policy under which insurers agree to pay a claim without requiring the insured to prove that he has an insurable interest. By s4(2) of the Marine Insurance Act 1906 such a policy is deemed to be a gaming or wagering contract and is therefore unenforceable in a court (*see* **tonner**).

Policy year
1 The calendar year in which a policy becomes effective.
2 The year that a policy runs, commencing with the inception or renewal date.

Pool
A pool is created when several insurers agree to share all insurances of a defined nature in specified proportions.

Pooling
Practice of sharing all business of an affiliated group of insurance companies among the members of the group. All premiums written by the subsidiary companies are customarily ceded to or reinsured by the parent company; then, after provision for any required outside reinsurance, the total premiums are in turn ceded back to the subsidiaries in agreed ratios. Claims, loss expenses, commissions and other underwriting and operating expenses (excluding investment expenses) are similarly treated, with the net result that each of the members of the affiliated group will share in the total business of the group (but usually in varying percentages) and all will achieve similar underwriting results.

Portfolio
1   The totality of the business of an insurer or reinsurer.
2   A segment of the business of an insurer or a reinsurer, e.g. fire
    insurance business is called his fire portfolio.

Portfolio consideration
The premium payable for the reinsurance of a portfolio of insurance or
reinsurance business, to which may be added an extra payment to cover
losses already outstanding or other charges.

Portfolio entry
At the outset of a reinsurance treaty a definition is necessary of the
insurances to be included, namely whether the treaty applies to business
in force at its inception or only to subsequent insurances and renewals.

Portfolio mix
The constituents of an insurer's portfolio of insurance or reinsurance.

Portfolio premium
The premium payable for the reinsurance of a portfolio of insurance or
reinsurance business.

Portfolio reinsurance
The cession by way of reinsurance of a portfolio.

Portfolio return
The procedure when a reinsurance treaty is terminated and the reinsurer returns the proportion of premium relating to insurances in force
and has no liability for claims thereunder.

Portfolio run-off
The procedure when a reinsurance treaty is terminated but continues to
apply to premiums and further losses in respect of insurances in course.

Portfolio transfer
1   The transfer of the portfolio of one direct insurer to another.
2   A term used in treaty reinsurance. The reinsurer undertakes to
    accept the whole portfolio of an existing reinsurance from a speci-
    fied date. He accepts not only the premiums due on risks attaching
    from that date but also the losses payable after that date in respect of
    premiums paid to the previous reinsurer. He is, of course, also
    entitled to recoveries paid after the inception date of the treaty
    even though these may be in respect of claims paid by the previous
    reinsurer, but is equally liable for returns of premium payable after

the treaty inception date even though the premium was originally paid to the previous reinsurer.

3 The term can also be used in connection with long-term premiums when a risk spans more than one period of account and part of the premium is carried forward to subsequent years of account.

Pre-debit
The debiting of a renewal premium at a rate of premium not yet agreed by the agent or the insured.

Premium
The consideration payable by the insured for a contract of insurance.

Premium advice note
A note sent to an insurer or a policy signing office by an insurance broker when the broker's client is debited with the premium or credited with a return premium.

Premium income
The income of an insurer from premium.

Premium income limit
The maximum amount of premiums that may be accepted on behalf of an underwriting member of Lloyd's. The limit is governed by the underwriter's means and the amount of the premium deposit he has made (*see also* **member's syndicate premium limit** and **gross premium underwriting limit**).

Premium reserve
A sum deposited by a reinsurer with the reassured to cover business in force at a given moment.

Premium transfer
Method used at Lloyd's where a risk is insured for more than 12 months. The premium for a period in excess of 12 months is paid over as an internal transaction by the original syndicate to its successor syndicate as reconstituted for the ensuing year.

Premiums trust fund
The trust fund into which all premium monies received by a Lloyd's underwriter must be placed in accordance with s83 of the Insurance Companies Act 1982. The fund is available for the payment of claims and syndicate expenses and, when an account has been closed, for the payment to the Name of his profit.

Professional indemnity insurance
The insurance of professional people against claims by clients or third
parties for damages for error and negligence.

Products liability insurance
Insurance against the liability of a producer, supplier, tester or servicer of
goods for injury to third parties or loss of or damage to their property
caused by a deficiency in the goods.

Profit commission
A commission based on profit (as defined in an agreement). Two specific
cases are:

(a) the commission received by a Lloyd's underwriting agent as part of
his remuneration from the Names; and
(b) the commission received by a cedant where business ceded to a
particular reinsurer has been profitable.

Proof of loss
A sworn statement furnished by the insured to the insurer setting forth
the amount of claim. This form, which is usually used in the settlement
of first-party claims, includes the date and description of the occurrence,
amount of claim and interested insurers. In law, the way of proving a loss
has occurred and that it was caused by an insured peril rests with the
insured.

Proportional reinsurance
Reinsurance of a part of an original insurance, premiums and losses
being shared proportionately between reinsurer and insurer.

Proposal
Request for insurance submitted to the insurer by or on behalf of the
insured, often on a printed proposal form. The proposal usually includes
sufficient facts for the insurer to determine whether or not he wishes to
accept the risk.

Pro rata reinsurance
Same as **proportional reinsurance**.

Pro Rata Temporis
In proportion to time.

Protection
1 Measure taken to guard against loss.
2 The financial safeguard given by the existence of insurance.

Protection and indemnity risks (P & I)
Certain risks have in the past not always been readily insurable in the
marine insurance market, and shipowners have formed mutual associations (clubs) to cover them. Protection risks include quarantine expenses,
liabilities to crews and, for collision and impact damage, wreck removal
expenses, liability under towage contracts, and liability for damage to
other vessels apart from collision. Indemnity risks include shipowners'
liability for cargo lost or damaged, and fines for inadvertent immigration
or customs offences.

Public liability
Same as **third party liability**.

Pure burning cost
Same as **burning cost**.

Pure year figures
Figures (of premiums, claims and so on) which relate only to business
written in a particular underwriting year. Figures relating to any element
of earlier years reinsured into that year are excluded.

Quasi-managing agent
At Lloyd's, a members' agent who has placed Names on a syndicate
managed by a managing agent but retains for that syndicate the rights
and duties regarding the investment of the premiums trust funds of such
Names.

Quota share reinsurance
A form of pro rata reinsurance. Treaty reinsurance providing that the
reinsurer shall accept a certain percentage of all, or certain classes of, or
parts of the business of the reinsured.

'R' account
A Lloyd's brokers' Canadian dollar account with Royal Bank of Canada
in London designated **Lloyd's Canadian Trust Fund**.

Rate
The charge for insurance for each unit that is used as a basis for the
calculation of premiums, e.g. per £100 of the value of property or per
capita.

Rebate
A reduction or discount.

353

Reciprocity
The exchange of reinsurances between two reinsurers.

Recovery
Money received by an insurer in respect of a loss, thus reducing the loss, by way of subrogation, salvage or reinsurance.

Registered person(s)
Individuals approved under the IBRA. Only such individuals may call themselves insurance brokers.

Reinstatement
1 A non-marine practice, whereby the amount of cover which has been reduced as a result of a claim is reinstated in the policy on payment of an additional premium, thus reverting the cover to the original sum insured.

This practice is generally unnecessary in the marine market because:
(a) cargo is seldom insured on a time basis and any loss is calculated at expiry of the policy; and
(b) repairs are carried out on hulls, thus reinstating the actual value of the vessel to its sound value.

Reinstatement is therefore automatic in the marine market and no additional premium is charged, with the exception of excess loss reinsurance, where it is common to apply the principle of reinstatement of losses by payment of an additional premium. Hull policies, nevertheless, always contain a clause providing that no claim is recoverable in respect of unrepaired damage if the vessel becomes a total loss before expiry of the policy.
2 Making good. Where insured property is lost or damaged, a policy may give the insurer the option to replace it or make it good rather than pay the loss in money.

Reinstatement clause
1 A clause in a fire insurance policy setting out the liability of the insurer if he elects or is legally obliged to reinstate the insured property in the event of a loss.
2 A clause in a reinsurance treaty that provides for a premium to be payable to replenish the sum insured after a loss.

Reinsurance
Insurance protection taken out by an insurer to limit its exposure to losses on original business accepted. The reinsured may be referred to as the original or primary insurer or the ceding party.

354

Reinsurance assumed premiums

All premiums (less return premiums) arising from policies issued to assume the liability, in whole or in part, of another insurance company which is already covering the risk with a policy.

Reinsurance broker

A professional intermediary between insurers wishing to place reinsurance and those willing to accept it.

Reinsurance ceded premiums

All premiums (less return premiums) arising from policies or coverage purchased from another insurer for the purpose of transferring the liability, in whole or in part, assumed from direct or reinsurance assumed policies.

Reinsurance to close

In syndicates, an agreement under which underwriting members (the reinsured members) who are members of a syndicate for a year of account (the closed year) agree with underwriting members who comprise that or another syndicate for a later year of account (the reinsuring members) that the reinsuring members will indemnify the reinsured members against all known and unknown liabilities of the reinsured members arising out of insurance business under-written through that syndicate and allocated to the closed year, in consideration of:

(a)   a premium; and
(b)   the assignment to the reinsuring members of all rights of the rein-sured members arising out of or in connection with that insurance business (including without limitation the right to receive all future premiums, recoveries and other monies receivable in connection with that insurance business).

Reinsurance treaty

Reinsurance of a block of business or whole account in accordance with the terms of a contract between cedant and reinsurer.

Renewal

The continuation of an existing contract of insurance for a further period.

Reserve

A fund set aside out of assets for general or specific purposes after provisions have been made.

Reserve basis
The particular set of assumptions as to interest and mortality or morbidity on which reserves are calculated.

Reserve premium
That proportion of a premium, payable under a contract of reinsurance, which is retained by the ceding insurer under the terms of the policy to help finance the reinsurer's share of the cost of settling claims.

Respondentia
The making of the cargo on board a ship security for the repayment of a loan.

Restricted premium
A transaction in respect of a convertible currency amount payable in US dollars (and to a lesser extent sterling) taken down by LPSO at a notional amount before the actual rate of exchange is known. Restricted premiums are not included in LCA for settlement.

Retained premium
See **reserve premium**.

Retention
1 The net amount of any risk which an insurer does not reinsure but keeps for his own account.
2 The amount of premium retained by an insurer after paying claims and expenses, i.e. profit (USA).

Retroactive (*or* **Retrospective**)
With effect from an earlier date; looking backward.

Retrocedant (*or* **Retrocessionaire**)
A reinsurer who reinsures some of the risks he has agreed to bear.

Retrocession
Reinsurance of indirect business.

Return commission
The commission returnable by an agent to an insurer on the cancellation of an insurance.

Return premium
A premium refund due to the insured, arising from an endorsement or cancellation.

Revenue year
The accounting year during which business is booked, as reflected in the annual accounts.

Riesco
In syndicates, a basis of allocating calendar year investment income and capital appreciation to two or more years of account.

Risk
Used in insurance in many senses, notably:
1 The subject matter of insurance.
2 Uncertainty as to the outcome of an event.
3 Probability of loss.
4 The hazard or peril insured against.
5 Danger.

Risk excess
Any excess of loss reinsurance where the contract is expressed 'excess of each and every loss, each and every risk' (note that risk is an individual exposure).

Rollover policy
A type of reinsurance policy which used to be effected by Lloyd's syndicates prior to 1984 in the form of a whole account stop loss policy, whereby in the event of a claim not being made by a particular year of account the whole, or substantially the whole, of the available cover is 'rolled forward' to be available under a subsequent policy.

Room, the
The room at Lloyd's in which underwriters sit at their boxes to do business.

Run-off account
A year of account of a Lloyd's syndicate which has been left open after the date at which that account would normally have been closed by reinsurance.

Run-off liability
Liability that remains to be met after insurance has terminated.

Run-off statement (of claims)
A statement comparing the provisions for outstanding claims at any particular date with the total of the payments on such claims from the initial date to the accounting date plus the estimated provisions for claims still unpaid at the accounting date.

Run-off statistics
An analysis by calendar year of claims paid per underwriting year on a pure basis.

Salvage
1 Amount received by an insurer from the sale of property (usually damaged) on which he has paid a total loss to the insured. For example, when an insurer has paid the insured the actual cash value of a car damaged (usually extensively by collision), the insurer takes title to and sells the damaged vehicle for his own account. Salvage is applied by insurance companies to reduce the amount of claim paid.
2 Remuneration payable independently of contract to an outside party who takes part in a successful rescue operation to save life or property at sea.

Salvage guarantee
An agreement whereby a guarantor agrees to make good a salvage award if the party responsible fails to pay it to the salvor. The salvor (termed 'Contractor' in the form) will discharge the maritime lien which he is entitled to attach to the salved property, in exchange for such an agreement subscribed by an acceptable guarantor or guarantors. Lloyd's may issue such an agreement for use in conjunction with Lloyd's Standard Form of Salvage Agreement. Payment in relation to the Lloyd's form is guaranteed by the Corporation of Lloyd's, who require to hold a policy written by acceptable insurers or an indemnity subscribed by syndicates at Lloyd's whereby they will be reimbursed if they have to make good any sum under the guarantee.

Schedule
The part of a policy containing information peculiar to that particular risk. The greater part of a policy is likely to be identical for all risks within a class of business covered by the same insurer.

Self-insurance
When an organisation bears some or all of a risk itself.

Settlement
1 The payment of an account or claim.
2 An agreement to resolve a difference of opinion.
3 An instrument by which property is settled on a person or persons.
4 A lateral movement, as opposed to **subsidence**.

Settlement date
The date specified in a market for the periodical settlement of accounts by brokers.

Settlement sheets
1 Statistical records showing separate cumulative totals of net premiums and claims for any one year of account. Where computer systems are used, the term is not usually relevant.
2 Lloyd's Central Accounting statements, produced weekly, are often referred to as Settlement Sheets (*see also* **special settlements**).

S.G. policy
Ship & Goods policy

Short closing
The act of a broker, when closing a line, in allotting to an underwriter less than the line he has written, either because more than 100 per cent of the insurance has been subscribed, or because the insurance is for a smaller amount than was expected at the outset. Short closing, unlike overclosing, is permissible.

Short rate
The rate of premium on a time policy is agreed, as a rule, on an annual basis. A short premium rate, pro rata of the annual premium rate, is the rate charged for a period of less than 12 months.

Short-tail
Business on which claims are known and settled quickly.

Signed line
The proportion of a risk to which an insurer is liable following any signing down of written lines (*see also* **full signed line** and **closed line**).

Signed risks
A Lloyd's term for risks signed by their central office, signing often taking place after the date business is accepted.

Signing down
The pro rata reduction of written lines applied where a slip has been more than 100 per cent subscribed (*see also* **closed line**).

Signing slip/(off slip)/signed slip
A slip copied by a broker from an original slip, and containing underwriters' lines and references. The copy is initialled by the leading underwriter and is used by the policy signing office.

Single premium
A lump sum consideration received by a life company in accordance with an assurance or annuity contract.

Slip

A document submitted by a broker to underwriters and containing particulars of a risk proposed for insurance. The underwriter signifies his acceptance by initialling the slip and indicating on it the share of the insurance he will take. The share may ultimately be scaled down by the broker, but it cannot be increased without the insurer's agreement.

Small claims pool

A pool of funds contributed to by all Lloyd's syndicates, out of which all small claims (amounting to less than £2 per syndicate) are paid.

Solvency margin

1 The extent to which the realisable assets of an insurance company, syndicate or an individual member of Lloyd's exceed its liabilities.
2 Brokers are required to be 'solvent' at three levels: 'IBA' accounts, net current assets, and overall. IBA solvency means the broker has an excess of IBA designated assets, including bank accounts, over net insurance creditors. Net current assets are carefully defined and the broker must monitor an excess of assets over liabilities (both including the IBA accounts). Overall the broker must maintain a minimum specified margin of net tangible assets. The broker's auditors must report on the solvency each year, both on the year-end position and on an 'any day' basis. Lloyd's brokers have more stringent rules.

Solvency test/audit

An audit of syndicate affairs involving verifications and tests partly based on mathematical formulae, culminating in a test of each Name's solvency as laid down in the Instructions for the Annual Solvency Test of Underwriting Members of Lloyds.

Special Reserve Fund

A fund that an underwriting member of Lloyd's is permitted under the Taxes Act to accumulate out of his underwriting income to provide against future losses. The fund is subject to favourable tax treatment.

Special settlement

A transaction through Lloyd's Central Accounting where quick settlement is required by brokers or underwriters, with the result that the normal credit terms have to be bypassed.

Stamp

The official annual list of members of a syndicate (Lloyd's Syndicate Constitution) showing each member's share by members' agents and bearing the signature of the leading active underwriter, and the total number of shares for a given year of account. It must be registered at Lloyd's.

Standard slip
A standardised form of broker's slip used by brokers for placing business with Lloyd's or with insurance companies.

Stop loss reinsurance
A form of reinsurance under which the reinsurer pays the cedant's losses in any year to the extent that they exceed a specified loss ratio or amount, subject as a rule to some specified limit. This reinsurance can be taken out by a company, syndicate or individual member of Lloyd's.

Sub-agency agreement
In Lloyd's, the agreement entered into between a members' agent and a managing agent when the former places Names on a syndicate managed by the latter.

Subrogation
In contracts of indemnity, the right of an insurer to stand in the place of the insured and exercise all the rights of and remedies available to the insured, whether already enforced or not.

Subsidence
Damage to buildings by subsidence is a peril covered by modern house-owners' policies. Subsidence is strictly a vertical downward movement, but has been held to include settlement (a lateral movement).

Sub-standard
Insurances that have some unfavourable feature making them unaccep-table on standard terms. An extra premium is charged for the extra risk, thus making the total premium higher than on standard insurance.

Sum insured *or* **assured**
The limit of liability of the insurer under a contract of indemnity, or the amount payable on the occurrence of an event insured against under a benefit policy.

Surplus line
1 The amount of reinsurance required after the maximum line has been declared on a reinsurance treaty or cover.
2 A risk which a broker is unable to place with insurers in his own state and for which he must therefore seek cover outside the state (USA).

361

Surplus reinsurance
Reinsurance of amounts over a specified amount of insurance, premiums and losses being shared proportionately between insurer and reinsurer.

Surplus treaty reinsurance
A proportional treaty under which an insurer cedes, in respect of each risk covered by the treaty, the amount surplus to the specified retention. Ceding companies very frequently have several layers of surplus treaties so that they may accommodate very large risks, as usually the reinsurer's participation in any one surplus treaty is limited to a certain multiple of the ceding company's retention. Premiums and claims are shared by the reinsurer and the ceding company on a pro rata basis in proportion to the amount of the risk insured or reinsured by each. This is one of the oldest forms of treaty reinsurance and is still in common use in fire reinsurance.

Surrender
Cancellation of a long-term policy before it reaches maturity, usually involving the payment by the insurer of a surrender value. The surrender value will amount to the total premiums paid under the policy less an allowance for expenses and the cost of providing cover up to the date of cancellation. Depending on the length of time the policy has been in force there may be some allowance for interest earned by the premiums.

Syndicate
A grouping of Lloyd's underwriters. Each syndicate has an active underwriter who is authorised to accept business on behalf of each underwriting member participating therein. A member of a syndicate is still a principal in his own right and is personally liable for his agreed share of each risk that is accepted by the syndicate. He is not liable for the debts of other syndicate members and thus the liability is several but not joint.

Syndicate allocated capacity
In relation to a Lloyd's syndicate, the aggregate of the member's syndicate premium limits of all the members for the time being of the syndicate.

Syndicate list
A list of the syndicates subscribing a Lloyd's policy, showing each syndicate's signed lines, pseudonym, syndicate number and reference.

Syndicate sheet
A large sheet showing the composition of each syndicate at Lloyd's.

Syndicate stamp (*or* Constitution)
See stamp

Syndicate solvency
The asset positions of a syndicate, after providing for:

(a) estimated future liabilities; and
(b) disallowed assets, at the gross level.

Taking down
In Lloyd's, the presentation by a broker of details of an insurance transaction to LPSO for recording and processing.

Tariff company
An insurance company that is a member of an association, such as the Fire Offices' Committee, for an insurance of a particular class.

Technical profit
Profit on underwriting calculated without allowance for expenses or investment earnings.

Technical reserves
The reserves that an insurer must hold to enable him to discharge his eventual liabilities on the insurance he has written.

Term
1 A period of insurance.
2 The time for which anything lasts.
3 A word used in an understood or defined sense.
4 A condition or stipulation in a contract.

Term assurance
Assurance providing for a death benefit only if the assured dies within the period of time specified in the contract. Coverage is for level or reducing amounts for stated periods, such as one year, ten years, or to a stated age. It provides life assurance protection for a temporary period of time and is therefore the least expensive. There are generally no loan or cash values. A term policy may be convertible (i.e. it may grant the privilege of exchange without medical examination for permanent assurance on the whole life or endowment plan). It may also be automatically renewable.

Third party
A person claiming against an insured. In insurance terminology, the first party is the insurer and the second party is the insured.

Third party liability
The indemnity against all sums which an insured shall become legally liable to pay to third parties on injury, loss or damage that is accidentally caused.

Three-year accounting
A system of insurance accounting under which profits (or losses) for a given year are not determined until the end of three years.

Time and distance policy
An unofficial term for a type of reinsurance policy entered into by an underwriter to provide cover for a loss that would be payable at some time in the future, whereby the cover is provided substantially by the premium paid plus interest thereon, thus maximising the interest earnings on the premium. This type of policy has no legal definition but is likely to have one or more of the following characteristics:

(a) the premium is substantial compared with the cover;
(b) the reinsurer is offshore, usually in a tax haven, and is usually a company specialising in these policies;
(c) there is only one reinsurer on the contract;
(d) the reinsurer has no risk, or very little risk, as his liability is restricted to the premium receivable plus interest thereon;
(e) the cover is secured by letter of credit; and
(f) claim payments are due on particular dates, irrespective of the dates of losses of the insured; alternatively, in the event of losses occurring to the insured in excess of a certain figure or in advance of a certain date, an additional premium is payable under the time and distance policy.

Time on risk
A period, during which insurance has applied, used for the calculation of premium when for some reason the insurance has been discontinued.

Title insurance
Insurance in respect of loss arising from a defect in title to real property.

Tonner policy
Originally a form of total loss only reinsurance of vessels over or between specified tonnages, it can be any form of policy where the policyholder has no direct insurable interest. Tonner policies are normally effected on a policy proof of interest basis and without benefit of salvage to the insurer, and may not be a legally enforceable form of insurance contract. In June 1981 the Committee of Lloyd's introduced rules prohibiting Lloyd's underwriters from placing or accepting tonner policies, which it regarded as purely gambling policies with no legitimate commercial interest.

Total loss
1   A loss of the subject matter of insurance such that it is totally lost, destroyed or damaged beyond economic repair.
2   A loss that gives rise to payment of the full sum insured.

Total loss of part
A marine cargo policy may provide that a loss of a whole package in loading or discharge, or the loss of a whole craft load, shall be treated as a total loss of that part of the cargo and hence will not be subject to a franchise (*see* **franchise**).

Total loss only (TLO)
A term used in marine hull insurance and reinsurance limiting cover to payment for a total loss. A clause is likely to define whether the cover is to include arranged or constructive total losses and whether legal and labour charges and salvage charges are recoverable.

Transfer of portfolio
The substitution of a new insurer for the original one in respect of all insurance business of a particular class.

Treaty
See **reinsurance treaty.**

Tribunal
In Lloyd's, a body operated by the Lloyd's association for the purpose of vetting potential holders of binding authorities in certain countries outside the United Kingdom.

Trust corporation
Defined by s68 of the Trustee Act 1925 as the Public Trustee, the Treasury Solicitor, the Official Solicitor, other officials prescribed by the Lord Chancellor, or a corporation either appointed by the court in any particular case to be a trustee, or entitled by rules made under s4(3) of the Public Trustee Act 1906 to act as custodian trustee.

Trustee security
A security in which trustees are empowered by the Trustee Investment Act 1961 to invest trust funds with no restrictions, unless the trust deed otherwise directs.

Twenty-fourths method
A basis used for calculation of unearned premiums involving the assumption that the average date of issue of all policies written during a month is the middle of that month.

US Dollar Trust Fund
See **Lloyd's US Dollar Trust Fund**.

Uberrimae fidei/uberrima fides
'Utmost good faith'. Insurance contracts are one of a limited class that requires the parties (insurer and insured) to exercise the utmost good faith in their dealings with each other. Specifically, the proposer of an insurance must disclose all material facts. The contract is voidable if this is not complied with.

Ultimate net loss
A ceding insurer's loss calculated for the purpose of a claim under an excess of loss reinsurance. It is usually defined as the sum paid by the ceding insurer in settlement of the loss, less deductions for recoveries, salvage and claims on other reinsurances, and including adjustment expenses but not the ceding insurer's office expenses and employees' salaries.

Umbrella arrangement
An arrangement between a Lloyd's broker and a non-Lloyd's broker whereby the Lloyd's broker permits the non-Lloyd's broker to use the name, LPSO number and pseudonym of the Lloyd's broker for the purpose of placing insurance business with or on behalf of underwriting members. It is different from the Direct Dealing arrangement under which non-Lloyd's brokers are enabled to place motor insurance directly with motor syndicates.

Umbrella cover
1 Cover providing excess limits over the normal limits of liability policies and giving additional excess for perils not insured by the primary liability policies.
2 In reinsurance, cover against an accumulation of losses under one or more classes of insurance arising out of a single event.

Underinsurance
Insurance that is not adequate in terms of the sum insured to provide for full payment of a loss.

Underwriters
1 Insurers (e.g. companies, Lloyd's syndicates or Names).
2 Those individuals performing the underwriting for a company, or underwriting agency (the Active Underwriters).
3 A person soliciting business on behalf of an insurer (USA).

Underwriting
The acceptance of insurance business by an underwriter.

Underwriting account
A revenue statement, included as part of a Lloyd's syndicate annual report, setting out cumulative transactions in respect of a year of account.

Underwriting agent
1   A person authorised to accept insurance on behalf of an insurance company as its agent.
2   An agent appointed by a Name under the terms of an underwriting agency agreement to manage his underwriting affairs at Lloyd's on his behalf. There is a distinction between a managing agent (who manages one or more syndicates) and a members' agent (who acts for his Names in other capacities and may place them on syndicates run by a managing agent), although many have complied with the requirements of the Council of Lloyd's for conducting an underwriting agency at Lloyd's (*see* **agent, Lloyd's underwriting**).

Underwriting agency agreement
A contract between a Lloyd's underwriter and an underwriting agent which lays down the duties, powers and remuneration of the agent.

Underwriting profit
The profit derived from the transaction of insurance or reinsurance exclusive of interest or capital gains on investments.

Underwriting year
The calendar year to which business is allocated for the purpose of monitoring underwriting statistics.

Unearned premium
The proportion of a premium which relates to the portion of a risk which has not yet expired.

Unearned premium insurance
Insurance added to an aviation hull policy to provide for a return of part of the premium if the policy terminates prematurely on the occurrence of a total loss.

Unearned premium reserve
The fund set aside as at the end of the financial year by a non-life insurer out of premiums in respect of risks to be borne by the company after the

end of that year under contracts of insurance entered into before the end of that year.

Unexpired risks reserve
The amount set aside as at the end of a financial period in addition to unearned premium in respect of risks to be borne by the company after the end of that year under contracts of insurance entered into before the end of that year, in order to provide for additional costs of claims. This may be necessary because certain business is expected to be loss making or, for example, to cover claims whenever they may arise in the future under contingency insurances paid for by single premiums.

Use and occupancy
Insurance of loss of use of plant or machinery or occupancy of a building.

Utmost good faith
See **uberrimae fidei**.

Voluntary excess
An excess which the insured agrees to bear in consideration of a reduction in premium.

Voyage policy
Insurance operative from the port of departure to destination irrespective of any time element.

Waiter
A uniformed attendant at Lloyd's.

Warranty
A statement made by the insured as absolutely true. Also a very strict condition in a policy.

Whole account treaty
A reinsurance treaty covering all the insurances written in a section of the ceding insurer's business. Thus if an underwriter had reinsured his marine account on a whole account basis, the reinsurance would apply also to incidental non-marine business written to his marine account.

Winding up fee
The fee paid by a Name to his members' agent to wind up his affairs when he ceases underwriting.

Working layer
A layer of excess of loss reinsurance in which frequent claims are likely to arise.

Working name
A person who works at Lloyd's or with a Lloyd's organisation and who is an underwriting member.

Write
Same as 'underwrite', i.e. insure (*see* **underwriting**).

Written line
The amount of insurance that an insurer has agreed to accept when signing a slip. It may be more than the amount actually insured, which is known as the closed line or signed line (*see* **full written line**).

Written premium
The cumulative amount of premium income due to be received by an insurer.

Year of account
Same as **underwriting year**.

Year free of premium
Some insurers offer insurance, especially household, under which a free year is granted from time to time, usually as a no claims bonus.

Bibliography

Part I

Chartered Insurance Institute Tuition Service *Management II: Insurance Broking Study Course 311*, 1983

Clews, R. (ed.), *A Textbook of Insurance Broking*, 2nd edn, Woodhead Faulkner, 1987

Cockerell, H. and Shaw, G., *Insurance Broking and Agency: The Law and the Practice*, Witherby, 1979

Dickinson, G. C. A. and Steel, J. T., *Introduction to Insurance*, M & E Business Studies, Macdonald & Evans, 1984

Hansell, D. S., *Elements of Insurance*, 4th edn, Macdonald & Evans, 1985

The Lloyd's Act 1982, HMSO, 1982

Lloyd's: a route forward (Report of the Rowland Task Force), Lloyd's, 1992

A new structure of governance for Lloyd's (Report of the Morse Working Party), Lloyd's, 1992

Regulatory Arrangements at Lloyd's: Report of the Committee of Inquiry (The Neill Report), Cm 59, January 1987

Self-regulation at Lloyd's: Report of the Fisher Working Party, Lloyd's, May 1980

Williams, G., *Understanding Insurance*, Waterlow, 1983

Part II

Financial Services Act 1986, HMSO, 1986

Gee's Compliance Factbook (looseleaf), Gee's

How to become a Lloyd's broker, Lloyd's, February 1989

Insurance Brokers (Registration) Act 1977, HMSO, 1977

Insurance Brokers Registration Council Annual Report, 1993

Lloyd's Brokers Byelaw (No. 5 of 1988)

Lloyd's Brokers (Amendment) Byelaw (No. 8 of 1989), together with *The Associated Explanatory Notes and Code of Practice for Lloyd's Brokers*, November 1988

Lloyd's Brokers (Amendment No. 2) Byelaw (No. 13 of 1989)

Money Laundering: Guidance Notes for Insurance and Retail Investment Products, Joint Money Laundering Steering Group, 1993

Morgan, C. and Patient, M., *Auditing Investment Business*, Butterworths, 1989

Neville Russell's Financial Services Compliance Manual, Butterworths, 1988

Personal Investment Authority (PIA) Adopted Rules (looseleaf)

Personal Investment Authority (PIA) The PIA's approach to regulation, 1994

Personal Investment Authority (PIA) Prospectus, 1994

Personal Investment Authority (PIA) Rule Book (looseleaf)

Practice Note 2: *The Lloyd's Market*, Auditing Practices Board, 1992

Umbrella Arrangements Byelaw (No. 6 of 1988)

Whittaker, A. and Morse, G., *The Financial Services Act 1986*, Butterworths, 1987

Part III

Brainin, J. J., *A costing policy handling by brokers*, British Insurance & Investment Brokers' Association, April 1989

Part IV

Amendment to FRS 5: *Reporting the Substance of Transactions Insurance Broking Transactions and Financial Reinsurance*, Accounting Standards Board, 1994

Auditing Guideline 309: *Communications between Auditors and Regulators under Sections 109 and 180 (1)(q) of the Financial Services Act 1986*, Auditing Practices Board, 1994

Loney, K. E., *Accounting Standards and How they Affect Insurance Companies*, Insurance Institute of London, 1983

McGrindell, A. L., *A Guide to Insurance Accounting*, Buckley Press, 1981

Neville Russell's Form and Content of Financial Statements, Tolleys, 1994

Oakes, R. G. and Drummond-Tyler, D. N., *Insurance Brokers* (Briefing 5 of *Business Briefings* looseleaf), Accountancy Books

Practice Note 5: *The Auditors' Right and Duty to Report to Other Regulators of Investment Business*, Auditing Practices Board, 1994

SAS 620: *The Auditors' Right and Duty to Report to Regulators in the Financial Sector*, Auditing Practices Board, 1994

Part VI

Andrew, S. L., *Insurance Brokers* (Briefing 10 of *Tax Briefings* looseleaf), Accountancy Books

Business Economic Notes BEN 20: *Insurance Brokers and Agents*, Inland Revenue

HM Customs & Excise VAT leaflet No. 701/36/92, HMSO, 1992

VAT Act 1994, HMSO, 1994

Index